D1474843

LOUIS MACNEICE
AND HIS INFLUENCE

ULSTER EDITIONS AND MONOGRAPHS
General Editors
Robert Welch
Joseph McMinn

Ulster-Editions & Monographs Series
ISSN 0954-3392

LOUIS MACNEICE
AND
HIS INFLUENCE

Edited by
Kathleen Devine
and Alan J. Peacock

Ulster Editions and Monographs: 6

COLIN SMYTHE
Gerrards Cross, 1998

Copyright © 1998 by Michael Allen, Terence Brown, Neil Corcoran,
Alan Heuser, Edna Longley, Peter McDonald, Alan J. Peacock,
Jon Stallworthy, Robert Welch, Richard York

First published in 1998 by Colin Smythe Limited
Gerrards Cross, Buckinghamshire SL9 8XA

British Library Cataloguing in Publication Data

A catalogue record of this book is available from the British Library

ISBN 0-86140-391-6

Distributed in North America by Oxford University Press,
198 Madison Avenue, New York 10016

Printed in Great Britain
by T. J. International Ltd., Cornwall

CONTENTS

INTRODUCTION

It is possible that Louis MacNeice's standing and reputation as a major Twentieth Century literary figure may be about to settle into due perspective. At last now, with the publication of Jon Stallworthy's biography,[1] we have the long-needed comprehensive survey of the full familial, social, educational and historical background to the career of a writer whose work has, in the past, tended to receive piece-meal consideration according to the particular points of access to it that individual critics have either chosen or been able to achieve. Limitations of outlook in MacNeice's interpreters too often masqueraded as alleged limitations of the work, in a process that did not begin to be seriously reversed until a decade after his death in 1963.

Consideration of his status as a Thirties Poet, for instance, for many years tended to occlude his identity as an Irish and Northern Irish poet. On the other hand, in spite of his Irish status (for MacNeice, however defined, emphatically something more than a mere geographical designation), his schooling, career and adult domicile in England have sometimes for some put him beyond the Pale of a certain Irish conception of an 'Irish Poet'. As Brendan Kennelly has observed, 'he has, apart from a few loyal followers among the poets of Ulster, such as Longley, Mahon, Heaney, Ormsby, Hewitt and Muldoon, as well as the distinguished critics, Terence Brown and Edna Longley, been largely ignored in Ireland, particularly in the Republic. He is still the outsider, still "banned", not only from the "Irish poor", but from the anthologies which help to educate the vast majority of Irish children.'[2]

As was said, however, things are changing and disjunction and fragmentation are giving way to a more rounded, synoptic approach. Peter McDonald, for instance, in his *Louis MacNeice: the Poet in his Contexts*,[3] has stressed the multi-contextual importance of MacNeice's work in a thoroughly documented study, following closely on Edna Longley's acute, succinct and similarly well-balanced 1988 study.[4] In 1988 also, Michael Longley produced an excellent *Selected Poems* for Faber[5] to replace Auden's more idiosyncratic 1964 volume. Moreover, with the publication of the *Selected Literary Criticism* (1987), the *Selected Prose* (1990) and the *Selected Plays*, (1993)[6] other facets of MacNeice's versatile talent are better positioned for appreciation and study. Twenty years of rehabilitation, beginning effectively with three critical studies of the early 1970s by W.T. McKinnon, D.B. Moore and Terence Brown,[7] have built towards an available textual and critical *corpus* commensurate with the reach, complexity and quality of the work. It is strange now though, over three decades after MacNeice's death, to be discussing the establishment of a rounded critical and scholarly base for the due appreciation of his work.

The fact is that the course of MacNeice's reputation has been persistently enigmatic. When, in 1965, David Wright anthologised for Penguin Books *The Mid Century: English Poetry 1940-1960*, the recently dead MacNeice was allotted only one short lyric, 'Brother Fire' from the early 1940s. Close on two decades of output is ignored. Patrick Kavanagh is given nine poems in a conscious and deserved counterbalance to relative neglect. MacNeice however is (among the contemporaries in his section) offered only a fraction of the space allotted to, for example, John Betjeman, Norman Cameron or Vernon Watkins. Presumably, MacNeice is a casualty of the Introduction's policy of 'cutting down or excluding better-known writers whose ambience, and best work, seems to belong to the thirties rather than the period covered by this anthology.'[8] On the other hand, MacNeice's late, outstanding achievement in *The Burning Perch* (1963) was well in currency in 1965, and the exclusion from the anthology of the build-up, through *Visitations* (1957) and *Solstices* (1961), to this late flowering utterly distorts the shape of his career. More acutely, in 1963 and with only the volumes up to *Solstices* for consideration, Maurice Wollman gives MacNeice (and Kavanagh) substantial representation in his anthology *Ten Contemporary Poets*: 'Although of an earlier generation, he accepts the life of today ... '[9]

This unevenness of recognition derives from the fact that, even in the 1960s, MacNeice's reputation was still patchily suffering from the hangover of a run of conceptually (and ideologically) blinkered criticism dating from the 1940s, where he is treated as a 'thirties also-ran, operating in the shadow of Auden, and hence categorised and assessed by criteria and a prescriptive aesthetic which are no more than partially applicable. The course of MacNeice criticism in this vein is a bizarre example of an aesthetic limited by period and context being applied to a writer who, centrally, is *not*. As late as 1988, Michael Longley, in his

Introduction to the *Selected Poems*, remarks how 'In England critics still respond mainly to those bits of his work which superficially resemble Auden.'[10]

The syndrome was indeed remarkably durable. In 1976, for instance, Samuel Hynes, while pursuing his Auden-centred view of the 1930s in *The Auden Generation*, could encapsulate MacNeice as a poet who, given to 'habitual sentimental melancholy', would 'clearly if the time [of Munich and *Autumn Journal*] allowed ... have been content to go on as he was, a charming Irish classicist with upper-class tastes and a gift for making melancholy poems.'[11] That such a formulation was possible at such a late date[12] is testimony to the stubborn tendency towards reductive categorization in the history of MacNeice criticism. There is no impression here of the crucial disquietudes and uncertainties always attaching to MacNeice's sense of nationality, of his unconventional classicism (on which, see Peter McDonald in the present volume), or, in the inadequate 'melancholy', of the vibrant, uncompromising, self-critical vein of philosophical quest and scepticism which runs dialectically through MacNeice's work from the earliest years.

Constantly there is, in this Anglo-centric tradition, a sense of MacNeice being sold short for his failure (more exactly, disinclination) to order his aesthetic priorities according to a particular phase in the course of modern English literature. Closer to the event, for instance, Francis Scarfe in his (again significantly titled) *Auden and After* (1942) decides at a late stage to include MacNeice in the volume, ascribes him to 'The Auden Group', but side-lines him as one who 'is not single-minded' and 'can be considered a very good representative of many of the young poets ... who have failed to make up their mind about society, philosophy and religion ... ' Moreover, he lacks, unlike Auden, 'understanding and love of England'.[13] The application of the latter criterion is piquant in a critique which jovially paints MacNeice as 'damnably Irish'. To say however that the author of *Autumn Journal* did not 'understand' England is odd from any perspective. Whether or not MacNeice 'loved' England according to some unspoken standard is not a tractable question. For someone who was not English, however, he did in fact achieve a remarkable degree of empathetic follow-feeling in *Autumn Journal* and elsewhere (particularly during the war years) – balanced of course by typically MacNeician counter-feelings: 'understanding' and 'love' can be subtly conflicting elements as MacNeice demonstrated in his complex attitude (or rather attitudes) to his native Ireland as well as his adoptive England.

In the broader political sphere, far from being a poet who 'failed to make up his mind', MacNeice was in fact notable as a 'Thirties Poet' who did not need to change it in the post-'thirties fashion of Left-wing recantation. His humanistic, philosophically circumspect, brand of socialism proved durable and constant in his life; and to the extent that he had found a strictly moderated fellow-feeling with the more callowly doctrinaire programme of some of his associates, he was able to defend the *aggregate* value of the trends they effected in, for instance, his reply to Virginia Woolf's attack on the poetry of the 'thirties (including, in particular, MacNeice's) in her 1940 essay, 'The Leaning Tower':[14]

We may not have done all we could in the Thirties, but we did do something. We were right to throw mud at Mrs Woolf's old horses and we were right to advocate social reconstruction and we were even right – in our more lyrical work – to give personal expression to our feelings of anxiety, horror and despair (for even despair can be fertile).[15]

MacNeice's reserve vis-à-vis the ideological naivety of *some* 'thirties colleagues is not allowed to blur a reasoned sense of overall gain. The position is typical of his considered, moderated, non-doctrinaire attitude to allegiance or commitment.

Nevertheless the implication of indecisiveness was a constant in criticism of MacNeice over three decades and is a charge which runs, in variant formulations, like a litany in the titles of articles written about him at different times. 'Evasive Honesty' is G.S. Fraser's term;[16] 'Louis MacNeice and the Line of Least Resistance'[17] is the title of Stephen Wall's 1964 article – formulations which do no justice to the principled independence, steadfastness and rigour of MacNeice's political and philosophical position. These tags from the 1950s and 1960s echo Scarfe's 1942 presentation of MacNeice as lacking a 'sense of direction' or 'single-mindedness' – a poet limited by a 'common-sense attitude to life and poetry'.[18] Rigorous philosophical scepticism, and a classicist's profound sense of the Horatian 'middle way' were thus reduced to an outlook whereby the poet may, in a philosophical poem such as 'Plurality', be deemed simply to 'not bother to pursue the deeper implications of his theme'.[19]

The stereotype of a talent responding essentially to the surface aspects of life and somehow lacking, however susceptible and responsive his evocation of sense-experience and phenomena, a deeper 'sense of direction' became a reflex topos of MacNeice criticism, memorably exemplified in Conrad Aiken's version of it:

For sheer readability, for speed, lightness, and easy intellectual range, Mr MacNeice's verse is in a class by itself. Open it anywhere, whether in narrative, eclogue or lyric, and at once you are swept away by the tireless and effortless enumerative pace, the bright rush of nominal images, the gay prodigality of scene, the so easily caught tune and mood. Yes, this is the world we know, all right, and this too is a fellow we can like ... And so, in we go; and out we come; and it is only then that we find how little of all this has stuck to us. Not a thing – practically not a thing. For the trouble is, it is *too* topical, *too* transitory, *too* reportorial ... [20]

That final exclamatory triad, consigning MacNeice's work to the category of 'reportage' is given unfortunate authority by the brilliance and energy of the preceding celebration of his vibrant response to the minute-by-minute, quotidian world of sensory experience. What is missing is any suggestion of the simultaneous sense of philosophical quest and scepticism which leads MacNeice to put such a premium on phenomena (and human sensory response to them) as a 'given' – something to hang on to in the midst of philosophical incertitude. This lapsed Christian who revised his undergraduate idealist tendency to 'drag in ultimate reality everywhere'[21] is, significantly, also the enthusiast, from school-days, of the Roman materialist Lucretius, who makes phenomena and access to them through the five senses the epistemological bedrock of his Epicurean *credo* (cf., in the same connection, MacNeice's disposition to favour Aristotelian empiricism over Platonic idealism). MacNeice's sharp, luxuriant and excitable response to sensory and, in particular, visual experience is not at odds with 'deeper' preoccupations, but an integrated part of a complex outlook. His purview as a 'concrete' poet interested in 'concrete living'[22] takes in all these polarities, just as it embraces all the experienced particulars of the socio-political world.

It is perhaps only in a particular critical tradition influenced, from the 'thirties onward, by the question of a poet's declared political beliefs and allegiances that the depth and persistent philosophical seriousness of MacNeice's poetry could for so long (really until the early 'seventies) be drastically underestimated. It is essentially an historical accident rather than an intrinsic difficulty. Moreover, MacNeice himself was aware, in 1935, of the

Louis MacNeice and his Influence

process. Commenting on the 'revolutionary, or communist attitude' in the poetry represented by Michael Roberts' *New Signatures* anthology, he presciently remarked how: 'We are now in danger of a poetry which will be judged by its party colours. Bourgeois poetry is assumed to have been found wanting; the only alternative is communist poetry. This seems to be an over-simplification. I doubt whether communist and bourgeois are exclusive alternatives in the arts and, if they are, I suspect these would-be communist poets of playing to the bourgeoisie.'[23] The political and psychological insight of this would be invisible to those demanding ideological 'commitment' and unaware of how testing, morally and intellectually, the 'middle way' can be. Asked in 1934, in a *New Verse* 'Enquiry', 'Do you take your stand with any political or politico-economic party or creed?', MacNeice replied: 'No. In weaker moments I wish I could'.[24] Such urbane, ironic wisdom requires a corresponding respect for individual sceptical integrity on the part of the reader and a sensitivity to irony and understatement in the elucidation of a position. It is the antithesis of doctrinaire rigour, sectional partisanship and intellectual self-indulgence or arrogance.

In this respect, there is an inescapable connection with the situation of a later generation of poets such as Michael Longley, Derek Mahon and Seamus Heaney. They too, as their careers developed in parallel with the escalating 'Troubles' of 1968 and after in Northern Ireland were subject to calls for 'commitment'; and both popular and critical exegesis combed their works for degrees of loyalty and affiliation to this or that socio-political grouping. Similarly, there was a tendency in the earlier years to lump them together as members of a literary 'Group' (though in practice they maintained, like MacNeice in respect of the 'Auden group', distinctive individual degrees of affiliation to Philip Hobsbaum's famous reading and discussion sessions).[25] In all these cases, the preoccupation of many critics with issues of political and socio-religious allegiance, fuelled by particular historical circumstance rather than any overwhelming proclivity or predisposition on the poets' part towards such themes (the first volumes are, across the board, relatively a-political), tended to mask their individuality and wide literary and cultural purview. Too often they were grouped together as 'Poets of the Troubles' or sub-categorised as Protestant or Catholic exhibits in this same context. If they gained by this in terms of securing international notice in their earlier years quite beyond what recent precedent in Ulster might have seemed to promise, they perhaps, like

MacNeice, suffered by constriction within convenient, but inadequate, critical categories. All three have provided humane, moving and analytical rather than partisan treatment of themes and issues generated by the 'Troubles'. They took them up reluctantly and non-exploitatively as they became part of their, and others' lives; and herein in fact lay their value as poets of the Troubles rather than 'Poets of the Troubles'. The parallel with MacNeice is obvious, and it is not surprising that he proved, in the decade after his death, an invaluable model and inspiration to his successors. As Derek Mahon put it in 1971: 'For a long time it seemed that Louis MacNeice was Irish only by an accident of birth, but in recent years his reputation, never at the highest in Britain, has come to rest in the country he could never quite bring himself to disown.'[26] If such recognition of his importance was being voiced in Ireland, the picture remained more equivocal in England.

When G.S. Fraser wrote an Introduction to D.B. Moore's 'pioneer study' of MacNeice in 1972, he was very much aware of the fact that nine years had elapsed between the poet's death and this 'book-length study' of a manifestly important talent; he refers to 'this comparative critical neglect of such a versatile, prolific, and piercingly intelligent poet'[27] (he had drawn attention to the accumulating studies of Auden and Dylan Thomas). Fraser goes on to note that 'Some of the reasons are ... to MacNeice's credit. Many of the books that have been written about Auden and Dylan Thomas are concerned, so to say, less with placing a poet than with cracking a code. There is no code to crack in MacNeice. He had his eye on the outer world, he observed things that we all observe, but more sharply and more vividly. His tone is conversational. His rhythms and stanza forms are often popular ones, owing something to jazz or nursery rhymes or folk poetry ... He is very much the poet as an urban man, speaking to urban men.' Aware however that this kind of argument may only confirm prejudices, Fraser immediately adds: 'Yet clearly, all the same, he is not a mere entertainer. He was acutely, sometimes delightedly, sometimes painfully, aware of the contradictoriness of life. He saw the outer world clearly but had to grope for his own deepest inner motives and responses, which always remained ultimately mysterious to him. He looked all his life for a unifying vision, but was too honest to persuade himself that he had ever quite found one.' These are acute observations which begin to plumb the complexities and depth of MacNeice's poetry. They are framed however in defensive terms, as if the full case has still to be made.

Fraser proceeds to note how it is 'difficult to find a formula for him' or to 'find an over-all pattern'. It is a career which, in this kind of account, seems to resolve itself into adversative encapsulations: if MacNeice is a 'liberal humanist', he is also one 'whose view of the state of our culture was a melancholy and ominous one'. If he was a 'hedonist', then there was also 'a kind of iron harshness in him, something puritan ... ' It is not however obvious why such contrasts should be the cause of any particular critical difficulty. Reducibility to 'a formula' is surely the mark of a minor talent, and the great lyric poets have immemorially traded in antinomies such as life-death, love-hate, pleasure-guilt etc. Fraser's critique is responsive and suggestive. Behind it however is the ghost of that familiar wish for an encapsulable core in MacNeice's poetry – an ideology, a belief around which generalisations might comfortably be manufactured. Fraser's comments strain against this tendency, but his rhetoric is conditioned by it. His essay occurs at a pivotal juncture however in criticism of MacNeice in its implicit recognition that, as Alan Heuser puts it, 'Louis MacNeice is a multi-dimensional writer who cannot be, refuses to be, pigeon-holed.'[28]

D.B. Moore's book, with Fraser's Introduction, was published in 1972. Its outlook is, significantly, England- and even Birmingham-centred. By this time, in another context, Michael Longley and Derek Mahon, having 'gutted the collected Louis MacNeice' in the 1960s as undergraduates at Trinity College, Dublin,[29] were firmly establishing themselves as significant figures consciously in a line of development from MacNeice. Seamus Heaney had purchased the same volume with the book-token he received as a graduation prize at Queen's University, Belfast – though his developing sense of identification with MacNeice was to prove, as Neil Corcoran shows in the present volume, a slower process. It is no accident therefore that the (still continuing) renaissance in MacNeice criticism was set in motion in the early 'seventies by critics with an informed, instinctive sense of the complexities in MacNeice's outlook which become apparent as soon as his Irish background is given full consideration. William T. McKinnon's *Apollo's Blended Dream* (1971) shows a broad grasp of MacNeice's familial and educational background, and stresses the philosophical and metaphysical elements in his poetry. Terence Brown's *Louis MacNeice: Sceptical Vision* (1975) similarly does full justice to MacNeice's cultural background in Ireland, and provides further appreciation and analysis of how subtly and pervasively MacNeice's philosophical seriousness informs the poetry. The idea of 'sceptical vision' is a quantum leap forward from Fraser's 'evasive honesty', and sets the debate on a footing commensurate with the vital, dialectical mix of questing impulse and balancing sceptical caution of the work. In 1982 Robyn Marsack's *The Cave of Making* provided a further overview of MacNeice's work, making extensive use of archival and manuscript material to elucidate the techniques and evolution of his art.[30] His classicism (a major aspect of MacNeice's outlook and poetic 'conditioning' still to be set on a comprehensive critical base – but see Peter McDonald's essay in the present volume) is the subject in this volume of some informed comment. In the later 'eighties, Edna Longley produced her already mentioned Faber volume which provided a popularly accessible account of the reach and complexity of MacNeice's work. Through the 'eighties, then, with the *Selected Literary Criticism* (1987: followed by the *Selected Prose*, 1990) becoming available, the furtherance of the study of MacNeice as a major poet on an informed and scholarly basis proceeded steadily.

For a critic in the 1990s, who is aware of MacNeice's placing in Irish Literature both as regards his predecessors and his successors, the picture is of a central, pivotal talent. As Edna Longley has put it:

Louis MacNeice has influenced redefinitions of Irish poetry and Irish identity in the North of Ireland. He has done so not only by virtue of what he 'says' about Ireland, but because he is such a good poet. It may also be significant that his poetry mediated between traditionalism and Modernism at an important juncture in twentieth-century poetry. MacNeice's relation to Ireland and England, to Yeats and Eliot, and to his 1930s contemporaries makes his poetry a remarkably broad conduit for the materials and techniques of twentieth-century poetry.[31]

Clearly a revolution has occurred and been consolidated in MacNeice studies. This kind of formulation appropriately reflects the cultural forces running through and from a major talent. It is this 'remarkably broad conduit' which forms, essentially, the subject-matter of the present volume. In terms of anthologies of Irish poetry, Paul Muldoon's 1986 *Faber Book of Contemporary Irish Poetry*[32] emphatically makes amends for past neglect of the kind we saw Brendan Kennelly regretting earlier. MacNeice's intelligent recognition of the accommodation to be made (under the compelling example of in particular Eliot and Yeats) between traditionalism and modernist imperatives, his measured subscription to the programme of the 1930s 'Auden' school and, above all, his avoidance of any callow, limiting allegiance in any of these connections, provide a model of scrupulous, non-doctrinaire and informed discrimination. In the terminology of Michael Longley's ironic poem on this subject with reference to his own work, he is fully aware of the difficult question of 'Options'.[33] Moreover, his willingness to revise, re-think and reassess in such areas echoes his shifting, evolving attitude to Ireland, England and the whole spectrum of issues of identity, belonging and loyalty evoked by them. It is his incisive scepticism, his determined pursuit of a rational course between extremes which has provided a challenging 'option' for successors such as Longley, Mahon and Muldoon in historical circumstances where the issues of 'commitment', 'loyalty' and bearing adequate witness to social or national upheaval or conflict have once again tested the mettle of the writer. Above all, though, it is the sheer quality of his work which, in an Ulster of scant literary distinction in the quarter-century or so preceding the 'sixties Northern 'Renaissance', made him the inevitable model or stimulus for talents such as Mahon and Longley in one generation and Ciaran Carson and Paul Muldoon in another.

Key aspects of the achievement and influence of this multi-dimensional writer are dealt with in the individual essays of the present volume. As was suggested at the beginning of this Introduction, the conditions are probably now in place, the framework of critical, historical and textual desiderata established, for the adequate prosecution of the kind of many-sided, on-going literary and cultural debate set in motion by a major talent; and the present volume is a contribution to this open-ended process. Within the following pages, established experts on MacNeice's work, including the authors of important full-length critical studies, continue their involvement with a writer whose authority and importance have been, and continue to be, endorsed by the pattern of influence traced in what follows. A major talent is never finally 'placed' – least of all that of the mercurial, questing, perpetually transient MacNeice, but the terms of the debate can at least continue to strive, progressively, to hold his achievement within something like a just perspective.

Alan J. Peacock

ACKNOWLEDGEMENTS

The editors would like to express their thanks to the Research Committee and to the Dean and Faculty of Humanities of the University of Ulster for financial support towards the present volume; to the Cultural Traditions Group of the Community Relations Council of Northern Ireland for a grant towards the 1994 session of the Ulster Symposium at the University, from which the essays in the present volume derive; to Professor Jon Stallworthy who was unable to attend the Symposium, but who has nevertheless provided an additional essay, and to the staff of the University Library.

Special thanks are due to the General Editor of the Series, Professor Robert Welch, for his generous interest and practical support.

Acknowledgment is made to David Higham Associates for permission to quote the extracts from the poems and prose of Louise MacNeice.

ABBREVIATIONS

CP   *The Collected Poems of Louis MacNeice*, ed. E. R. Dodds, Faber and Faber, London, 1966.

Other abbreviations are indicated in individual essays.

YEATS AND MACNEICE: A NIGHT-SEMINAR WITH FRANCIS STUART

ROBERT WELCH

Some weeks ago I dreamed of Francis Stuart. We were at a seminar. The theme was something like History and the Imagination. Yeats and MacNeice were the focus when Stuart started to talk. The argument was this: Yeats is one of the greatest of the poets because he realised exactly where he was in history. The world moves in great historical cycles and the one we are in, now, is drawing to a close. Yeats saw that

> Black out; Heaven blazing into the head,

and faced into it

> Gaiety transfiguring all that dread;[1]

and retained composure. Not only did he face the horror of the best lacking 'all conviction', and the worst being 'full of passionate intensity', he probed it. This exploration was conducted in faith and with the pulse of certainty: faith that even during nightmarish times there remained some kind of indescribable and permanent form, which could be known and experienced and revealed; and the certainty that effort and labour could bring a mind schooled in discipline and harsh thought into some form of sure knowledge.

Yeats knew that he had to have, like the Japanese courtier in 'Meditations in Time of Civil War', 'waking wits'; that is, a steady focus on a core of meaning underlying the phenomena:

> For the most rich inheritor,
> Knowing that none could pass Heaven's door
> That loved inferior art,
> Had such an aching heart
> That he, although a country's talk
> For silken clothes and stately walk,
> Had waking wits ...

1

The aching heart keeps the wits awake:

> only an aching heart
> Conceives a changeless work of art.
>
> ('Meditations in Time of Civil War')

Nothing less than total sorrow can drive the mind, no matter how vigorous it may be, to seek out those forms that are permanent and, as he describes them in 'The Moods', 'fire-born'. It is not the case, either, that any consolation is necessarily to be found in this essentially tragic conception of the work (or fate) of the artist or, indeed, of man. There is no collapsing with relief into the accommodating arms of some warmly-welcoming elemental being or white goddess. All there is is the effort and the search, the turning into the clamour of the night, as this cycle of time winds down, as the gyre loosens and spins wildly:

> Some moralist or mythological poet
> Compares the solitary soul to a swan;
> I am satisfied with that,
> Satisfied if a troubled mirror show it,
> Before that brief gleam of its life be gone,
> An image of its state;
> The wings half spread for flight,
> The breast thrust out in pride
> Whether to play, or to ride
> Those winds that clamour of approaching night.
>
> ('Nineteen Hundred and Nineteen')

'Clamour'; 'tumult'; 'dread'; 'a sudden blow'; 'rage-driven, rage-tormented, rage-hungry' – all words that bear witness to Yeats's utterly clear testimony to what he conceived of as manifestations of an inescapable historical reality about western civilisation as it was drawing to an end. This effort of Yeats, in facing the ragged tumult of the age, and in resolutely retaining a grip on some inner core, a mathematics of being itself, gave him a remoteness, a 'solitude', which made him, in a very crucial sense, indifferent to praise or blame. If we are to judge him, or to fault him, say for his so-called inhumanity, we had better be sure that we do so having first exercised ourselves fully to comprehend the sorrow, bleakness, and probable accuracy of his appraisal of the way we live now.

MacNeice, Stuart as seminar-leader went on to say, did not see he was in history with anything like the same clear gaze that Yeats was able to level at things. His was a more tentative, more circuitous, in a way more heart-smitten kind of absorption in the facts. Yeats's stare, like that which he attributes to Major Robert Gregory, his friend's dead son, is one in which the

> gazing heart doubles her might.

This isn't concentration on *things*:

> cold Clare rock and Galway rock and thorn
> … that stern colour and that delicate line
> That are our secret discipline …
> ('In Memory of Major Robert Gregory')

It is, as he makes clear, a secret discipline driving into the *heart* of things, from which the gazing heart takes sustenance and strength. The probe is matched by an equal and fortifying response out of the things themselves. The process is a live interchange engaged by the will in its (to use a word of Coleridge) 'irremissive' pressure. The discipline is one which visits the natural world with an intent and intensified consciousness, which then *responds*. This responsive interchange makes the art of imagination a *responsible* one: focussed, forceful, and steady. Only such well-governed behaviour of the imagination will do, in the Yeatsian universe, when all things are falling apart. The alternative, as he chillingly tells us in 'Nineteen Hundred and Nineteen' is to 'sink unmanned' into the 'half-deceit of some intoxicant / From shallow wits'. How differently MacNeice 'read the signs'.

And there, more or less, Stuart finished his exposition. Wherever such things come from, there is, I believe, something in the distinction made in my night-seminar, and I'd like to explore it under three interrelated aspects, to do with philosophy, moral outlook, and formal concerns. You will notice that I'm leaving Ireland out of the picture as a theme or concern, as an issue to be dealt with explicitly. Yeats's and MacNeice's relations with Ireland, are, I suppose, still of some interest, but I would suggest that we have now arrived at an understanding of their work, and its place in Irish or Anglo-Irish tradition, which allows us to take it for granted that each poet, in different ways, was utterly obsessed with Ireland and her history, and that this concern animates almost every line they wrote in form, phrasing, political and moral awareness, and the kind of philosophical weather their poetry creates.

Autumn Sequel (1954) is generally regarded as an example of the prosy MacNeice; the poetic energy is regarded as too dispersed, the commentary and philosophising too intrusive. Mostly it is unfavourably compared to its predecessor, *Autumn Journal* (1939), MacNeice's remarkable fusion of his day-to-day impressions of life in England and Ireland immediately before the war, his own emotional and intellectual concerns, and his sense of impending crisis, all brilliantly focussed in a poetic language which is at once both accommodating and compressed. Yet *Autumn Sequel* has its own power. Thomas Kinsella, so says John Montague,[2] actually prefers the later poem. I'd like to home in on one of the less prepossessing and less remarkable passages, in Canto XVII, set at Halloween and All Saints' Day, 1953, in Norwich and London. Having evoked the enjoyment and terrors of Halloween at Carrickfergus Rectory during his childhood, when the Catholic cook from Fivemiletown, Co. Tyrone, would get them to bob for apples and would read the tea leaves for Louis and his sister down in the kitchen, he describes waking in Norwich in the post-war present. This is typical MacNeice, a poet turning over in his mind, with an effortless confidence and skill, his concerns and preoccupations:

> So now I wake
> To find that it is Norwich and All Saints' Day,
>
> All devils and fancy spent, only an ache
> Where once there was an anguish. The tall spire
> In harsh grey rain stands grey while great gales shake
>
> The trees of Tombland; every man's desire
> Is washed away in what is a record fall
> Of rain, as the gay colours of nave and choir
>
> Were washed away long since. The church bells call
> Forlornly from their cages within cages,
> Oak beams within blind stone; a similar wall
>
> Immures for each of us the Middle Ages
> Of our own childhood; centuries of rain
> Have made the colours run and swilled the pages
>
> Whether of missal or chapbook down the drain
> In one conglomerate pulp ...
>
> (CP 399)

It is easy to overlook the virtues of this as verse: it is steady, lucid, and clear, a perfect vehicle for a mind anatomising its contents. Even the terza rima, with its onward push and backward echo, is perfect for the attempt at reflecting a tension between the moment of realization as it occurs, and the 'irremissive' (again Coleridge) pressure of the inquiring will. Musically too – look at the mesh of assonantal vowels driving through the terse rhyme: 'grey', 'rain', 'gales', 'shake', 'away' etc. – there is much going on, but the technique is a part of the kind of patient, alert *watchfulness* MacNeice is so good at. There is, it seems to me, a philosophical base to this quality of nervous attentiveness. This linking of empiricism and humanism has been discussed by Edna Longley;[3] it might be called an absorbed phenomenology. I don't want to lose complete sight of the contrasting method of watching in Yeats: the calm and resolute *stare* or *gaze*. MacNeice's way of looking involves a kind of surrender to the thing or the occasion, or the moment, a form of Keatsian negative capability, as he recognises himself in the following passage from *The Strings Are False*:

I have never steered myself much. An American friend once said to me rebukingly: 'You never seem to make any positive choice; you just let things happen to you'. But the things that happen to one often seem better than the things one chooses. Even in writing poetry, which is something I did early choose to do, the few poems or passages which I find wear well have something of accident about them … or, to put it more pretentiously, seem 'given'. So Magilligan Strand was like falling in love. For such occasions the word 'falling' is right; one does not step into love any more than one steps asleep – or awake. For awake, like asleep, is what one falls, and to keep falling awake seems to me the salt of life much more than existentialist defiance. We cannot of course live by Keats's Negative Sensibility alone, we must all in E.M. Forster's phrase, use 'telegrams and anger'; all the same what I feel makes life worth living is not the clever scores but the surrenders – it may be to the life-quickening urge of an air-raid, to nonsense talked by one's friends … to woods, or weirs, or to heat dancing on a gravelled path, to music, drink or the smell of turf smoke … or to the curve of a strand which seems to stretch to nowhere … [4]

In another autobiographical sketch, 'When I was Twenty-One',[5] MacNeice tells us that while he was at Oxford he spent a good deal of time wandering about, pondering the significance of things, like, for example, a cylinder of brawn in a butcher's window, thinking that appearances were more real than what Plato would have called reality, his ideal forms. This strict emphasis on the solid, tactile reality of actual things gives MacNeice's work its phenomenology and its moral texture. His work is crammed with a sense of the uniqueness of each passing moment, the variety and plurality of every aspect of what we see, apprehend and understand, and the insufficiencies of human systems of thought or organization to encapsulate this utter mobility. For this reason he is drawn to long discursive poems, such as *Autumn Journal* and *Autumn Sequel*, because this kind of writing can focus on the significance of the quotidian, explore the complexion of what it is like to be alive and to be in a traffic jam in Birmingham, or in a train going to London in the 1930s or 1940s; and yet move on, not allowing the wilful ego of symbolist impulse to stop and freeze that moment or situation. 'World is suddener than we fancy it', as he writes in the early lyric, 'Snow'; going on, 'World is crazier and more of it than we think', and MacNeice's continuous effort is to hold his poetry open to this 'drunkenness of things being various'. This is not a simple matter of trying to be as realistic as possible; nor is he ever really attracted to the easy option of abandoning formality and strictness and purity of diction and syntax in his writing in a nerveless attempt to accommodate variousness by becoming formless. The world is more 'spiteful and gay' than one supposes, he also says in 'Snow', indicating that watchfulness is required, that the world is 'dangerous' to use G.M. Hopkins's ominous yet excited word, to describe this same sense of threat. To be a writer in MacNeice's world is to be involved in exploring the 'incorrigibly plural' nature of things and that requires the discipline of code, form, and manners. Technique, Pound once said, is sincerity; it is also good manners, which are required in a world where wrong choices or inaccurate evaluations can have disastrous consequences.

In *The Strings Are False* the passage in which he writes in praise of surrendering or 'falling awake' follows an account of one of MacNeice's definitive experiences, and is obviously related to it. All people probably have such experiences, where the particular weather and form of their world are revealed to them. What makes artists artists perhaps, is their ability to recall these moments, and separate them out from the welter of multitudinous impressions. He is remembering his first sight of Magilligan Strand, one of the largest and smoothest in Ireland. No-one told him they were going there, but

... we suddenly came round a corner and there it was, unbelievable but palpably there ... I had the sense of infinite possibility, which implied, I think, a sense of eternity.

This is like, he says, his experience of the unfelt wind beyond the wall which he also recalls from a holiday on the North

Antrim/Derry coastline, and which he also writes about in *The Strings Are False*. He calls it, tersely and exactly, a revelation of space. He and his sister were walking along a road near Portstewart between high walls:

I could see nothing but the road and the air on the road was quiet and self-contained. On the top of the walls, on the contrary, there were long grasses growing in the stonework and these were blown out, combed, by a wind which I could not see. I wondered what was over those walls and I thought that it must be space.[6]

These passages, about the strand and the wild grasses blowing, register a shock of recognition, of thinking again, when the known and seen world is charged by a realization that there is something other: 'more of it than we think'.

It is not that the shock of something other, the more, empties this world: rather does the visitation of a multi-dimensional possibility beyond the here and now make the things, the wild grass, the strand, stand out even more radically in their given presence. And that presence is given by the something beyond, an eternity, an absence. This is brilliantly said in a Marvell-like metaphysical quatrain in 'Suite for Recorders':

The windblown web in which we live
Presumes a yawning negative,
A nothing which cries out to see
A something flout its vacancy.

(CP 286)

The off-hand, graceful manner in which the thought is nonchalantly engaged masks the startling and abrupt economy of the realization. For all of Yeats's longing for sprezzatura he never achieved anything as remotely and serenely relaxed as this assured confidence. Yeats was never nonchalant, it was one of those masks he strove for. Whenever Yeats is priming himself to deliver a startling and outrageous thrust of thought, he does so with all rhetorical flags flying, delivering cannonades of assertion, contempt, vulnerability on all sides, as he works himself up to the (often brilliantly terse) statement, such as the extraordinary and poignant

Man has created death.

This wonderful statement comes after these lines:

> A great man in his pride
> Confronting murderous men
> Casts derision upon
> Supersession of breath;
> He knows death to the bone –
> Man has created death

('Death')

MacNeice's own comment on this is:

... he builds up from his own pride in man and his belief in ... reincarnation this astonishing statement.[7]

But in MacNeice's own luminous, deeply appreciative, and generous study of Yeats there is no mistaking his reverence and affection for the older poet. His comments are extremely enlightening about Yeats's world-view and method; but they also serve to point up both the similarities and differences between them; and to indicate a philosophical and indeed moral standpoint which is an alternative to Yeats's apocalyptic if courageous vision. In Yeats, MacNeice says:

Thought at its highest merges into spirit, Yeats being an idealist who assumes that spirit is the primary and ultimate reality. The descent into time means a splitting of this primary reality into those secondary half-realities opposed to each other whose mutual antagonism implies their mutual dependence. This metaphysical dialectic underlies much of Yeats's later poetry and is involved with his doctrine of reincarnation as well as with that of historical cycles.[8]

This quite superbly summarises a good deal of Yeats's imaginative dynamics: the interplay of opposite forces; his love of England torturing his nationalist hatred; the natural face opposing the mask; and the golden bird and bough of Byzantium rebuking 'common bird or petal'. Even simple lines like

> ... send imagination forth
> Under the day's declining beam ...

('The Tower')

are marked by a characteristic Yeatsian challenge: the activity of the imaginative thrust is pushing against a declining passivity: will is pressing against dull impenetrability to awaken the mutuality of antagonism and dependence. How different is MacNeice's 'falling awake' into fresh realization. Where Yeats drives at the phenomena, fixing them with that gaze in which the heart can double its 'might' (note the word), MacNeice is prepared to let them be.

Now there are certain moods of Yeats's in which he blesses the accidentality of given things as in 'The Long-Legged Fly', when the young Helen practises a tinker shuffle in a street thinking no-one is looking, but even then there is a sense of impending threat, of the huge wheel of fortune turning and carrying this beautiful girl towards Troy. This sense of inescapable tragedy gives Yeats's poetry its chill, electrifying his syntax by his intimations of fate. Part of the thrill of Yeats is his pitilessness, his relentless and unswerving focus on doom. This mood of steady concentration on the determinism of history – as he sees it – is occasionally enlivened by uprushes of joyous force, but these surface in and are channelled through the self when it achieves or discovers a harmonious correlation with spiritual reality:

> I am content to follow to its source
> Every event in action or in thought;
> Measure the lot; forgive myself the lot!
> When such as I cast out remorse
> So great a sweetness flows into the breast
> We must laugh and we must sing,
> We are blest by everything,
> Everything we look upon is blest.

('A Dialogue of Self and Soul')

The discipline that underlines this correlation between events and their source is a secret discipline, and he elsewhere calls it magic. Spiritual reality may suffer fragmentation and may resolve into opposing antinomies when it comes into time; but for the ardent disciple, the master adept (and Yeats, by virtue of Madame Blavatsky, George Russell, MacGregor Mathers, Annie Horniman, Lady Gregory, Capt. Dermot MacManus and Georgie Hyde-Lees, his wife, was such) it was possible to gain direct contact with and knowledge of the whole thing. In any case, the self, properly re-searched, contained all other selves, and so the adept could realise, within himself, the whole, the one:

> I asked if I should pray,
> But the Brahmin said,
> 'Pray for nothing, say
> Every night in bed,
> "I have been a king,

> I have been a slave,
> Nor is there anything,
> Fool, rascal, knave,
> That I have not been,
> And yet upon my breast
> A myriad heads have lain."'

('Mohini Chatterjee')

Against this, place, from MacNeice's 'Mayfly':

> ... when this summer is over let us die together
> I want always to be near your breasts.

(*CP* 14)

Or from earlier in the same poem, describing the movement and sound of water near a public house, people outside in the sunshine, drinking beer:

> Gulp of yellow merriment; cackle of ripples;
> Lips of the river that pout and whisper round the reeds
> The mayfly flirting and posturing over the water

'Incorrigibly plural'; but also content to work in the here and now, where Yeats wants his statements and images to be oracular and begotten of the One:

> One is animate,
> Mankind inanimate fantasy.

('A Meditation in Time of War')

Again, an extreme statement, a throwing down of the gauntlet to reason. As if to say, all of the life commonly known as life is pure inanition, only to be energised by a voice capable of the incantations necessary to enliven it, or a stare that is so concentrated that it can bring life to stone, an anti-Medusa, or anti-Gorgon.

MacNeice, probably because of his particular ecclesiastical background (his father became a Church of Ireland bishop, and like many members of that church had Puritan leanings), is always very careful to draw a clear line between what can be seen and known and understood, and what can not. A boundary exists between the world of phenomena, which can be spoken of, and the world beyond the wall, of which it is foolhardy to speak recklessly. Of that which cannot be known it is best not to speak is a good Puritan dictum, and one which applies to MacNeice as much as to Bunyan or Marvell. The beyond is there – the wind

combs the long wild grass on the wall in Portstewart; eternity lies
somewhere at the back of what one sees as Magilligan Strand –
but it does not yield its secrets to sage, philosopher, or poet. That
something lies beyond makes the tendrils of the 'windblown web'
in which we live all the more beautiful, fragile, and worthy of our
care. This caring instinct in MacNeice is reflected in the infinite (I
do not use the word loosely) courtesy he bestows on language,
things, people in his formally gestured poetics, his reverent and
spacious meditative procedures in longer poems, and in a
revelling in the physical uniqueness of people, things, places,
elements. This 'carefulness' gives a moral tenor to MacNeice's
world, a combination of humanity and seriousness, and a sturdy
reasonableness. 'The Gardener', commemorating the Orangeman
who tended the rectory garden in Carrickfergus, is full of heart-
smitten affection, but there is also something else going on; there
is an honouring of the man's unique individuality, and a
recognition that, as a gardener, he keeps borders clear and is
keeper of that liminal area between the known and owned
territory, and that which is out there. He is both human and
parabolic at once:

> … between the clack of the shears
> Or the honing of the scythe
> Or the rattle of the rake on the gravel
> He would talk to amuse the children,
> He would talk to himself or the cat
> Or the robin waiting for worms
> Perched on the handle of the spade;
> Would remember snatches of verse
> From the elementary school
> About a bee and a wasp
> Or the cat by the barndoor spinning …
>
> He believed in God –
> The Good Fellow Up There –
> And he used a simile of Homer
> Watching the falling leaves,
> And every year he waited for the Twelfth of July,
> Cherishing his sash and his fife
> For the carnival of banners and drums.

(CP 172–3)

This is no Olympian transmogrification of a person into a symbol;
this is the simplicity of the very old device of making a certain

type of person a parable for a set of moral values. It is Langland, Spenser, Bunyan; and bardic poets such as Gofraidh Fionn Ó Dalaigh, Eochaidh Ó hEodhasa and Tadhg Dall Ó hUiginn. MacNeice everywhere has an eye for the living colour to be found in people, a colour with larger resonances and vibrations; it is part of the whole concept of falling awake. There is, too, perhaps, yet another dimension to his characterisation of the gardener, which relates this genial and humane tribute to a moral seriousness and qualities of tact and reserve. It may be that a Protestant vision cherishes borders: it is necessary to know where to draw the line between ceremony and sacrament. Above the wall there are those wild and beautiful spaces but what can be said with certainty of them? Liberty is protected by drawing a line between what is known and what may be spoken of only with great circumspection, if at all. One needs continually to fall awake into the ordinary. MacNeice describes Jack MacGowran, the actor, miming the famous Cork hurler, Christy Ring, in a wine bar in Baker Street in London:

He swung his non-existent stick (or hurley or camán) and everyone in the bar watched the non-existent ball soar through the wall and away into Regent's Park. But brilliant mime though MacGowran is, this is no more remarkable, and certainly less dangerous, than what a real hurling player does with a real ball.[9]

Engaging in art or in any coherent activity involves a plunge of trust into the thick of the given, the here and now, which is utterly mysterious in itself – so MacNeice would say – mysterious and bafflingly various. This view of the world of 'things being various' involves a kind of philosophical scepticism (sceptical vision in Terence Brown's phrase), an unwillingness too readily to presume any definite *conceptual* (as distinct from *intuitive*) knowledge of it. In other words this philosophical persuasion becomes a form of moral praxis in the actuality of day-to-day existence, in which all of MacNeice's writing roots itself. The progress through the challenges, abrupt shocks and terrors of ordinary life (where the 'fanged pit' waits, as well as the 'geyser suddenly of light') involves choice, will, and the application of effort. All of life is seen as a place in which the moral integrity of a person can be made and unmade through the variety of accidents waiting to occur, or the laxity of purpose which calls them down. Making a garden is all effort, but curiously therein also lie joy and 'grace abounding'. It is not surprising, given this moral tenor, that MacNeice should have been drawn, in his plays, prose-works, and poems, to the theme of the quest (where the person proves himself against all odds) and to the form of parable (which gives fabling a purposive, practical, and applied focus). But just in case this sounds all too hymnal and preachy (in itself of course not necessarily a bad thing) MacNeice's writing also accomplishes another synthesis, in that it combines a seriousness of purpose with a celebration of a set of human qualities frequently in abeyance in twentieth century writing: valour, courage, honesty, and dignity, summed up possibly in the word, virtue. These qualities MacNeice found and admired in the English, especially the English during the Second World War. There is, incidentally, a sense in which all real poets, or male poets at least, are war poets, in that it is the condition where conflict is out in the open which really tests human nature, unlike say, the condition of uneasy peace, so excoriated by Samual Daniel the Jacobean, which conceals the true situation and often prevents us from seeing how bad things really are. In this sense both Yeats and MacNeice are classic war poets, but whereas Yeats is at war with nature, ordinariness, and the things of time, save where he surrenders to them, overwhelmed by their sheer ungainsayability, MacNeice combines a form of continual surrender to life's data with a steadiness of resolve to be alive to its dangers and complexity, as well as watchful for its good. In *The Dark Tower* he mixes a mood of Roman stoic sadness with profound admiration for the human capacity for effort, knowing full well that effort will, eventually, like all expenditures of fortitude, fail. Childe Roland, before he sets off to confront the Dragon, a journey/quest his father and brothers have undertaken before him and not returned from, receives advice from his tutor:

> A man lives on a sliding staircase –
> Sliding downwards, remember; to be a man
> He has to climb against it, keeping level
> Or even ascending slightly; he will not reach
> The top – if there is a top – and when he dies
> He will slump and go down regardless. All the same
> While he lives he must climb. Remember that.[10]

Evil never dies, Roland is told by the Sergeant who teaches him the trumpet-blast that will summon the Dragon when he comes to the final place, but he is instructed that he must hold the note in defiance even when the Beast appears in all his terror. It is a stirring play and one that should be explained to all young people in these islands (and beyond), but it is stirring because it is so simple and so true. This is how it is for us on this 'bitch of an earth' as Beckett (another Protestant parablist whom MacNeice admired, along with Bunyan and Spenser) has it; who also, Seneca to MacNeice's Horace, wrote: 'I can't go on, I'll go on'. Life is arduous and calls forth our ardour, our virtue. Whether it is the hurler venturing into the variousness and danger of the game, or the gardener keeping the borders clear so that nature can thrive, effort, valour, and unceasing vigilance are required.

Where Yeats uses rhythm and rhyme to hammer rivets into his thought so that the whole machine can become animate with the frenzy of the self proclaiming itself to the moon, for MacNeice formal devices are a means of ever-finer differentiation and discrimination between 'things being various'. Rhythm is the activity of the will in its seeking mode; rhyme is the discovery of simultaneity and change. Take the following couple of extracts from what is often regarded as an example of the uninspired and 'tedious' MacNeice, 'The Stygian Banks'. This is philosophical, meditative verse, as in a good deal of Wordsworth which is very highly valued. If anything MacNeice is much the stronger poet because he is a more exacting thinker. In this passage he is talking about walls, gardens, limits, effort, will, queues of people in post-war London, and so on; all our themes so far. The garden is all gardens, but especially and originally that of the rectory in Carrickfergus: all men, even apparent ciphers

> Rough out their own best moments. Moments too rare
> For most of these in the queue. Granted the garden,
> There are distinctions in soil and in what comes out of it ...
>
> (CP 263)

There are distinctions, between all that lives on the earth, and to lump all together, in one anonymous clump at the service of a concept, is to accept the miserable inanition of those who view the mass of people as a mass (the snobs, intolerants, reactionaries) or of those who maintain that all human beings are the same (the left-wing agitators, Stalinists, reactionaries):

> To raise a value gardens must be gardened
> Which is where choice comes in. Then will. Then sweat ...
> Many will tell you that is what protects us,
> What makes in fact the garden, saves it from not-being
> So that, now it is there, we need not think beyond it;
> But look at the eyes of that tired man in the queue
> In whom fatigue dulling the senses has rendered

> Some other part of him sensitive – Intake of distance.
> What is it that comes in? Can it be that the wall
> Is really a stepping-stone? So that what is beyond it
> (That which as well perhaps could be called what is Not)
> Is the sanction itself of the wall and so of the garden?
> Do we owe these colours and shapes to something which seems
>   their death?
> It does not bear thinking of.

And yet it does 'bear thinking of'; this 'intake of distance' seen or imagined in the tired man's eyes is the endlessness and scope of being as it shows itself to us now, as long as the garden continues to be made, and as long as Childe Roland goes forth ready to hold the note even as the Dragon grows, and expands in size and seemingly unassailable power. These openings, 'intakes of distance', flashes of genius, occur where the intellect and intuition are schooled to receive them; hence MacNeice's diction, so spare and receptive; and his rhythm, which often, when seeking out intimations, moves towards and sketches in a kind of 'distance – seeking' (remember Magilligan Strand) anapaestic, *rocking* rhythm that draws upon the Greek and Latin hexameter and English and Anglo-Irish balladry. It's as if this rhythm impulsively moves forward on the intuition that discovery is out there in the distance if the momentum is sustained. It is more securely based in the feel, texture, and multiplicity of language than the harsh daring, acrobatics, and incantations of Yeats's middle and later styles. MacNeice's style is utterly unferocious; the thrills are there, but they emerge slowly, surprising one in their amazing strangeness, when, to begin with, all seemed fairly well composed. Take 'The Cyclist', where the meaning is entirely contained within the experience, which the poem completely – perfectly, I would say – articulates. It recalls five minutes of freewheeling down a hill past the chalk horse in the Downs near Marlborough, the school he attended. The central idea is that the experience of freewheeling is like poetry itself, an intense realization of the total variousness of being, a realization bracketed by and a part of the ordinariness around it:

> Freewheeling down the escarpment past the unpassing horse
> Blazoned in chalk the wind he causes in passing
> Cools the sweat of his neck, making him one with the sky,
> In the heat of the handlebars he grasps the summer
> Being a boy and to-day a parenthesis
> Between the horizon's brackets; the main sentence

Waits to be picked up later but these five minutes
Are all to-day and summer. The dragonfly
Rises without take-off, horizontal,
Underlining itself in a sliver of peacock light.

And glaring, glaring white
The horse on the down moves within his brackets,
The grass boils with grasshoppers, a pebble
Scutters from under the wheel and all this country
Is spattered white with boys riding their heat-wave,
Feet on a narrow plank and hair thrown back

And a surf of dust beneath them. Summer, summer –
They chase it with butterfly nets or strike it into the deep
In a little red ball or gulp it lathered with cream
Or drink it through closed eyelids; until the bell
Left-right-left gives his forgotten sentence
And reaching the valley the boy must pedal again
Left-right-left but meanwhile
For ten seconds more can move as the horse in the chalk
Moves unbeginningly calmly
Calmly regardless of tenses and final clauses
Calmly unendingly moves.

(*CP* 229–30)

This is MacNeice at his best – the verse crammed with life, the rhythm reaching out, searching variousness, the moment completely there, bracketed within the poem, as life is bracketed between one silence and another, as the horse on the downs is bracketed in the parenthesis of time.

There is a brilliant passage in MacNeice's study of Yeats in which he describes Yeats's attitude to history as one of 'cosmic pride', which is, says MacNeice, 'common among artists'. The artist is proud to be in the world, and to be able to shape its materials or work upon them with thought or language or sound, but the artist also is 'enraged' (MacNeice's word) to know that he is such a small part of it. This takes him to a consideration of the geometry of *A Vision*, which he characterizes as a view of history seen

as an enormous kaleidoscope where each man in the changing but recurring patterns can play all the different rôles: only there must be no fusion, the pattern is always pattern.[11]

In so far as I understand this, what MacNeice seems to be saying is that for Yeats all art is indeed a wearing of a mask, through which the basic patterns (or mathematics as I've called them elsewhere) of being come through. Poetry is a mediumistic activity to release those inner selves which have their authority by virtue of their conflict with one another. Hence Yeatsian drama, with its impersonality, its mythological dimension, its deliberate evocation of atavistic powers (as in *Cathleen ni Houlihan*), its hatred of placid realism, and the centrality of those moments when a character is invaded by a passion, mood, or energy from another life, or some past life. This theatrical method derives from the same concept of personality or character that informs the poetry: that is that what isolates the self, and gives it distinctiveness, is its capacity to be possessed, animated, and yet retain control. Then the words 'can accomplish fate'. ('Under Ben Bulben')

Again the thinking is shamanistic and magical, and although Yeats used it to develop an oracular and hieratic quality of voice and pronouncement, it is part and parcel of international folk belief that humans can be invaded by forces that can take them over. Time after time he returns, in his writings on folklore, to stories, gathered in Sligo, Galway, and Clare, of the 'others' waiting for an opportunity to gain access to this world through a weakness of personality, or a propensity to extreme emotions of rage, love, or jealousy.

MacNeice's theatre, on the other hand, and of course his poetry, is much more 'normal', if we can use the word in such a way as to divest it of all pejorative associations. His theatre and all his writing is concerned with the pity, sadness and valour of ordinary people, the elements that go to make up 'normal' experience. Even *The Mad Islands*, his version of the early Irish *Imraim Curaig Maile Duin, The Voyage of Maeldun*, uses the various strange encounters Muldoon has on his sea-quest of revenge to separate out normal human experience into distinct components. At the end, when the seal-woman who has been his guide and protector swims off into the vast ocean with her partner because 'human beings are too difficult', all the strangeness of the sea, and the pity of human life in our separateness from nature is encapsulated in the lovely line that Muldoon speaks over the sound of the waves:

Two round heads swimming away.[12]

MacNeice is most strenuously exercised by the pity of things; Yeats not really. MacNeice's comment on this matter is again most telling:

... for Yeats, as for Hegel, apparent frustration and failure are part of the eternal process and, if seen from outside – from some eternal auditorium – purposive. ... The pity of it, of course, is that the frustrated and the men who fail cannot themselves see the logic – or the harmony – of their own misfortunes. But neither Yeats nor Hegel was much worried by pity.[13]

I think MacNeice was. This pity, or empathy, or outgoing of the active virtue of charity – love – is what motivates MacNeice's engagements in and with things and people. It animates his rhythm and gives it a moral exactness and force. His Hiberno-English balladic hexameter probings reach out towards the mysteriousness inherent in others, things, nature, but, most of all women, making him, in my view, one of the finest love poets in the Irish tradition. In 'Déjà Vu' his beloved is sitting opposite him in a train; she scratches her elbow, and suddenly the poetry re-enacts an experience of 'falling awake', which unites the immersion in the moment, there and then, in that particular place, with a feeling that this has all happened before, that what happened once is occurring again, and that at some future time, aeons distant, this miracle of recognition will happen once more. Notice the rhythm, a beautiful Hibernian rhythm which is visited, in ghostly fashion, by Homer, Virgil, the ballads, and the sound of the train itself floating through time, but also thundering over real metal rails. As John Ennis has said, describing poetry, it is 'Plato's ghost and heavy metal':[14]

> It does not come round in hundreds of thousands of years,
> It comes round in the split of a wink, you will be sitting exactly
> Where you are now and scratching your elbow, the train
> Will be passing exactly as now and saying It does not come round,
> It does not come round, It does not come round, and compactly
> The wheels will mark time on the rails and the bird in the air
> Sit tight in its box and the same bean of coffee be ground
> That is now in the mill and I know what you're going to say
> For all this has happened before, we both have been through the
>   mill,
> Through our Magnus Annus, and now could all but call it a day
> Were it not that scratching your elbow you are too lovely by half
> So that, whatever the rules we might be supposed to obey,
> Our love must extend beyond time because time is itself in arrears
> So this double vision must pass and past and future unite
> And where we were told to kowtow we can snap our fingers and
>   laugh

And now, as you watch, I will take this selfsame pencil and write:
It does not come round in hundreds of thousands of years.

(CP 517)

The MacNeice 'turn' may be summed up in an extract from 'Flowers in the Interval', in which he celebrates his lover as part of the world, which he reveres for itself, and also because she is in it. The opening phrase packs all this meaning in:

But to turn in on the world, you are all the places
That I have been in with you, blacked-out London,
Polperro's blue braided with gulls or Nephin
Striding beside us always on the right
While we were trudging west, you are the Tessin
Fuddled with oleanders … you are the miles
On miles of silence down Magilligan Strand …

(CP 322)

'To turn in on the world', MacNeice; 'I hail the superhuman', Yeats.

In his night-seminar Stuart calmly and deliberately outlined the inevitability of Yeats's vision of life as continual conflict, given the need for the imagination always to triumph over circumstances, which are always antithetical to the self as it seeks to secure itself and become whole. MacNeice knew much less clearly where he stood. He remains 'Fuddled with oleanders', ready to be baffled, heading for the grave, trying to be normal, to be decent, to be a man.

MACNEICE AND THE PURITAN TRADITION

TERENCE BROWN

In 1935 MacNeice in his essay 'Poetry Today' declared that 'Whatever the "true function" of poetry is, there is something idolatrous or fetishistic about our pleasure in it'.[1] It was a daring admission in a decade when poetry was widely reckoned only admissible if it served some obviously ethical function. MacNeice in contrast to the prevailing political puritanism of the period was unwilling to deny that poetry gives pleasure and he knew that this fact to the puritan mind must seem a kind of idolatry, a worshipping of a false god, the making of a fetish of something insignificant and unworthy. But for MacNeice the matter is, in the end, quite simple: 'poetry *qua* poetry is an end and not a means; its relations to "life" are impossible to define; even when it is professedly "didactic", "propagandist" or "satirical" the external purport is, ultimately, only a conventional property, a kind of perspective which many poets like to think of as essential'.[2]

MacNeice in his twenties and early thirties, when he wrote his most searching essays on the rôle of poetry in such articles as the one quoted above, 'Subject in Modern Poetry' and in his book *Modern Poetry: a Personal Essay* was well-equipped to resist all those who would have made poetry subject to ethics or even to political necessity. For as an Ulsterman he well understood that the impulse of the puritan sensibility is to suspect art and the pleasure it affords. And the poet who had escaped the utilitarian 'Attempts at buyable beauty' of Belfast (excoriated in the poem of that name) was unlikely to submit to any dogma which would have reduced poetry to a merely functional activity in the service of ideology. In his recollective account of his youth, 'When I Was Twenty-One', published in 1961, he recalled a need felt in his early manhood to 'escape from the puritanism and mud of my Ulster surroundings to the honey-coloured finials and gilded understatements of Oxford'.³ This polarity between a puritanical Ulster and the escapist attractions of sensuous immediacy governs almost all of MacNeice's autobiographical prose writings about his childhood, even if as in *Zoo* he remembers to submit a recantation:

A harassed and dubious childhood under the hand of a well-meaning but barbarous mother's help from County Armagh led me to think of the North of Ireland as prison and the South as a land of escape. Many nightmares, boxes on the ears, a rasping voice of disapproval, a monotonous daily walk to a crossroads called Mile Bush, sodden haycocks, fear of hell-fire, my father's indigestion – these things, with on the other side my father's Home Rule sympathies and the music of his brogue, bred in me an almost fanatical hatred for Ulster. When I went to bed as a child I was told: 'You don't know where you'll wake up'. When I ran in the garden I was told that running was bad for the heart. Everything had its sinister aspect – milk shrinks the stomach, lemon thins the blood. Against my will I was always given sugar in my tea. The North was tyranny.⁴

What stimulates MacNeice to second thoughts about Ulster in this extract from *Zoo* is a weekend in Belfast which 'was all sunshine'. 'I could not', admits MacNeice, 'remember Belfast like this, and the continuous sunshine delighted but outraged me. My conception of Belfast, built up since early childhood, demanded that it should always be grey, wet, and repellent and its inhabitants dour, rude and callous'.⁵ That delight in the unexpected sunshine in the city alerts us to a characteristic of MacNeice's sensibility – its instinctive relish for the pleasure of sensory experience set against the rigours of a puritan sense of life. It is almost as if the memory of Belfast which the poet carried with him is the energising spring which releases a new vision of the place he had hitherto only known under the guise of tyranny. So where he had recently written of

> ... the end of the melancholy lough
> Against the lurid sky over the stained water
> Where hammers clang murderously on the girders
> Like crucifixes the gantries stand⁶

now he evokes Belfast Lough in a passage of delighted sensuous zest:

As we went faster, crinkling the water a little, the reflections squirmed like tadpoles, the double reflections from the sheds regularly and quietly somersaulting. Two cranes facing each other conferred darkly. In the widening channel the lines of reflected lights behind us stretched in uncertain alleys like the line of floating corks set out for swimmers. A black motor-boat cutting across them threw out shooting stars behind it. A buoy skated rapidly backwards winking periodically red. Then the cranes and quays fell away and the channel opened into the lough – a single line of lights on each side – like a man stretching his arms and drawing a breath. Cassiopeia was tilted in her deck-chair over Antrim; Arcturus over Down.[7]

It is impossible, in this little prose poem of dark and light, not to open to the images of pleasurable expansion and enlargement of vision which it exploits. The relish of the occasion is physical, somatic, sensuous. Note 'squirmed', 'somersaulting', 'stretched', 'swimmers', 'skated', 'winking', 'drawing breath'.

It is in those terrible two-and-half pages which are given as section seven of *The Strings Are False* (MacNeice's unfinished autobiography) that this juxtaposition between what the poet, at the head of the immediately succeeding section, calls 'puritan repression' and sensuous delight, is most deliberately represented in MacNeice's work. There we are told of the death of Louis's mother, of the dark night-terrors which followed as his father mourned his wife, of the boy's guilt and the steady encroachment of religion. Set against such a backdrop of gloom and shadow, the sensory brilliance of the visible world is in recollection surprisingly vital:

That Christmas we got a great many presents; they were marshalled on the nursery hearthrug by the crackling of the early morning fire. Everything was gay with colour, there were coloured chalks and coloured wooden rattles and striped tin trumpets and tangerines in silver paper, and a copy of the *Arabian Nights* with princesses in curly shoes and blue-black hair.[8]

And MacNeice was always to be responsive to a world of surprising sensation that must be rendered in terms of a strongly verbal lexicon. The 'crackling' fire of this passage finds frequent echo in the poetry as in the grass which 'boils with grasshoppers' (*CP* 230) in 'The Cyclist' or 'the rumpled/ Tigers of the bogland streams' which 'Prowl and plunge through glooms and gleams' (*CP* 446) in Poem I of 'Donegal Triptych', or the coffee which 'leaps in a crystal knob/ Chugs and glints while birds gossip' (*CP* 488) in 'Country Week-end'. But what of course this passage most precisely brings to mind, with its tangerine and evocation of the exotic range of epicurean possibility, is one of MacNeice's most remarkable poems, the sensationally intense *aperçu* 'Snow', with its snow, pink roses, fire, and tangerine. The poem as a celebration of the pleasures of perception and of the senses which make that possible, is the delighted response of a poet who knows such things arrive of a sudden, excess given added spice by our customary expectation of altogether less. For the poem expresses pleasure unburdened by guilt, is even perhaps self-consciously ostentatious about so doing, but is also, in its insistent comparative tone, aware how freakish (only after a snowfall, when snow and roses are collateral?) is the possibility of such drunken zest:

> The room was suddenly rich and the great bay-window was
> Spawning snow and pink roses against it
> Soundlessly collateral and incompatible:
> World is suddener than we fancy it.
>
> World is crazier and more of it than we think,
> Incorrigibly plural. I peel and portion
> A tangerine and spit the pips and feel
> The drunkenness of things being various.
>
> And the fire flames with a bubbling sound for world
> Is more spiteful and gay than one supposes –
> On the tongue on the eyes on the ears in the palms of one's hands –
> There is more than glass between the snow and the huge roses.
>
> (CP 30)

MacNeice is in fact a considerable poet of pleasure. He is certainly no mere hedonist, but he unabashedly relishes the gifts of sight, sound, texture, smell and taste as they make life livable. He is especially exhilarated by the effects of sunshine on water ('The dazzle on the sea' (*CP* 86), the mayfly's 'dance above the dazzling wave' (*CP* 14)) but he is attentive too to moments of bodily sensation and sexual impulse. In 'The Stygian Banks' for example he remembers how 'Munching salad/ Your child can taste the colour itself – the green –/ And the colour of radish –the red'. (*CP* 264) In Poem I of 'Trilogy for X' images of wind and of trains evoke a powerful, intimate physical passion:

> But now when winds are curling
>   The trees do you come closer,
> Close as an eyelid fasten

> My body in darkness, darling;
> Switch the light off and let me
> Gather you up and gather
> The power of trains advancing
> Further, advancing further.

> *(CP 89)*

Nor does MacNeice neglect the lesser pleasures of drink, bawdy talk, gossip, habitual satisfactions – what he identifies in his late poem 'Memoranda to Horace' as 'the tangles'. (*CP* 542) Few twentieth century poets could have written with such enthusiasm of sociability, with booze and crack:

> In the road is another smile on the face of day.
> We stop at random for a morning drink
> In a thatched inn; to find, as at a play,

> The bar already loud with chatter and clink
> Of glasses, not so random; no one here
> But was a friend of Gwilym's. One could think

> That all these shots of whisky, pints of beer,
> Make one Pactolus turning words to gold
> In honour of one golden mouth, in sheer

> Rebuttal of the silence and the cold
> Attached to death ...

> *(CP 412)*

Few others could have responded with such vital pleasure to a glass of water on a wiltingly hot day: 'tower of liquid light ... / Which the sun coins and cool from ice/ It spears the throat like an ice-cold sun'. ('Our Sister Water'). (*CP* 301)

MacNeice in his poetry is constantly alert to the palpable givenness of the material world in which he takes such pleasure. He is a poet for whom things exist undeniably distinct from the poet's designs upon them – beautiful, attractive, desirable, pleasure-giving in their own right. In 'Train to Dublin' he salutes 'the incidental things which pass/ Outward through space exactly as each was' (*CP* 28) and his poetry is rich in the quiddity of a world of such inscapes. It was indeed a capacity for responding to things as well as people that MacNeice admired in his friend Graham Shepard of whom he wrote in his fine elegy 'The Casualty': 'For above all that was your gift – to be/ Surprised and therefore sympathetic, warm/ Towards things as well as people' (*CP* 247); the poem accordingly evokes the dead man in a proliferation of brilliant and precise visual as well as emotional epiphanies –' here the Wiltshire sleet/ Riddles your football jersey – here the sack/ Of night pours down on you Provençal stars'. (*CP* 247)

MacNeice the Ulsterman in flight from a grim Puritanism found in the material world a pleasure that he allowed to inform his art. Of course he knew that poetry had to be more than a celebration of sensuous experience. But reading Hopkins' *Note-Books and Papers* in 1937 he noted that poet's 'voracity for objects'[9] and observed: 'his zeal in recording the visions of his bodily eye I find extremely refreshing and salutary'.[10] He found it so in a period when what he identified as a 'ruthless puritanism' had tended to make 'the human subject ... of supreme importance'.[11] MacNeice reflects plaintively of this situation: 'We might remember ... that man is a [living animal] as well as [citizen] and that quite a number of people have an organic sympathy with trees, mountains, flowers, or with a painting by Chardin'.[12]

Yet for all his willingness to admit pleasure to his poetry and to acknowledge that pleasure is certainly an aspect of poetry's attraction for us, MacNeice knew that art for pleasure's sake is as unproductive an aesthetic as *l'art pour l'art*. He shared his generation's suspicion of mere aestheticism. In 1936 he advised: 'Art for Art's Sake has been some time foundering. A masthead or two even now show above the water ... but on the whole, poets have ceased showing themselves off as mere poets. They have better things to do; they are writing *about* things again'.[13] And he evinced a distaste for a poetry that is all sensuous beauty and the indulgence of a life of sensation rather than thought in a remarkably grudging introduction he published to a selection of Keats's poetry in 1941. The times of course were urgent and furthermore MacNeice had been at work on his study of W.B. Yeats, published in the same year, so some of the elder poet's antagonism to Keats may have rubbed off on him. He does in fact argue that had Keats lived he might, like Yeats, have become less 'poetic'. Be that as it may, in a volume which includes C.S. Lewis on Spenser, Tillyard on Milton and Auden on Byron, all sympathetic advocates of their writers, MacNeice takes Keats on what he regards as his own terms as 'an adolescent writing for adolescents'.[14] Keats's poetry draws from MacNeice the judgement that 'there is no such thing as a merely sensuous poet'[15] and an acknowledgement that even Keats was more complex than his most self-indulgent lines would suggest. He was, admits

MacNeice, a 'mystic through the medium of the senses'.[16] MacNeice insists, 'few major poets, however, have lived by mysticism – or by the senses – alone'.[17]

MacNeice's curiously 'puritan' estimate of Keats may, I would like to argue, originate in more than his reading of Yeats or the exigencies of the hour in war-time London. For he himself, as he certainly knew when he penned his essay on Keats, had a good deal of the 'sensuous mystic' (his own term for Keats) in him. The man who in 1957 would write

We cannot of course live by Keats's Negative Sensibility alone, we must all in E.M. Forster's phrase, use 'telegrams and anger'; all the same what I feel makes life worth living is not the clever scores but the surrenders – it may be to the life-quickening urge of an air-raid, to nonsense talked by one's friends, to a girl on top of the Empire State building, to the silence of a ruined Byzantine church, to woods, or weirs, or to heat dancing on a gravelled path, to music, drink, or the smell of turf smoke, to the first view of the Atlantic or to the curve of a strand which seems to stretch to nowhere or everywhere and to ages before and after the combustion engine which defiled it[18]

was one who in 1940 had insisted in the preface to his study of Yeats, dated September, 1940, 'The faith in the *value* of living is a mystical faith. The pleasure in bathing or dancing, in colour or shape, is a mystical experience'.[19] MacNeice, I think knew there was a Keatsian sensuous mysticism in his own attitude to life. He knew that his own first volume, *Blind Fireworks*, could be accused of sensuous excess and that he, as he puts it in 'Dedicatory Poem to *Collected Poems, 1925–48*', published in 1949, had been at one time 'content if things would image/ Themselves in their own dazzle'.[20] Indeed one of the prevailing excitements of MacNeice's poetry and prose throughout his career is the way it can suggest consciousness being roused to pleasure by the world of material objects as they swim, unbidden, into awareness. This is 'Morning Sun' from March, 1935:

> Yellow sun comes white off the wet streets but bright
> Chromium yellows in the gay sun's light,
> Filleted sun streaks the purple mist,
> Everything is kissed and reticulated with sun
> Scooped-up and cupped in the open fronts of shops
> And bouncing on the traffic which never stops.

                                                              (CP 26)

This is 'Country Week-end' from the late 1950s:

Wild grass in spate in a rainy wind,
We have come from London to stay indoors
With paraffin on our hands, our eyes
Watching through glass the trees blown east.

As if hypnotised, as if this wet
Day were the sum and essence of days
When such spinning shafts of steely water
Struck to numb, or revive, the mind.

(*CP* 490)

What inhibits the mystical streak in MacNeice and his epicurean delight in pleasure is his social awareness and commitment to communitarian social values. In his introduction to Keats's poetry he cites that poet's famous assertion that 'A Poet is the most unpoetical of anything in existence, because he has no identity' only to comment:

That a poet has no identity is a useful half-truth, for it counteracts the common opinion that a poet is someone hawking his own personality. Many poets, however, have had an identity as spokesman for a congenial community or for a tradition that was still functioning.[21]

This is entirely of a piece with the MacNeice of the final section of 'Autumn Journal' who, in the face of the collapse of the Republican Government in Spain, the betrayal of the Czech Republic and impending war against Hitler, dreams of and prays for

a possible land
Not of sleep-walkers, not of angry puppets,
But where both heart and brain can understand
The movements of our fellows;
Where life is a choice of instruments and none
Is debarred his natural music …

(*CP* 152)

It is a collective Utopia that the poet envisages, anti-capitalist:

Where nobody sees the use
Of buying money and blood at the cost of blood and money,
Where the individual, no longer squandered
In self-assertion, works with the rest …

One senses that it is such a community that MacNeice as poet wished himself to serve as spokesman, when he considered how Keats was bereft both of community and tradition.

There has been a marked tendency for MacNeice's critics, and I include myself among their number, to underestimate his political and social commitments. Anxious to exonerate him from the charge that he worshipped with his naive generation the god which failed, MacNeice's critics have too readily identified his view-of-life with an unexceptionable liberal humanism, or just haven't bothered to examine what his poetry is about – even when MacNeice's own essays tell us that poetry is always about something. Perhaps fifteen years of Tory government in the United Kingdom and the depredations of Thatcherism, which MacNeice would have found appalling, now allow us to read him as a much more political poet than when he was reckoned by his contemporaries merely the voice of a conventional set of left-of-centre social opinions.

MacNeice it must be remembered, although no Marxist, stated of his politics in 1942: 'distrust all parties but consider capitalism must go ... Would normally vote Labour in England, but think the Labour Party won't get anywhere till they have got rid of their reactionary leaders'.[22] In 1955, updating this biographical entry, which appears in a dictionary of modern literature, MacNeice was not moved to amend his earlier statement. Through his poetry and prose writings in the 1930s, although he is watchfully suspicious of the political nostrums of the comrades, there is a concern to address the social issues of the day – unemployment, human degradation in an industrial society, the challenge of fascism. What stirs him is the idea of community as he seeks to break out of the privileged cocoon his background and education have spun for him. It must be noted of MacNeice's work in general that he is one of those modern poets who do not scorn or patronise common life. This is a poet who can write a tender elegy for Florrie Forde (a music hall songster), can salute the quotidian satisfactions of pub games, sport, the world of domesticity, 'routine work, money-making or scholarship' (*CP* 76), cliché, small talk, the potency of cheap music, those songs that come to us 'off the peg' and 'made to measure' (*CP* 545) and can affectionately recall the lives of an illiterate gardener, an elusive, forgetful godfather and bear testimony to the quiet dignity of the men and women of unsung integrity who comprise, what he calls in one poem, 'The Kingdom':

> Under the surface of flux and of fear there is an underground
>   movement
> Under the crust of bureaucracy, quiet behind the posters,

Unconscious but palpably there – the Kingdom of individuals.

(*CP* 248)

His relish for the pleasures of life is tempered too by an awareness that much which makes life agreeable for the few in the modern world, luxury and comfort, is bought at the expense of the poor:

> We slept in linen, we cooked with wine,
>   We paid in cash and took no notice
> Of how the train ran down the line
>   Into the sun against the signal.
> We lived in Birmingham through the slump –
>   Line your boots with a piece of paper –
> Sunlight dancing on the rubbish dump,
>   On the queues of men and the hungry chimneys.

(*CP* 115)

In fact MacNeice's impulse to delight in the presence of objects, things, sensations, to relish common life, co-exists with a slowly intensifying distaste for mass-production. More and more in the post-war period (as the consumer society replaced the austerity of the war economy and the welfarism of socialist reconstruction under Labour), he becomes assailed by a sense of meaning, vitality, being drained from things as they proliferate in the endless repetitive availability which is the motor of modern commerce. The alienation that he expressed with increasing bitterness as he grew older may have its sources in psychological, religious and metaphysical anxieties but its significant social content must not be disregarded. This is a poet (the poet of 'Snow') who deprecates a world of 'Roses with the scent bred out,/ In lieu of which is a long name on a label'. (*CP* 522) In place of community has emerged a voracious capitalism which has made of citizens consumers of unreality, addicts of false consciousness. In 'New Jerusalem' from 1962 he advises in sardonic anger:

> Bulldoze all memories and sanctuaries: our birthright
> Means a new city, vertical, impersonal,
> Whose horoscope claimed a straight resurrection
> Should Stimulant stand in conjunction with Sleeping Pill.
>
> As for the citizens, what with their cabinets
> Of faces and voices, their bags of music,
> Their walls of thin ice dividing greynesses,
> With numbers and mirrors they defy mortality.

(*CP* 529)

MacNeice's late poetry is in fact a poetry of pained revulsion at what modernity has done to the human potential of ordinary life. In this respect his work represents a striking break with the ethos of the literary Modernism which as a young man he could not have failed to have encountered as the definitive response to the century's modernity. Indeed MacNeice himself admitted in the 1930s that 'the history of post-War poetry in England is the history of Eliot and the reaction from Eliot'.[23] It is a testament to the imaginative and ethical strength of MacNeice as an artist that his own poetry is an impressive re-orientating of English poetry's fundamental concerns in the common life of a community rather than in the high culture, under threat from modernity, which was the source of so much Modernist imagining and anguish.

However, MacNeice was not a man to wear his beliefs on his sleeve. In 1953 he did respond nevertheless to a request by Ed. Murrow to answer the question 'What do I believe?'. In this brief statement he insists that belief is a matter of values and is always belief in something. But he is at pains to insist that this is not merely a matter of individual whim. His sense of life is ineradicably communitarian:

Apart from the fact that, whether we want to or not, we have to live in communities, I think that human individuals are much more like each other than they are unlike each other. One may live on bread and another may live on meat but they all feel hunger when they're hungry. And on a much higher plane than that of hunger I think that all human beings have a hankering for pattern and order; look at any child with a box of chalks. There are of course evil patterns or orders – which perhaps is the great problem of our time. What I do believe is that as a human being, it is my duty to make patterns and to contribute to order – good patterns and a good order. And when I say duty I mean duty; I think it is the turn of enjoyment, I believe that life is worth while *and* I believe that I have to do something *for* life.[24]

Notable here is the democracy of feeling, the lack of élitism, the recognition of duty and the relish for living. For this is a poet who values pleasure but who also wishes to live in a community for which he feels an obligation.

For MacNeice of course the question of community loomed ambiguously because of his nationality. I have written elsewhere of his complex relationship as an Irishman with both Irish communities north and south of the border and of his early interest in islands as metaphors of possible modes of community which might offer an alternative way of thinking about human order in an era of transnational capitalism.[25] What must however be said is that MacNeice only sporadically felt truly a part of any community and that when he did it was an English one. Much of the best recent criticism of MacNeice, and its authors are with us today, has been somewhat Hiberno-centred. And MacNeice's influence has been marked in contemporary Irish poetry. I sense that as a result the English MacNeice has been rather neglected. I am thinking in this respect of the poet who experienced an English classical education and whose literary formation and preoccupations throughout his life were predominantly English.

The exact nature of MacNeice's classicism is, I hasten to add, as complex as his relationship with Ireland and intriguingly has its Irish aspect, not least through his friendship with E.R. Dodds. For MacNeice the classical world represented a literary resource that offered models of artistic integrity in evil times (Horace, whom he translated skilfully, on his Sabine farm was his imaginary confederate). He rejected the malign symbiosis of English classicism and imperial service (he was sufficiently concerned about the matter, we note, to include in his autobiographical entry to the dictionary of modern literature, cited above, the statement: 'Think the present English system of teaching the classics is bad').[26] He provided an acute diagnosis in *Autumn Journal* of a syndrome which combined a classical education with an élitist assumption of the English right to govern – 'the classical student is bred to the purple'.(*CP* 126) But he made his knowledge of classical and English prosody the basis of some of his own metrical proficiency (strikingly evident in *Autumn Journal*), giving to modern English verse a tone of lucid, conversational communicability, which enabled him to forge an instrument of precise, sane, communal immediacy, colloquial and colourfully direct, urbane and elegant by turns. It was a tone admirably suited to broadcasting in the period when the B.B.C. under the influence of Lord Reith took its public service duties completely seriously.

Radio in the war years and in their aftermath offered MacNeice (he was employed by the B.B.C. from 1941 until his death in 1963, restricting himself almost entirely to radio) the opportunity to work in a small community of creative people who hoped they might make a contribution to the cultural life of the general community. This was the period when the radio feature and the radio play were in the process of development and MacNeice became an accomplished practitioner in both forms. What characterised his radio work, I believe, was a capacity to deal in serious, even 'highbrow', matter, without patronising a popular audience. One senses, in his plays and features, that MacNeice knew the people for whom he was writing and could address his predominantly English, adequately-educated, middle-class constituency in precisely the tones and emotional timbre they would find congenial.

In the period MacNeice was at work in the B.B.C., English public discourse, it must be remembered, was undergoing significant changes. To listen now to the speeches of politicians in the radio archives, to read their parliamentary effusions, to watch Pathe News films, is to be reminded that the English élite, in church and state, addressed the commonality in the 1940s in a language of high-flown sentence, grandiloquent fustian, and mannered reserve. Churchillian *rodomontade* was only possible because of the generally rhetorical verbal climate. By the early 1960s and the television age such public discourse had come to seem impossibly pompous, bullying and ridiculously complacent. The Goons and Monty Python put paid to it. By contrast MacNeice as broadcaster employed a version of plain style, supple, judicious, not without its own colour and energy, its metaphorical suasions. In so doing he helped to make available a tone and a mode of address that might be termed the house-style of the B.B.C. in its hey-day, a style remote from the imperial rumble of establishment authoritarianism or the crass *Sunese* of the contemporary sound-bite.

It was a style which increasingly came to prominence in MacNeice's own post-war poetry, in such pieces as 'Beni Hasan' (1955), or 'Figure of Eight' (1956) or 'Selva Oscura' (c. 1960). Cool, intelligent, elliptical, it disguises deep feeling in syntactical finesse. It assumes it will find a readership in a community of equally thoughtful individuals:

> A life can be haunted by what it never was
> If that were merely glimpsed. Lost in the maze
> That means yourself and never out of the wood
> These days, though lost, will be all your days;
> Life, if you leave it, must be left for good.

(CP 512)

Among the sources for this communitarian style are the poets and prose writers of what might be termed an English puritan tradition. I mean poets such as Spenser and Herbert (both poets with beliefs, something to say, a message to communicate), whom MacNeice greatly admired; the tradition would also include the morality play *Everyman* (MacNeice noted its 'spare and undecorated and sometimes colloquial'[27] style) and the Bunyan of *Pilgrim's Progress*, whose plain-style quest romance with its double-level significance so influenced MacNeice's own remarkable parable, the radio play *The Dark Tower* (1946).

In writing in this way MacNeice was engaging with a mode of English feeling and self-understanding which has its distinctively democratic aspects. MacNeice himself observed: '*Everyman*, like *Pilgrim's Progress* later, came from the people and was addressed to them'.[28] He was identifying too, in his frequent employment of quest motifs in poetry and drama, with a still potent English tradition which, from Langland and Malory onwards, had seen, in a myth of quest, an image of life lived purposefully and self-forgettingly. It was a way of feeling, English and communal, that found expression for example in the music of Vaughan Williams whose *Fantasia on a Theme of Thomas Tallis* (1910) had been adapted by the composer for a stirring wartime radio version of Bunyan's famous work. Williams had always associated his own composition with *Pilgrim's Progress* (like MacNeice he was also an admirer of George Herbert) and had welcomed the opportunity to blend his music with Bunyan's prose at a time of profound English national crisis. MacNeice must surely have had this important collaboration in mind, and have been aware of working in a specific tradition, when his own quest play, *The Dark Tower*, was given an added 'dimension'[29] by the music of that other composer of the English musical renaissance in the twentieth century, Benjamin Britten.

So the MacNeice who adapted the English classical tradition in which he had been trained to his own egalitarian, communitarian purposes, as a communicator also built on an English style and exploited an essentially puritan English tradition of writing and imagining to give his beliefs a valency in the public sphere of post-war British life. The resulting work and achievement were admirably consistent with the political and social commitments which MacNeice made as a man who believed, for all his valuing of sensory pleasure, that he was obligated to do something '*for* life'.[30]

'WITH EYES TURNED DOWN ON THE PAST': MACNEICE'S CLASSICISM

PETER McDONALD

In a short comment on *The Burning Perch* submitted to the *Poetry Book Society Bulletin* a week before his death, Louis MacNeice noted the new book's formal developments from his earlier work – that 'a good third' of the poems there were without rhyme, and that rhythmic change also was underway in the poetry:

[...] I notice that many of the poems here have been trying to get out of the 'iambic' groove which we were all born into. In 'Memoranda to Horace' there is a conscious attempt to suggest Horatian rhythms (in English of course one cannot do more than suggest them) combined with the merest reminiscence of Horatian syntax. This technical Horatianizing appears in some other poems too where, I suppose, it goes with something of a Horatian resignation. But my resignation, as I was not brought up a pagan, is more of a fraud than Horace's: 'Memoranda to Horace' itself, I hope, shows this.[1]

The evocation of Horace here brings with it important reservations; while the Latin poet's name is raised as relevant to the volume's advances in technique, any claims of affinity are severely qualified: against 'technical Horatianizing' MacNeice balances the reminder that 'I was not brought up a pagan'. The poet's proximity to and his distance from a classical model are involved both in matters of technique and content, and this double-sided statement of position is of some importance for reading MacNeice. If, on the one hand, it is easy to recognize in the poet the techniques and resources of a trained reader of Greek and Latin, it is necessary on the other hand to acknowledge that his poetry puts such training to a very severe test and, indeed, almost finds it wanting in the end. In the poems of *The Burning Perch*, the poet Horace in particular is a focus for MacNeice's sceptical engagement with a whole body of knowledge, and habit of mind, which was being put under enormous pressure. In *The Burning Perch*, as I shall argue, this pressure bears on MacNeice's writing in formal and other respects, and has a part to play in the late triumph which that volume represents.

It is a less troubled idea of classicism which features in an early puff for the thirty-two year old MacNeice provided for a New York audience in 1939 by W.H. Auden. This brief introduction is worth quoting in full:

Mr. Louis MacNeice is an Irishman with a classical education. Ireland gave him a love of the gracefully individual, the odd amusing detail, the disorderly charming; Latin and Greek a linguistic discipline and a distrust of vagueness in expression.

This marriage of a wayward anarchist nature to a precise technique has been happy; his nature prevents him from becoming academic and pedantic, his technique from romantic excess.

He is perhaps the only poet today whose work is directly in the classical tradition. Both as a person and as an artist, the first descriptive adjective he suggests to one is 'Elegant,' and the first writer of whom one is reminded is Horace (from whom he has made some beautiful translations). The one Horatian quality he lacks is content, but, in view of the world we live in, that lack is a positive virtue.[2]

Does Auden mean 'content', as in the matter of his poetry, or 'content', a maintained state of contentment with things as they are? Perhaps the ambiguity is of little importance, since for Auden (it seems) Horace's content is one which, however it is to be judged in the world of Augustus, would have been culpable in 1939: Horace's content, in this sense, was a form of contentedness. MacNeice's 'elegance', on the other hand, is being presented by Auden as a style with contemporary meaning, verbal control and 'linguistic discipline' with a point. Auden's identification of classicism with 'precise technique' does help to clarify the way in which MacNeice's 1930s poetry related to other writing at the time, and the ways in which this cultivation of precision itself related to a content of dis- or un-content (as it were) in his poetry.

Another element to which Auden draws attention is MacNeice's Irishness, something which seems to pull in another, unclassical direction, that of the 'disorderly charming' and 'wayward anarchist' in the poet. Two years earlier, in a radio talk later printed in *The Listener*, MacNeice had himself brought Irishness to bear against classicism – or at least Hellenism – while reminding his audience that 'All of us seem vulgar to someone':

It isn't surprising that the Greeks – who never stopped saying one ought to know where to stop – had a word for vulgarity. For my own part, though my job is lecturing about the Greeks, I have two traditions behind me which encourage me to rush into very un-Greek extremes or excesses. First of all, I am an Irishman, and the Irish are notorious for not knowing where to stop, either in conversation or in action. (By the way, many of the Irish think the English vulgar, and vice versa.) Secondly, I am a writer in the English language, and English literature is notorious for its lack of classical shape, its uncontrolled irrelevances.[3]

It may be that the 'wayward anarchist' in MacNeice is speaking here, and certainly the lighthearted talk attempts to play fast and loose with generalizations and stereotypes which, in other contexts, might be much more problematic. Even so, it is interesting to see MacNeice pitting English literary energies (which are themselves made to seem more Irish than English) against notions of classical measure and moderation. In the 1930s as later, classicism for MacNeice is distinct from the kind of golden mean to be detected in Victorian notions of the classics: Matthew Arnold is far away, and the Graeco-Roman literary world is involved with more complex interactions between 'English' and 'Irish' habits.

The earlier phase of MacNeice's classicism, that of the 'wayward anarchist' playing the Greeks off against the Irish and the English, reaches a climax in *Autumn Journal* (1939). MacNeice's choice of an autobiographical mode in that poem enables him to write at length on his profession as a lecturer, an 'impresario of the ancient Greeks', as well as allowing him to recall the conventionally classical education he received at Marlborough and Oxford. There is little room left in *Autumn Journal* for contentment of any kind, and MacNeice is as strict in his sceptism with regard to Greece and Rome as he is unsparing in his comments on the Munich crisis or Irish politics elsewhere in the poem. In section IX, rejecting the late-Victorian idea of the classics as 'Models of logic and lucidity, dignity, sanity,/ The golden mean between opposing ills', MacNeice sets himself apart from the kind of academic humanist who 'Chops the Ancient World to turn a sermon/ To the greater glory of God':

> But I can do nothing so useful or so simple;
>   These dead are dead
> And when I should remember the paragons of Hellas
>   I think instead

Of the crooks, the adventurers, the opportunists,
   The careless athletes and the fancy boys,
The hair-splitters, the pedants, the hard-boiled sceptics
   And the Agora and the noise
Of the demagogues and the quacks; and the women pouring
   Libations over graves
And the trimmers at Delphi and the dummies at Sparta and lastly
   I think of the slaves.
And how one can imagine oneself among them
   I do not know;
It was all so unimaginably different
   And all so long ago.

                                     (CP 118–119)

MacNeice's disavowal of the utility of his version of Greece should not, perhaps, be taken quite at face value, for the bathos of the conclusion here is not without its point in the scheme of *Autumn Journal* and that poem's particular angle on events in 1938, in a world with no shortage of crooks, opportunists, trimmers or dummies. By taking the shine off 'The Glory that was Greece', MacNeice adds another system of myth and self-indulgent pretence to a collection which includes Ireland and London, Spain and Munich and even the personal life (a failed marriage and a failing love-affair); *Autumn Journal* takes stock of lost illusions, public and private, past and present, and shapes its narrative around the relics which all these things represent at the end of 1938. However important the classics may be within this scheme, the poem itself disavows any 'classical' intention in terms of either form or content; indeed, MacNeice makes a virtue out of his ability to 'run to very un-Greek extremes or excesses', to push things as far as they will go without regard for any acceptably general sense of coherence other than that which time and accident supply. While the verbal 'precision' and tight technical control identified by Auden as classical elements are used constantly in *Autumn Journal*, classical affinities, so comforting to those looking for a secure 'classical tradition' of cosy intertextual dialogue, are made to seem (at best) irrelevant to the poem's immediate business.

   MacNeice had, of course, reserved to himself the right of what he called 'overstatement' in *Autumn Journal*, and the poem is hardly the final word on the poet's classical or other concerns.[4] Nevertheless, it does represent a point in his work at which rejection of the supposed lessons of the ancient world reaches expression. Yet, this disavowal of classicism is not quite the same thing as a disavowal of the poet's *own* kind of classicism; indeed, it is part of a whole system of sceptical and learned reflexes which MacNeice identified, at this stage, as the product (or gift) of his particular kind of education. The result, in *Autumn Journal*, is a voice which is charged with intensity, precision, and authority in accounting for the fear and horror of its immediate contexts; and yet, it is precisely because MacNeice's classically-formed reflexes (as identified by Auden) are serving him so well in *Autumn Journal* that the poetry there does not incorporate and embody fear and horror in the way that the poems of *The Burning Perch* will do more than twenty years later. If technique and content come together in *Autumn Journal* to both work and argue for lucidity, they fuse also in *The Burning Perch* to make lucidity a grim joke. In the process, classical models have been both more completely absorbed and more comprehensively transformed.

It is possible to look at three aspects of MacNeice's changing involvement with classicism separately, though they are not finally distinct: first, the development of what Auden called 'verbal discipline' and 'precise technique' through MacNeice's experience of the form of English lyric; second, the poet's contact through classicism with religious problems; and third, the refraction of classical influences through the medium of private nightmare in the poet's later work. In the light of these things, the entertaining and hard-hitting performance of the young classics don of *Autumn Journal* IX is a beginning for, rather than the consummation of, MacNeice's artistic classicism.

Like any other classically-educated person of his generation, MacNeice's earliest experiences of Greek and Latin involved translation; as a writer, MacNeice both experimented with translation and experimented *in* it, and several translation projects were to play significant rôles in the development of his writing, from the stage-version of Aeschylus' *Agamemnon* in 1936 to radio adaptations of Homer and Horace in the last years of his life. But from an early stage MacNeice treated the translation of ancient poetry as a task to which the more usual idioms of the translator were not on the whole equal, and for which the resources of English lyric would need to be stretched. Reviewing a translation of Aeschylus by Gilbert Murray in 1935, MacNeice insisted on the good effects of literalism in avoiding weak poeticisms in English, recommending that 'a translation should start from the Greek, preferably line for line', then noting that 'A touch of Gerard Manley Hopkins might have helped Professor Murray': 'His Greek original is so real to a scholar like Professor Murray that it is probably never out of his mind, and so he cannot see what the English looks like just as English.'[5] The reference to Hopkins is interesting, for MacNeice was willing to run similar stylistic risks in translation to those taken by Hopkins in his poetry in the hope that this would – like Hopkins's work – be part of a final clearing-away of the late-Victorian legacy of poeticism and mannerism, something which persisted much longer in the world of literary translation than it had in that of contemporary poetry.

In an undated series of notes for a lecture or essay on the classics, which seem to have been written in the 1930s (though it is possible that they date from MacNeice's Oxford years), the poet sets out some principles of translation which suggest ways in which his own practice would develop. Praising Milton's uncompromising innovation, MacNeice commends a degree of unfamiliarity in translation:

What I want to say is that if only translators & paraphrasers & hellenizers had taken Milton's hint they wld not have ruined the Gk choruses & Gk lyric poetry by putting them into pat English metres & slick English rhythms but they would have done something severe & intricate & probably irregular in English to convey what is severe & amazingly intricate in Greek. If you are translating Gk verse into English verse, you must not use any sustained & regular English metre, for the more regular & the more specific a metre it is, the more will it obsess the ear of the hearer & keep out the Gk atmosphere from the mind.[6]

Severity, intricacy, and irregularity are not in any simple sense translatable values in poetry, as MacNeice acknowledges, but they are incompatible with 'slick English rhythms', and the beginnings of an ambition to escape from the 'iambic groove' are perhaps visible here. For MacNeice, the ancient original must be almost a disruptive presence in the stylistic formation of an English version, and again literalism will be necessary in conveying the force of this linguistic otherness:

I don't know that I believe in paraphrasing. That may give a good poem but it may only be an English poem. The method I shd adopt myself wld be to try translating line for line (& if poss word for word) as literally as possible (1stly) with the merely negative object of avoiding all grossnesses which will distract the reader & (2ndly) with the object of imposing rhythm on the words you are left with. It doesn't matter if the order of the words is odd; it will give the reader to think & will not lull him asleep by reminding him of Herrick.

This sounds like fairly rough-and-ready advice; but its apparent crudity is belied by the kinds of results MacNeice was capable of achieving in, for example, the choruses of the *Agamemnon*, when he allowed some at least of the oddness of the original to enter the stylistic texture of the English verse. The influence of Ezra Pound on the formation of MacNeice's ideas here is at least possible, but the kinds of discipline and experiment which MacNeice put into practice differ widely from Modernist precedents.

In his volume *The Earth Compels* (1938), MacNeice included a version of Horace's Odes I.4., 'Solvitur Acris Hiems' (*CP* 549). Here, the poet works to combine unusual rhythms with the more familiar recurrence of rhyme, writing in quatrains with their second and fourth lines rhyming, and their first and third lines being longer, unrhyming, and with feminine endings. Within this scheme, MacNeice achieves a great degree of rhythmic variation, playing off the longer, sometimes dactylic, first and third lines against the rhyming, predominantly iambic lines that follow them (Horace's metre, the fourth Archilochian, also alternates longer and shorter lines). At the conclusion of the poem, MacNeice manages a precarious balance between English and Latin registers:

> Equally heavy is the heel of white-faced Death on the pauper's
>   Shack and the towers of kings, and O my dear
> The little sum of life forbids the ravelling of lengthy
>   Hopes. Night and the fabled dead are near
>
> And the narrow house of nothing, past whose lintel
>   You will meet no wine like this, no boy to admire
> Like Lycidas, who today makes all young men a furnace
>   And whom tomorrow girls will find a fire.

The self-enacting play of 'the ravelling of empty/ Hopes' here (where the Latin vocabulary is more plain) forces an effect from the verse which MacNeice uses only sparingly in his original poetry. Similarly, the English idiom of the last line, 'And whom tomorrow girls will find a fire', plays a straight iambic pentameter against a stretched syntax, at the same time holding on to the literal meaning of an expression already metaphorical in Horace's Latin ('et mox virgines tepebunt', the verb rendered as 'glow with love' in the Loeb edition). More interestingly, MacNeice finds at the end of Horace's poem a vista opening on to a place which was to return in his later poetry: 'Night and the fabled dead are near/ And the narrow house of nothing'. In finding a phrase for Horace's 'domus exilis Plutonia' (the wretched house of Pluto, god of the Underworld – where 'exilis' (wretched) develops from the root meaning 'narrow'), MacNeice comes upon a property which his later poems also visit, and the alternative which he finds here as a translator to the mythological reference of his original belongs to the world of what he would later identify as parable. For all its virtuoso stylistic display, and its faithfulness to the text of Horace, MacNeice's poem most comes to life when 'Night and the fabled dead are near'.

If Horace in particular, and classical poetry in a more general way, were significant forces operating on the style of MacNeice's poetry, the issue of style itself was never distinct from that of content. And in the 1930s especially, content was something of a pressing issue for a poet of MacNeice's generation. In *Modern Poetry* (1938), recalling his reading while at Marlborough, the poet brought style and content together in his appreciation:

At this same time I began reading some of the 'Odes of Horace', who also would be disallowed as a poet by many modern critics and is sometimes even disallowed by name. 'It does not ring true' people say of him as they say of Villon. What should be remembered is that the *attitude* in Horace, as in many Latin poets, is something consciously applied – one more convention within which the poet has to work. People misunderstand Horace because they miss the grain of salt and because they demand of him the directness and simplicity of a purely lyrical poet, whereas Horace is a contemplative poet writing odes which have something of the involved pattern of Pindar, though on a much smaller scale. As a boy I liked the glitter of Horace – O fons Bandusiae splendidior vitro – and admired his tidiness, realizing that English with its articles and lack of inflexions could hardly ever equal Horace either in concentration or in subtlety of word-order.[7]

For MacNeice, Horace 'rings true' because his verse rings so piercingly clear; the Bandusian fountain's glitter, brighter than crystal, perhaps adds to the passage's ringing endorsement. The values which are present here – tidiness, concentration, subtlety of word-order are, like the 'severe and intricate' virtues of Greek poetry, only approximately possible in English: MacNeice's appreciation of classical style always re-inforces his sense of the *difference* of English style. Nevertheless, the new inflexion given to the idea that poetry should 'ring true' is of some relevance for the poet who is soon to write *Autumn Journal*.

MacNeice's poetry of the 1930s is as indebted to the formal challenges posed by classical poetry as W.H. Auden's writing of

the time is under an obligation to German, Norse, Icelandic, and
Old English models. Both poets found their styles altered by the
alien examples: for Auden, gnomic habits of expression along with
alliterative rhythms fed into his verse, as well as an impatience
with the definite article, while for MacNeice the value of sinuous
and precise syntax was increased, and rhythms moved, if not in
mock-classical measures, in longer, more subtle and flexible line-
lengths. A poem like 'Birmingham', so powerfully original in its
procedures, has learned even so from classical technique as
MacNeice understood it, and strings complicated clauses across
long lines in which different kinds of rhythm are at work. In the
last stanza, the morning traffic is presented in a 'severe and
amazingly intricate' way, through one involved (but unforced)
sentence, and with subtle changes of rhythmic pace:

> On shining lines the trams like vast sarcophagi move
> Into the sky, plum after sunset, merging to duck's egg, barred with
>   mauve
> Zeppelin clouds, and Pentecost-like the cars' headlights bud
> Out from sideroads and the traffic signals, crême-de-menthe or
>   bull's blood,
> Tell one to stop, the engine gently breathing, or to go on
> To where like black pipes of organs in the frayed and fading zone
> Of the West the factory chimneys on sullen sentry will all night
>   wait
> To call, in the harsh morning, sleep-stupid faces through the daily
>   gate.

> (*CP* 18)

MacNeice's technical command here is something quite distinct
from a virtuoso display, and the long, rhyming lines bring
together syntactic complexity with a precision in the matter of
timing. The effect is not mock-classical, but neither is it entirely
'English', and the 'daily gate', at which the poem's syntax and
rhythms come to their measured destination, has acquired a
faintly Homeric tinge in MacNeice's defamiliarization of the scene.

The technical intricacy of MacNeice's 1930s poetry, and the
ways with rhythm, rhyme, and syntax which are developed there,
have a great deal to do with the successes of *Autumn Journal*.
While the forms used by MacNeice in the 1940s and early 1950s
are as various, and in their way as experimental, as those
employed in the 1930s, the sense of discovery, of the pressure of
classical forms moving an English line into an unexpected
rhythmic or syntactic configuration, is more rare after the War.

Effects like those achieved in the last couplet of 'Now that the Shapes of Mist' (1936), 'Mingling, my dear, your breath with the quiet breath/ Of sleep whom the old writers called the brother of Death' (*CP* 76), where the long breath of the lines is precisely paced in the slow rhythm, were less easy to repeat, especially if repeated according to formula. Although MacNeice uses a variety of long lines in his volumes *Holes in the Sky* (1948) and *Ten Burnt Offerings* (1952), their effects are often too visibly engineered, and too repeatedly enacted. The unfortunate decision to compose *Autumn Sequel* (1954) entirely in a regular *terza rima* took MacNeice's poetry into an 'iambic groove' in which the vitality of the 1930s writing was almost completely lost.

The impression given by a good deal of the poetry written in what MacNeice referred to as his 'middle stretch', that the 'severe and amazingly intricate' had declined into a technical habit, or at least had been replaced by the not so severe and the predictably intricate, is not the impression which much of MacNeice's last three volumes make. The affinity of this late work with aspects of his 1930s writing was noticed by MacNeice himself; and one aspect of the affinity is to be found in a return to technical adventurousness, informed again, though perhaps now in rather a different way, by classical models. The poems of *Solstices* (1961) take new risks, and the shapes made by syntax begin to move to the foreground, with line-length and emjambement again playing more than subsidiary roles in the poems' effects and meaning. Where the long line had often in the past been for MacNeice a vehicle for slow, delayed effects, in a poem like 'Variation on Heraclitus' it allows for speed and quick transformations:

> Even the walls are flowing, even the ceiling,
> Not only in terms of physics; the pictures
> Bob on each picture rail like floats on a line
> While the books on the shelves keep reeling
> Their titles out into space and the carpet
> Keeps flying away to Arabia nor can this be where I stood –
> Where I shot the rapids I mean – when I signed
> On a line that rippled away with a pen that melted [...]
>
> (*CP* 502–3)

MacNeice's habit of parataxis is put to a new use here, where it works alongside a line without any stable rhythm: the emjambement speeds up the voice, as do the frequent triple rhythms (dactyls or anapaests) within the lines. Where MacNeice's earlier work might have wound up the successive clauses to finish

with a syntactic resolution, the resolution now is rhythmic, and
deadly flat:

> And, all you advisers on this by the time it is that,
> I just do not want your advice
> Nor need you be troubled to pin me down in my room
> Since the room and I will escape for I tell you flat:
> One cannot live in the same room twice.

The effect MacNeice achieves here is akin to that he observed in
the rhythmically-charged Latin prose of Apuleius in 1946: 'an
arithmetical or cumulative technique, a succession of fairly short
phrases, roughly equal in length and often rhyming, often without
conjunctions, just adding up and adding up.'[8] In 'Variation on
Heraclitus' the rhythmic clauses add up and add up, but they also
add up to something: 'You cannot live in the same room twice'.

A writer like Apuleius would hardly have been considered the
best of classical models in MacNeice's classical education, whether
at school or university; but then, the kinds of ideas about the
classical world in the context of which MacNeice received his
education underwent considerable changes during his lifetime.
The ironic asperities of *Autumn Journal* IX announce their author's
reaction against the concept of classicism which transformed the
study of the ancient world into a training in the higher liberalism,
with the Greeks and Romans themselves being presented as
differing species of Victorian statesmen. However, one aspect of
the (admittedly complex) composite which made up a classical
education for MacNeice's generation stood in a more interesting
relation to nineteenth- and early twentieth-century orthodoxies:
the paganism of the ancient world had been interpreted with
varying degrees of sympathy and distortion by the traditions of
scholarship, and the issue of the light shed upon paganism by
Christianity, or upon Christianity by paganism, was often a major
concern of classical literary and philosophical studies. Matthew
Arnold's celebration of the moral values implicit in ancient
writing (most notably, perhaps, in his essay 'Marcus Aurelius')
was only one aspect of a broader tradition, with which the young
MacNeice was in contact, of locating religious values (of one kind
or another) in study of the ancient world.

In Arnold's tradition, the strength of moral thinking in the
classics went together with a profound rationality and clarity of
thought; these particular Victorian Greeks and Romans seemed to
have converted superstition into poetry. MacNeice was inclined to
reject such accommodations of the ancient world in their more

readily rejectable forms (Pater's *Marius the Epicurean*, for example), but this fairly conventional sniggering on a tour of the Victorian waxworks is not the whole story. The idea that religious values (or something to take the place of religious values) might inhere in the classics retained a certain interest for the poet. In *The Strings Are False*, written in 1940–41, MacNeice remembered a significant influence on his education at Marlborough, the master G.M. Sargeaunt, whose learning and life he contrasted with other masters, 'those pre-War devotees of reason who had whittled away their doubts with a razor and were left with nothing but a razor'. The account is worth quoting at length:

G.M. Sargeaunt, the master of the Classical Upper Sixth, was very different. Apart from his pupils few boys in the school had spoken to him. He was aloof and austerely Olympian, had a private religion of his own founded on ancient Stoicism. He had once been a housemaster but had resigned because he refused to give religious instruction to the boys in his house who were about to be confirmed. Tall and slim, with grey hair sweeping back from his forehead and suffering innocent blue eyes, he dressed with a lazy sophistication and spoke with a beautiful contemptuous drawl – as if he had one foot in Heaven and were just dragging the other foot after him. But could hardly be bothered to finish the sentence, left the other foot where it was because Heaven after all was perhaps a little crude.[9]

Sargeaunt's manner, appearance, and beliefs are brought together in MacNeice's account, and the glamour of the 'suffering innocent blue eyes' is associated here with the attractiveness of a 'private religion', itself disdainful of the orthodox rewards of faith. 'Sargeaunt was homesick for fifth-century Greece', MacNeice continues, recalling how 'He liked the Greek attitude to Fate, their refusal to bank on Utopias, their courage in going on living without the stimulus of heaven or heady idealism.' This recalls MacNeice's phrasing in *Autumn Journal* II, where 'the falling castle' which the poet – like others – helps to construct 'has never fallen, thanks [...] to the human animal's endless courage.' (*CP* 104) Sargeaunt, like MacNeice's persona in *Autumn Journal*, is more than just a rationalist; his humane values are rooted in something other than 'Reason', though they are also above and beyond the superstitious or traditionally religious. Closer perhaps to Pater than to Arnold, he is nevertheless celebrated by MacNeice for his distance from the conventional, and for the signs of consequent detachment in his achieved aloofness. The portrait of

Sargeaunt is reminiscent, in some respects, of impressions given later of MacNeice himself; certainly, Sargeaunt provides a figure against whom MacNeice will measure both himself and the classicism which the master and pupil have in common.

Two other figures come to loom large in MacNeice's gallery of classicists: the Dublin translator of Plotinus, Stephen MacKenna, and Professor E.R. Dodds, who was to become a close and trusted friend. MacNeice came to MacKenna's work through Dodds, who edited his *Journal and Letters* in 1936, and he gave his work a brief Yeatsian celebration in the poem 'Eclogue from Iceland':

> There was MacKenna
> Spent twenty years translating Greek philosophy
> Ill and tormented, unwilling to break contract,
> A brilliant talker who left
> The salon for the solo flight of Mind.

> *(CP 45)*

This glimpse of 'the human animal's endless courage' praises 'the solo flight of Mind', and MacKenna's work on Plotinus (again, in terms of conventional classical studies, deeply unorthodox) is seen as a form of heroic dedication which implies isolation. Reviewing the *Journal*, MacNeice praised MacKenna for having 'the courage of his instincts':[10] it is interesting to consider how far such courage led towards 'the solo flight of Mind' in a neoplatonism which, if at odds with conventional religion, was nevertheless part of a reaction against the values of 'Reason'. Like Sargeaunt's 'private religion', MacKenna's heroic scholarly persistence, and its consequent isolation and detachment, have something to do with a commitment to belief. In E.R. Dodds, MacNeice found a classicist whose work (which, like MacKenna's, began with study of an unfashionable neoplatonism) was out of step with the Victorian marriage of classicism and 'Reason'. While Dodds's major academic writings, such as his *The Greeks and the Irrational* (1951) or his edition of Euripides' *The Bacchae* (1944), made decisive scholarly inroads on the superstition and supernaturalism of ancient thought and writing, his other activities included work for the Society for Psychical Research. For MacNeice, Dodds was clearly another figure who had 'the courage of his instincts', something visible both in his academic work and in his sense of professional and political independence. What is more, those instincts made classicism part of a study of the irrational, and even the supernatural, a discipline with lines open to the haunted and the uncanny.

Of course, E.R. Dodds was no Yeats in the intensity (or gullibility) of his interests in the supernatural, and his autobiography *Missing Persons* (1977) depicts a man of many passions, scholarly and otherwise, in the service of a humane notion of the life of letters. MacNeice in his portrait of Dodds in *Autumn Sequel* (as 'Boyce') spends more time on his mentor's gardening skills than he does on his classical expertise, but the tone of admiration is unambiguous:

> Boyce with his schooling in the humaner letters
> Can spot the flaws in each inhuman purge
>
> Or measure of false security, knows what fetters
> Are forged in the name of freedom, still declines
> To defer to politicians as his betters.
>
> I find him among his books, his presence shines
> Like a straight candle in a crooked world,
> His eyebrows twinkle and the thoughtful lines
>
> On the high forehead run true [...]

(CP 382)

Dodds's 'high forehead' is just slightly reminiscent of Sargeaunt's air of detachment, though these eyes twinkle (or rather, curiously, the eyebrows do) instead of, like Sargeaunt's, suffering. Yet Dodds's wisdom in 'the crooked world' is founded on something different from Sargeaunt's 'private religion':

> He knows that Rome
> Absorbed rough wine and blood with the she-wolf's milk
> And the dogmas of each pompous dome
>
> In Moscow, Washington, and places of that ilk,
> Are largely based on some irrational urge [...]

(CP 381–2)

For MacNeice, Dodds's wisdom is founded on his willingness to admit the role of the irrational in both ancient and modern affairs. The 'private religion' of Dodds's garden, the 'specially printed blooms which he can annotate/ As well as his Greek texts', brings him into MacNeice's own private pantheon of classicists who create a kind of order out of a knowledge of disorder.

It would be unduly crude to suggest that Dodds's order, like Sargeaunt's or MacKenna's, was ultimately a religious value for MacNeice. However, these three classicists are celebrated by the poet in terms .which emphasize their distance from a conventionally rationalist, humanist idea of classicism. More to the point, MacNeice's own ideas of classicism became increasingly tinged by religious issues and symbolism in the middle years of his career, and poems such as 'Didymus' or 'Areopagus' in *Ten Burnt Offerings* make a habit out of the juxtaposition of classical motifs and references with Christian themes. The effect in these poems is often that of a forced amalgam; however, despite the limited success of much of the volume, it is apparent that MacNeice had become accustomed to associate classical material with (however broadly defined) religious questions. In the writing of his last volumes of poetry, religion shadows classicism, and classical subjects touch on a religious dimension which the poet recognized with increasing frankness.

In part, MacNeice's experiments in *Ten Burnt Offerings* and elsewhere brought the poet back to a point at which the basic elements of classicism, like the basic elements of Christianity, were encountered as general truths of experience. Such things slide easily into generalities, and the writing of MacNeice's 'middle stretch' is indeed marked by a fascination with generalities, often much to its disadvantage: timeless truths can be unexciting truisms. This problem is raised in a radio play of 1956, *Carpe Diem*, where the central character muses over his life in relation to the poetry of Horace, something which is adequate to his experiences, but also perhaps (as his wife suggests) a little too easily adequate. Responding to his wife's question, 'Doesn't your favourite poet rather go in for commonplaces?', this character, called (improbably enough) Quintus, replies with a defence of commonplaces:

Listen my dear. What is a commonplace? Being born, making love, growing old – what could be more commonplace activities, yet the human race still goes in for them. And feels – with all respect to Freudians and Marxists – and feels, I should think, very much the same about them. 'Naturam expellas furca, tamen usque recurret'. Throw out nature with a pitchfork, she always comes back, you know. No, Horace didn't live in Cloudcuckooland – nor in the Waste Land. He enjoyed himself on the earth – though he saw its drawbacks. *And* he had a sense of human decency. He was civilised in fact; like my father. Though Horace, of course, though he'd fought on the losing side, did become part of what they now call the Establishment.[11]

Quintus here finds himself defending the commonplaces handed on from Horace by his father, though in a world where they seem out of place – 'Commonplace *and* common sense – they do seem outmoded in a lunatic asylum'. *Carpe Diem* is not amongst MacNeice's best radio plays, partly because it leans so heavily on briskly-expressed, no-nonsense truism, and partly because its use of the dying man remembering his life and times is no more than a tired runthrough of a familiar formula. Yet in the very weakness (and perhaps fatigue) of MacNeice's writing here it is possible that something new is beginning to stir; moreover, the new element speaks with a Latin voice, and starts to turn commonplace into something more individual and distinct. Horace's poetry in *Carpe Diem* is not capable of being distinguished from either Quintus, the superannuated hero, or from his father, doubly superannuated in the background; the poetry is part of their failures and disappointments and survives along with those failures.

The last stage of MacNeice's classicism comes when inadequacy, disillusion and scepticism begin to take on palpable form in the fabric of his later poetry; here, the significance of Latin and Greek also becomes paradoxically more definite as its apparently positive elements begin to drop away. In a memoir of MacNeice, Kevin Andrews wrote of him as 'Someone profoundly frightened, therefore modern', but balanced the observation with 'Able to live with fear, and therefore classical'.[12] This summary does perhaps suggest a context for the classicism of MacNeice's later writing, in the opening-up of his poetry to elements of nightmare logic, where parables are twisted and distorted and there is the suspicion that sometimes, as Edna Longley has remarked, 'waking up from the nightmare was only part of the dream'.[13] In *The Burning Perch* classicism, like the religion of MacNeice's childhood, and that childhood itself, is often visible, but is as much a ghostly apparition as a living presence. Often, the sound of classical poetry is faintly audible in MacNeice's rhythms, as in the pacing and syntactic manoeuvres of the poems; the attempt to escape from the 'iambic groove' is indebted to ancient examples, though it does not merely mimic these.

The most elaborate poem in *The Burning Perch* is the five-part 'Memoranda to Horace', in which MacNeice's classicism, in full-dress (so to speak) considers both itself and its context. The figure of Horace, even while he is being celebrated, is also subject to challenge and opposition, not least from the 'creatures for you over-Gothic,/ Met only by twilight' who belong to the parable and nightmare worlds of MacNeice's writing:

With whom to hobnob is a mortification
Of self-respect, one's precious identity
Filtered away through what one had fancied
Till now were one's fingers, shadows to shadows.

(*CP* 543)

But the Horace whom MacNeice's poem addresses is also involved with 'shadows'. The classical poet is accessible only through his poems, 'your Aeolian measures/ Transmuted to Latin – *aere perennius*': the personality whom MacNeice addresses is, in this way, the illusion of a personality, or a personality's apparition in posterity. In this sense, Horace is another of the many ghosts that fill *The Burning Perch*, addressed not in the calm timelessness of the rational classical canon, but as a spirit lingering uncannily in a superstitious and haunted world:

Yet (another paragraph) I should correct myself
Though not for myself or my time but for the record:
Fame you no longer presumed on than pontifex
And silent Vestal should continue daily
Climbing the Capitol. Whether that proviso
Has been properly kept seems open to question
Even though a coiffed and silent figure
Has been seen by some on Michelangelo's piazza
With eyes turned down on the past

(*CP* 540)

This ghostly figure lingers in posterity, in a modernity to which MacNeice's poem is itself painfully exposed, 'With eyes turned down on the past'. Is it 'really' present? Part of the force of 'Memoranda to Horace' derives from the knowledge that MacNeice, like the Horace he addresses, is writing into a posterity in which any 'presence' will be textual presence, an illusion engineered in poetry. The poem's final turn is towards the idea of 'carpe diem', now something rather more than a commonplace:

To opt out now seems better than capitulate
To the too-well-lighted and over-advertised
Idols of the age. Sooner these crepuscular

Blasphemous and bawdy exchanges; and even
A second childhood remembering only
Childhood seems better than a blank posterity,
One's life restricted to standing room only.

(*CP* 543)

'Seize the day' has been transmuted into 'opt out'; and yet, like much else in *The Burning Perch* the grimness of this feels more like a victory than a defeat.

The three elements of MacNeice's classicism – its influence on technique, its connection with religious preoccupations, and its affinities with the darker side of the imagination in MacNeice's nightmare logic – come together in the poem 'Charon'. Here, a last journey takes place in the noisy London of 'Memoranda to Horace', but with a cock crowing as well as a dog barking (St. Peter as well as Cerberus?), to a place where natural and supernatural are no longer distinct. The poem's sound, its movement and repetition, and its final abrupt halt, have been developed from the techniques of poems like 'Variation on Heraclitus', and are fully escaped from any 'iambic groove':

Charon

The conductor's hands were black with money:
Hold on to your ticket, he said, the inspector's
Mind is black with suspicion, and hold on to
That dissolving map. We moved through London,
We could see the pigeons through the glass but failed
To hear their rumours of wars, we could see
The lost dog barking but never knew
That this bark was as shrill as a cock crowing,
We just jogged on, at each request
Stop there was a crowd of aggressively vacant
Faces, we just jogged on, eternity
Gave itself airs in revolving lights
And then we came to the Thames and all
The bridges were down, the further shore
Was lost in fog, so we asked the conductor
What we should do. He said: Take the ferry
Faute de mieux. We flicked the flashlight
And there was the ferryman just as Virgil
And Dante had seen him. He looked at us coldly
And his eyes were dead and his hands on the oar
Were black with obols and varicose veins
Marbled his calves and he said to us coldly:
If you want to die you will have to pay for it.

(CP 530)

This a classicist's poem, both in the sense that its technique is made possible only by an absorption of the sound of Greek and

Latin poetry, and in the sense that it is written by someone 'able to live with fear'. At the same time, the poem's classicism is without illusions: no mythology, however venerable, will brighten the dark vista that opens so convincingly, and so coldly, in this writing: 'Nightmares', MacNeice had written in 'Areopagus', 'are often just'. Nevertheless, MacNeice also knew that even 'the narrow house of nothing' could be 'a house/ He could not remember seeing before' where 'something told him the way to behave' ('The Truisms'); to this extent, classicism required a degree of trust from the poet, and perhaps repaid that trust.

'SOMETHING WRONG SOMEWHERE?': MACNEICE AS CRITIC

EDNA LONGLEY

I'll begin with a dozen quotations – some of MacNeice's *obiter dicta* about the limits and failings of literary criticism, especially in its response to poetry:

– The literary critic fails through being literary.[1]

– *Marxists* do not as a rule make helpful literary critics.[2]

– All that the critic can do is lay stepping stones over the river.[3]

– The critic's view of art is essentially static; the artistic process is essentially dynamic.[4]

– Literary criticism's great vice is that it will take any individual poet as a pure specimen of any one tendency or attitude.[5]

– Criticism based on the assumption that a poem is a mere *translation* of facts outside itself is vicious criticism.[6]

– the man who reads a poem and likes it, is doing something far too subtle for criticism.[7]

– Critics often tend to write as if a condition were the same thing as a cause.[8]

– the big critic, who writes whole books, is often plugging some perverse general theory of poetry which leaves no room for seven poets out of ten. The little critic, who writes book reviews, seems compelled, partly by lack of space, partly by laziness, to prefer the snap generalization, the ready-made label, to any decent down-to-earth analysis.[9]

– In a world where most of the sceptics are cold pike and most of the enthusiasts melting jellyfish, [Randall] Jarrell stands out as someone well equipped not only with a heart but with several grains of salt.[10]

– According to my reviewers, taken collectively (and I am confining myself to more or less favourable reviews), I am a writer they can place quite simply: I am a surprisingly feminine, essentially masculine poet, whose gift is primarily lyrical and basically satirical, swayed by and immune to politics, with and without a religious sense, and I am technically slapdash and technically meticulous, with a predilection for flat and halting and lilting Swinburnian rhythms, and I have a personal and impersonal approach, with a remarkably wide and consistently narrow range, and I have developed a good deal and I have not developed at all.[11]

– Quotations are too often used either to save thought or to show off.[12]

My penultimate quotation might cause a cold-pike sceptic to sneer that MacNeice's gripes stem from the critical reception of his own poetry. But he does cite 'more or less favourable reviews', and goes on to say (this is 1949): 'Most living poets have been similarly treated by reviewers. Can something be wrong somewhere?'

Discussion of MacNeice's criticism has mainly asked how it serves, and serves to explicate, his poetry. Recent commentary, for instance, links it to his central role in assimilating and challenging – from a combination of Irish and English perspectives – Yeats's aesthetic.[13] This essay is less concerned with the themes that plot MacNeice's artistic direction, or with the critical strategies that help him to negotiate anxieties of influence, than with his broader practice as a critic in a less specialised era. Practice generates theory (his usual order of priorities), when he thinks about poetry or when the conceptual inadequacies of poetry criticism provoke him. One subtext may be the encounter between a classicist/philosopher and the sloppiness of literary-critical language and categories. And, although he broaches other topics (fiction, translation from the classics, academic studies, any book to do with Ireland), poetry is always on his critical mind. In 'Pleasure in Reading: Woods to Get Lost In' (1961) he says: 'Of the works that I "turn to time and again" the great majority are in verse. It is like having a taste for distilled liquors, natural in someone who is in the distillery business.'[14] All creative artists are, deep down, self-serving critics, although some disguise it better than others. Yet the ratio between subjectivity, or the selfish gene, and objectivity varies from poet-critic to poet-critic. They may open a narrower or wider window on perennial questions. We do not trust them equally as guides to the best malt. Nor do MacNeice's irony and frank polemic seduce us into reading his critical writings naively, as melting-jellyfish scholars read the self-representations of contemporary poets. The current dichotomy, or perhaps collusion, between hard theory and soft criticism is not only a new guise for pike and jellyfish. It is a fulfilment of trends against which MacNeice warns.

I want to develop this proposition with reference to four related points: what the 'critical faculty' means to MacNeice; some literary-critical positions shared by MacNeice and Auden in the later 1930s; MacNeice's angle on the intertwined issues of tradition and literary generation (issues central to this symposium); and a recurrent motif in his writings about poetry – a motif which is dialectical, as he said all criticism should be: that is, the tension between his sense of shape and his openness to anarchism, to writing that breaks all the rules, including his own. Hence his delight in the eclecticism of Apuleius: 'It is hard to find a writer who combines such dissimilar qualities – elegance and earthiness, euphuism and realism, sophistication and love of folk-lore, Rabelaisian humour and lyrical daintiness, Platonism and belief in witchcraft, mysticism and salty irony.' Yet he continues: '[Apuleius] was predominantly an artist; the *Golden Ass* is not just a mixture but a blend.'[15] Like other critical formulations by MacNeice, this bears on post-modernism, form and meaning.

II

MacNeice's criticism is conditioned by a variety of material, literary and intellectual contexts. His most substantial essays and the two full-length critical books, *Modern Poetry* (1938) and *The Poetry of W.B. Yeats* (1941), are products of the decade when he was making his name and his early aesthetic, and during which he was briefly tempted to become a full-time writer. His Clark lectures, assembled in the posthumous *Varieties of Parable*, were delivered after he had left the BBC staff to become freelance. His more occasional reviews and articles of the 1940s and 1950s are the critical memoranda of somebody otherwise occupied – as poet, broadcaster, translator, adept of the George salon. The important essay 'Experiences with Images' (1949) is an exception, although that, too, seems to be required writing in Larkin's sense. But if the opening sentences respond to a commission, they also illustrate three characteristics of MacNeice's critical interventions: their analytical thrust, their dialectical structure, their self-consciousness about the kinds of authority they claim:

How do I use images? In trying to answer this question (and I shall merely scratch the surface) I find it hard to be honest. There are two such strong but opposite temptations – to oversimplify, make it all sound neat-and-easy (here comes the Master Craftsman counting his brass tacks) and to make it all sound alarmingly but glamorously mysterious (here comes Inspiration falling off her tripod).[16]

MacNeice wrote for periodicals whose very names now 'accentuate a thirst', to quote his 'Epitaph for Liberal Poets'. Alan Heuser's bibliography lists *New Verse, Horizon*, the *Listener* ... The *London Magazine* and the *New Statesman and Nation* (technically) still exist. Here he could count on a Left-liberal readership for whom literature, culture and politics interpenetrated, even after the 1930s. Nor were the vocabularies of 'big critic' and 'little critic' as distinct as they have since become. Hence his later lament – in the tone of one glad to be an academic manqué – that Yeats, Shaw and Joyce 'should now be at the mercy of the evergrowing tribes of humourless scholars'.[17] Further, the overlaps between Heuser's *Selected Literary Criticism of Louis MacNeice* and *Selected Prose* (not only the presence of reviews in both volumes) suggest that literary criticism is never a wholly separable category for MacNeice. His radio-scripts involved literary themes and adaptations; he put contemporary poetry on the air. Similarly, the literary-critical stratum of his poetry does not simply underline reflexiveness or intertextuality for the benefit of academe. I have written elsewhere about MacNeice's eclogues as contributions to the debate about literature and society in the 1930s.[18] *Autumn Journal* more obliquely mingles literary and social criticism as it rereads a variety of texts in the light of Munich. These include the classical canon, Auden's 'Spain', Yeats's 'Meditations in Time of Civil War', his own earlier poetry. A different example of literary-criticism holistically entering poetry is the gentle *Dunciad*, 'Elegy for Minor Poets': 'Who might have caught fire had only a spark occurred,/ Who knew all the words but failed to achieve the Word'. 'Woods' suggests how the landscapes, culture, traditions and reading of childhood have contingently produced the adult poet for whom Herrick's nymphs and Malory's knights must 'arras the room'. More pervasively, MacNeice's deepest imaginative structures debate the aesthetics, metaphysics and politics of 'flux' and 'pattern': all the problematics of achieving 'the Word'.[19] His autobiographical prose, as well as poetry, contains literary criticism; for example, the satirical passage on Spender's *Trial of a Judge in The Strings are False*. Conversely, *Modern Poetry*, subtitled 'A Personal Essay', incorporates 'literary autobiography, i.e. the history of my own reactions to and demands from poetry, in reading and writing it, over a number of years starting from early childhood'.[20]

This self-interrogating 'case-book' method reflects the empiricist bent of what Ellmann terms MacNeice's 'critical mind always discontented with its own formulations'.[21] MacNeice, philosophically trained, was not against theory, but against its propensity to arrogance, to absence of discontent: 'And oh how much I liked the Concrete Universal,/ I never thought that I should/ Be telling them vice-versa/ That they can't see the trees for the wood' (*Autumn Journal* XIII). In 'Poetry Today' (1935) he binds aesthetic theory to practical trial and error: 'To banish theory is as much of a half-truth and a whole lie as to make theory omnipotent. The functions of theory are propaedeutic, prophylactic, and corrective; just as in learning to play tennis. When it comes to the point, the work is done with the hands.'[22] By the same token, the critic should not be 'more interested in producing a water-tight system of criticism than in the objects which are his data'.[23] In *Modern Poetry* MacNeice maintains that a 'poem is not an abstracted circle but rather a solid ball'.[24] So if we, as critics, are to get our hands on that ball, we will have to 'descend from metaphysics into history'.[25] More new historicist than post-modernist in temper, MacNeice argues that the 'new similarities' produced by poetic conjunctions can only be appreciated with reference to the old similarities current 'at a particular time'.[26] He regards Marxist criticism as mostly too metaphysical for this task.

Perhaps owing to his intellectual tussles with Anthony Blunt, MacNeice invariably represents aestheticism and Marxist literary theory (1930s style) as inversions of each other. This is so when he calls for 'a responsible criticism' in 'Poetry, the Public, and the Critic' written for the *New Statesman* in 1949:

> most critics pass by on the other side. But then most critics, unlike creative artists, are snobs and will only preach to the converted. This is true not only of the aesthetic critic who prefers to leave the 'average reader' on the other side of a gulf, but also of the Marxist critic who says that nothing can be done about the gulf until there has been a revolution.[27]

In the same essay MacNeice insists that critics need to be *more* responsible than poets. Whereas anarchist poets may be allowable,

'there is not much place for the anarchist critic'. He approves E.M.
Forster's view of criticism's job as 'education through precision'.[28]
Elsewhere MacNeice calls verse itself 'a precision instrument'.[29] So
criticism should aim at being precise about precisions. Similarly, it
should be critical about a criticism: i.e., literature's 'criticism of
life'. MacNeice has no difficulty with Matthew Arnold's
definition, given sharper point by the 1930s. In *Modern Poetry* he
declares it 'part of a poet's legitimate business to say what he
thinks are the best or the next best goods for man'.[30] Accordingly,
it is part of a critic's legitimate business to evaluate such value-
judgements. This demand, however, is not met when critics
neglect their duty of precision towards the artistic matrix; when
they assume that there is 'a stock set of answers ... to a stock set of
questions'; and when they acquire the 'superficial habit of
fastening on something in a poem which can easily be labelled
and then making [their] own label the differentia of the poem'.[31] In
the Introductory chapter to *The Poetry of W.B. Yeats* MacNeice
contrasts Yeats and Rupert Brooke, as he ponders relations
between a poem, 'the life of the poet', and 'the life outside [the
poet]':

Brooke's paeans to war *are*, on analysis, self-contradictory; they are
a sentimental falsification that, unlike the lover's, has no profound
natural sanction. The fact that many of his contemporaries agreed
with Brooke does not vindicate his poems. It merely widens the
basis of the lie ... If we now turn to Yeats, we find that he also at
times – and also from sentimental motives – misrepresented the
world in which he was living. But it seems to me that there is an
important difference between his approach and Brooke's. Brooke,
under the mask of realism, flatly asserts that something which is
bad is good; what is more, he trumpets his mistaken belief in the
manner of one who wishes to convert others. Yeats, who repudiated
realism and does not use the tone of a crusader, may present certain
facts coloured or distorted by his own partisan feelings but he
allows the reader to see that this presentation is founded on an 'as
if'.[32]

   The Poetry of W.B. Yeats already corrects the 1930s half-truth that
'a poem must be *about* something'.[33] By 1960 MacNeice had
expelled the last traces of reportage or journalism from his
creative and critical systems. His Clark lectures conclude with a
salute to 'good parable writers' for being concerned with 'the kind
of truth that cannot be, or can hardly be, expressed in other
ways'.[34] Yet, if his stress has decisively shifted to parabolic 'inner

conflict' or 'inner light', he 'still hold[s] that a poet should look at, feel about and think about the world around him'.[35] Thus he does not anticipate, in both senses of the verb, the strange (back-to-aestheticism) gyre that led some Marxist theory to favour and encourage writing that 'foregrounds its own fictionality'. Despite his admiration for Beckett, he finds Golding's 'world of moralities and story-lines' a relief after the metaphysical extreme of *The Unnamable* (which he compares to Hindu esotericism and Christian 'accounts of the Negative Way').[36] At this yogi end of the spectrum there can be no criticism of life. Thus it seems valid to emphasise the lasting impact of the 1930s on MacNeice's critical attitudes and attitude to criticism. The well-known Preface to *Modern Poetry* declares the term itself integral to poetry. Here MacNeice sharpens up Arnold, as well as Horace's *utile* and *dulce*, as he envisages the critical spirit moving vigilantly between the aesthetic, ethical and socio-political spheres:

The poet ... is both critic and entertainer (and his criticism will cut no ice unless he entertains) ... Propaganda, the extreme development of 'critical' poetry, is also the defeat of criticism ... The writer to-day should be not so much the mouthpiece of a community ... as its conscience, its critical faculty, its generous instinct.

The asyndeton makes the last-named qualities permeate one another, with 'critical faculty' intermediary between conscience and generosity. Conversely, it is envisaged in *Autumn Journal* that the war and propaganda war against Hitler will mean becoming, like the enemy, 'uncritical, vindictive' – the latter a consequence of the former. 'Criticism' is, in fact, the last word of *Modern Poetry*: 'When the crisis comes, poetry may for the time be degraded or even silenced, but it will reappear, as one of the chief embodiments of human dignity, when people once more have time for play and criticism.'[37]

'Responsible criticism', then, continues the responsibilities of poetry itself; and its path, which never finally divorces aesthetics from ethics, seems contrary to the Negative Way. During the war he thought that Auden had sold out in saying: 'Others must be regarded aesthetically & only oneself ethically'. This is because 'Ethics presupposes not only judgement upon others but calculated interference with them'.[38] It is interesting to note why MacNeice warms to certain critics, literary and otherwise. He likes precision, real debate with other voices, communication, a refusal to pull punches. Thus he praises T.S. Eliot's criticism (despite its 'catchwords') for promoting a 'general movement towards clarity and rigour'; Honor Tracy for saying 'a great many things which few Irishmen would have the guts and few Englishmen the wits to put down in black and white'; Rosamund Tuve for setting Herbert in context and for bridging the 'pseudo-historical gulf' which had made it impossible to read Spenser; Randall Jarrell for sticking 'his neck out' and telling 'you exactly which poems by anyone he thinks are his best, he will quote from these abundantly, *and* he will tell you exactly why he admires what he quotes'.[39]

III

Years earlier this had been MacNeice's own method with Auden and other contemporaries. It exemplifies the MacNeice-Auden relationship – though not necessarily its balance of literary powers – that MacNeice's critique of Auden is on the record, whereas comparatively little runs the other way. Auden's *Selected Poems* of MacNeice is a significant – and, of course, post-dated – exception. His selection shows taste (in recognising that the late 1940s to the late 1950s was a dull stretch for MacNeice), but not always insight (in largely overlooking the Irish dimension). According to Craig Raine,[40] the Faber files disclose that MacNeice outsold Auden in the 1930s. However, it was not the common reader who canonised Auden, but a literary-Left coterie with a counter-establishment agenda that was itself informed by English national priorities. Of course, Auden's groupies misread Auden, just as they could not read some dimensions of MacNeice, and most critical reception during the decade missed the significant reciprocities and differences between the poets. Again, although Auden can write with magnificent precision about poetry – witness the essay on D.H. Lawrence – his characteristic form of critical utterance became aphorism rather than analysis. He also diversified into a greater range of cultural commentary after moving to the US. Even during the 1930s, MacNeice's essays and reviews, as contrasted with the prose in *The English Auden*, more often work with the hands and work on poetry. While Auden also generalised brilliantly about education and psycho-analysis, MacNeice was defining 'the new poetry', and defining it in more concrete terms than those emanating from the politically inflected Auden-worship, or self-worship, of other young poet-critics.

There is a tension between MacNeice's sense of where Day Lewis and Spender fail and his need to affirm a poetic dynamic not exclusively of Auden's making. Obviously one reason why he wrote about poetry was to rescue his own work from 'ready-made labels' and 'a stock set of questions': the reductionist abstractions that derived from reviewers' reading of Auden and of the times. Hence, in part, the autobiographical strategy of *Modern Poetry*. In the earlier essay 'Poetry Today' MacNeice calls Spender 'a naïf who uses communism as a frame for his personal thrills'; notes that Day Lewis 'has committed lamentable ineptitudes while preaching for the cause'.[41] Yet he also finds innovative qualities in their less pretentious work, and appreciates the pressures of the Zeitgeist on all the poets, including Auden himself:

Auden's great asset is curiosity … He reads the newspapers and samples ordnance maps. He has gusto, not literary gusto like Ezra Pound, but the gusto which comes from an unaffected (almost ingenuous) interest in people, politics, careers, science, psychology, landscape and mere sensations. He has a sense of humour. To say he is an Aeschylus as some people have done, is merely stupid and might encourage him to be pompous. His job is to go on observing things from his very unusual angle and recording them … in his very individual manner.[42]

In *Modern Poetry* this repositioning of Auden and the poetic movement in MacNeicean terms becomes more explicit. He stresses not politics but shifts in diction, rhythm, imagery, and relations with an audience, and concludes: 'it is desirable that poets like these should write honestly, their poetry keeping pace with their lives and with their beliefs as affecting their lives, neither lagging behind in an obsolete romanticism nor running ahead to an assurance too good to be true'.[43]

Modern Poetry also seems to ratify the aesthetic convergence between MacNeice and Auden as they 'rode and joked and smoked' in Iceland. (I am reminded of Robert Frost and Edward Thomas in August 1914.) Their consensus turns on the relation of poet to community, on the necessary fusion of entertainment and criticism (Auden's 'parable art'), and on how to read the history of poetry in the twentieth century. *Letters from Iceland* is a channel between MacNeice's mid-thirties essays and *Modern Poetry*. Its best-known critical text, Auden's 'Letter to Lord Byron', epitomises the book's multiple liaisons between literary and social criticism. In *Modern Poetry* MacNeice calls the poem 'a mass of contemporary criticism, autobiography and gossip' in an 'elastic form, able to carry … discursive comments … on a world of flux and contradictions'.[44] It influenced the different elasticity of

Autumn Journal, as did the tonal togetherness of 'Last Will and Testament'. After Iceland MacNeice reviewed Auden's *Look Stranger!* and *Oxford Book of Light Verse* (dedicated to E.R. Dodds). His review of the former praises Auden for his capacity to develop, for exhibiting 'that criticism of life which is the function of major poetry', for his 'eye which keeps the balance between emotion and intelligence', for his entertainment-value, and for having 'something to write about'.[45] He welcomes the *Oxford Book* as representing poetry's 'manysidedness', calls Auden 'one of the few living poets whose poetry can walk in the street without falling flat on its face', and concludes: 'As a comment on poetry or the nature of poetry or the function or anything-else-you-like of poetry, this book is worth a hundred laboured volumes of literary criticism.'[46]

But it was not a matter of MacNeice's criticism propagating Auden's values. Discussion of Auden's late-thirties re-alignment overlooks the exchange between the poets at this period: an exchange which also, up to a point, meant that they changed places. Their convergence helped MacNeice to become more political (critical) in his poetry, helped Auden to be less so. There are MacNeicean resonances in Auden's self-extrications from his false position as leader of the literary Left. To quote some of his apostasies: 'Poets are rarely and only incidentally priests or philosophers or party agitators. They are people with a particular interest and skill in handling words in a particular kind of way ... Apart from that they are fairly ordinary men and women'; 'We can justly accuse the poets of the nineties of ivory towerism, not because they said they were non-political, but because the portion of life which they saw as poets was such a tiny fragment.'[47] MacNeice's politics had long been informed by the irony of Auden's aphorism: 'That movement will fail: the intellectuals are supporting it.'[48] Unlike Auden, however, as their disagreement over Yeats shows,[49] MacNeice did not think that to give up on 'clever hopes', on particular utopian theories, meant that all had failed. In 'The Poet in England Today: A Reassessment' (1940) he writes: 'If the artist declines to live in a merely political pigeonhole, it does not follow that he has to live in a vacuum. Man is a political animal, not a political cog.'[50]

IV

Poetic movements may have greater stamina. This introduces MacNeice's interest, as a critic, in literary tradition and literary generation. By supporting and interpreting (in a more selfless way than his peers) the movement to which he belonged, MacNeice engaged with the crux which he identifies at the beginning of 'Subject in Modern Poetry' (1936): 'The literary critic includes the literary historian, but it is notoriously difficult to write a history of one's own times'.[51] Perhaps the effort to do so, culminating in *The Poetry of W.B. Yeats*, kept MacNeice in touch with history in general. If he overcame some of the difficulty, it was partly due to his belief in the existence of a poetic movement, in an imaginative collectivity. Here, like Christopher Caudwell, the Marxist critic whom he admired as an exception to the rule, MacNeice subscribes to a socialism of the creative process that contrasts with the 'Auden as leader' model. In espousing Caudwell's view of art as Communal Ego, rather than solo performance, MacNeice may have been partly influenced by his Irish literary and cultural affiliations. Certainly, the intersection between an Irish sense of genealogy and an English sense of collectivity gave him an unusually profound grasp of how tradition works. This may, in turn, have benefited his successors. Poets are coy about their links to contemporaries: X will say of Y and Z: 'I may have had a drink with Y after meeting Sam Beckett in Paris, and Z gave my first book a rave review, but I wouldn't call us a *movement.*' This disregards the commonality exerted by more impersonal pressures: by mechanisms of tradition, by the mutual awareness that shapes difference, and by the obligation, as MacNeice puts it, to 'do our duty by the present moment'.[52]

An example of MacNeice doing his critical duty in this respect is also one of the occasions when he speaks as survivor amid the ruins of the thirties Left intelligentsia. 'The Tower that Once', the most effective reply to Virginia Woolf's famous polemic 'The Leaning Tower', claims (as MacNeice does elsewhere) an authority that resides in 'my generation':

[Mrs Woolf] should not attack my generation for being conditioned by its conditions. Do not let us be misled by her metaphor of the Tower. The point of this metaphor was that a certain group of young writers found themselves on a leaning tower; this presupposes that the rest of the world remained on the level. But it just didn't. The whole world in our time went more and more on the slant so that no mere abstract geometry or lyrical uplift could cure it.[53]

This insists on the nexus between history and literary tradition. MacNeice emphasises that neither Woolf's high modernism nor

Georgianism could have been simply reheated in the 1930s. Yet he always denied that 'my generation' had thrown out tradition. In 'Poetry Today' he says:

All the experimenting poets turned their backs on mummified and theorized tradition, but the more intelligent realized that living tradition is essential to all art, is one of the poles. A poem, to be recognisable, must be traditional; but to be worth recognizing, it must be something new.[54]

In *Modern Poetry* he puts it more succinctly: 'All experiment is made on a basis of tradition; all tradition is the crystallization of experiment.'[55] A later essay, 'The Traditional Aspect of Modern English Poetry', written for an Italian audience in 1946, plays the European card against those traditionalists and anti-traditionalists for whom the term means the poetic traditions of the nineteenth century. MacNeice concludes: 'Most of the younger generation have returned to more regular forms while trying to be their masters, not their slaves ... believers in meaning (though not necessarily in a wholly rational meaning) they try, in the European tradition, to convey it by all the means at their command – and most of these means, on analysis, are traditional.'[56]

In 'The Tower that Once' MacNeice calls the 'mutual misunderstanding of the literary generations' 'one of the evils of our times', adding: 'my own generation has too often been unjust to its immediate predecessors'.[57] He was to experience such injustice himself. Reviewing two anthologies in 1957 he says: 'This game of pigeonholing literary generations has gone too far ... Posterity may find our generations closer to each other than we care to think'. His complaint is not just personal pique or loyalty to old comrades, but an objection to the myopia and amnesia of the 'little critic' and unhistorical anthologist: 'There have been too many anthologies of contemporary verse and much in their introductions has been either dull or ridiculous.'[58] MacNeice's readings of the poetic 'present moment' always imply long vistas and hence high standards, whether provided by the classics, by his touchstones in English literature, or by the foundational roles of Yeats and Eliot in the twentieth century. His alternative title for *Varieties of Parable* was *From Spenser to Beckett*. Similarly, he likes Randall Jarrell's habit of mentioning his contemporaries 'in the same breath as Dante, Shakespeare et al'.[59] If MacNeice had lived to edit the *Oxford Book of Twentieth-Century English Verse*, something exciting might have happened.

V

MacNeice's awareness of tradition stimulates his sense of proportion. His criticism consistently condemns one-dimensional readings of poetry and mono-rail literary trajectories. In 'Subject in Modern Poetry' he rejects the poles of 'psychic automatism' and 'pure propaganda', of 'visceral parrot-talk' and 'bill-plastering'.[60] But in desiring genuine complexity to crystallise out of 'the interflux of extremist principles', [61] MacNeice does not seek a safe middle way. When he calls most of the great poets 'compromisers', he means that criticism should 'try to work out in each poet a kind of Hegelian dialectic of opposites'.[62] In *Autumn Journal* IX he disparages the Hellenistic poets for turning out 'dapper little elegiac verses/ ... carefully shunning an over-statement/ But working the dying fall'. He brilliantly cuts through to the kernel of Yeats's self and anti-self by renaming them Jekyll and Hyde: 'the poet as he thinks he is or consciously wishes to be' *versus* 'his suppressed and subordinate self (or the self which, *as a poet*, he would wish to suppress or subordinate)'. He adds: 'Hyde complements and corrects Jekyll, sometimes indeed by sabotage'.[63] And when MacNeice attacks the disproportionate Pound of the *Cantos* (he appears to agree with Yeats in perceiving this art as 'opposite' in a sense probably beyond dialectic), it is because Pound's extremism has pushed poetry back into a nineties corner: 'For very many years he has been repeating, rather hysterically, that he is an expert and a specialist; but he has specialized his poems into museum pieces'.[64]

It is 'manysidedness', like Auden's, that over-specialised poets and critics resist or fear. Celebrating Yeats's transgressive 'little mechanical songs' in the persona of Crazy Jane, MacNeice deplores

the puritanical book reviewer who demands that any one poet should be all the time a specialist, confined to his own sphere (the reviewer allocates the sphere), and all the time self-consistent. If a poet has been labelled serious, he must never be frivolous. If the poet has been labelled 'love-poet', he is taken to be declining if he shows the Latin quality of 'salt' ... But the poet should not bother with this Procrustes who has to live by his bed. 'So I am to speak only as myself,' the poet might say, 'my whole self and nothing but myself?' If you know what my whole self and my only self is, you know a lot more than I do. As far as I can make out, I not only have many different selves but I am often, as they say, not myself at all. Maybe it is just when I am not myself – when I am thrown out of gear by circumstances or emotion – that I feel like writing poetry.[65]

Although relevant to Yeats and his masks, this outburst both defines MacNeice himself as a mask-poet, and expresses his weariness with being monotonously labelled in the 1930s. It may also reflect the problems that English critics have with the lyrical drama of Anglo-Irish poets in general. Yeats advertised his masks because he knew that they might puzzle Wordsworthian expectations. It is significant that MacNeice's interchangeably negative terms for bad critics are 'puritanical' and 'procrustean' – terms that evoke ways in which minds might be closed in two countries.

MacNeice subtly characterises the trap of repetition for both poet and critic when he asks 'whether any one mood or idea can valuably be expressed more than once with exactly the same emphasis'.[66] So proportion means continual dialectic – the gyres – rather than succumbing to an extreme of specialisation and therefore stasis. It means altering the angle, choosing a different canvas, and not, like Pound, using 'the same cadences again and again for glamour, and the same contrasts again and again for brutality (or reality)'. MacNeice's own poetry sometimes falls into the Procrustean trap. That it invariably escapes is connected with his internalisation of proportion. He says of Pound: 'Quantity must always affect quality. A metre of green, as Gauguin said, is more green than a centimetre, but a bucket of Benedictine is hardly Benedictine'.[67]

MacNeice's anatomy of criticism makes equivalent points. Pound, like the American Auden, helped the academy to assert greater control over the reception of poetry: buckets of literary-critical Benedictine. In *Learning to be Modern: Pound, Eliot, and the American University* Gail McDonald concludes by stressing Pound's compatibility with the 'Puritan inheritance [perhaps MacNeice sniffed this out] ... the nineteenth-century American college, the core curriculum, and Irving Babbitt'.[68] MacNeice, in contrast, inhabited a less rarefied literary environment, and wished for more balanced relations between 'Poetry, the Public and the Critic', for a situation in which there would not be 'an unbridgeable gulf between [a community's] poets and its readers'.[69] His own criticism moves from aesthetic manifesto to socio-cultural critique to review to academic article without violent changes of stylistic and tonal gear. Perhaps – among many other factors – it is partly because he never pandered to academic audiences, in his criticism as well as in his poetry, that the ascendant graph of his reputation has taken so long to accelerate. I have argued elsewhere that MacNeice's creative and critical endeavour to juggle the legacies of Yeats and Eliot is crucial to how we understand the evolution of poetic modernism on this side of the Atlantic, and that many consequences of his endeavour are to be seen in contemporary Northern Irish poetry.[70] This is one reason why MacNeice's criticism – how grateful we are to Alan Heuser – must not be neglected. Another reason centres on his appeal to 'honesty' as an objective for poet and critic alike. The term has been misread as recommending a form of 'honest Ulster' bluntness. Certainly, one of honesty's opposites is 'lies', but not in a merely factual sense. In *Autumn Journal IV* the protagonist tells his 'honest' lover that 'even your lies were able to assert/ Integrity of purpose'. He also praises her 'special strength/ Who never flatter for points nor fake responses'. Honesty, then, seems close to 'integrity': another favourite term, denoting not a static condition but the complex radar that prevents betrayal of creative instincts and critical principles. For the critic, honesty means not faking it, trying not to become an intellectual fashion-victim, never making fundamental compromises when a judgement might prove unpopular or imprudent. On this count, too, MacNeice's record looks better and better. There is, indeed, 'something wrong somewhere', if he fails to influence the vocabularies in which we talk about twentieth-century poetry.

LOUIS AND THE WOMEN

JON STALLWORTHY

Louis MacNeice loved women, and women loved MacNeice. We need no ghost from the grave to tell us that, but I want to suggest that we do need a ghost to lead us back into the heart of his darkness, the mystery at the heart of his life and work.

More than 20 years after his death, his widow distilled his life into a remarkable prose poem she called 'The House that Louis Built':

It was a handsome house with thick walls. The windows on the west side looked towards Connemara, Mayo and the Sea. Those to the south scanned Dorset, The Downs and Marlborough – the windows to the north overlooked Iceland and those to the east, India.

The front door was wide and always open

[... .]

Upstairs there were two rooms, the first, rather bare, received the casual lady encounter or the tentative relationship of short duration.

The second room contained paintings, flowers, a grand piano and was elegantly furnished – there, the five ladies of his life lingered, some more than others. The first, a young girl 'with whom I shared an idyll five years long'. Through her he finally escaped from the Anglican church, background of his father. The next four all had worlds of their very own, a painter, a writer, a singer to whom he was married for eighteen years and a talented actress.

Over the lintel of that door was written Love, Loyalty, Loneliness and Disillusion.

On September 3rd 1963, with the words 'Am I supposed to be dying?', he quietly closed the door of the house he had built.[1]

I think that is beautiful and true, but it is not the whole truth. When Hedli MacNeice speaks of 'the five ladies of his life' – Mary

68

of the five-year idyll, Nancy Coldstream the painter, Eleanor Clark the writer, herself the singer, and Mary Wimbush the actress – she omits two other women whom I wish to consider.

'The book of life begins in a garden', said Oscar Wilde, and that is where it began for Louis MacNeice. When he was three and a half, his father (a Church of Ireland clergyman) moved to Carrickfergus Rectory, a mile or so inland from Belfast Lough; and in *The Strings Are False*, we are told that this house 'was in a garden'.[2] The phrase is revealing in that it seems to ascribe priority to the garden rather than the house. Writing to his father in 1914 or 1915, he tells him 'I read some Genesis',[3] and this and other letters of that period suggest that Louis and Elizabeth MacNeice's rich fantasy life was centred in the garden rather than the house.

> In my childhood trees were green
> And there was plenty to be seen.
>
> (CP 183)

The retrospective view of the poem 'Autobiography' resembles that of his friend Dylan Thomas's 'Fern Hill': 'once below a time I lordly had the trees and leaves'. In these timeless Edenic gardens there is only one season until, as MacNeice puts it in his prose autobiography:

My mother became steadily more ill and at last she went away; the last I can remember of her at home was her walking up and down the bottom path of the garden, the path under the hedge that was always in shadow, talking to my sister and weeping.[4]

Whatever the actual circumstances of Mrs MacNeice's departure in August 1913, it is clear that her son has imaginatively ordered those events to conform to biblical paradigms – a dejected woman about to be ejected from a garden, and another woman weeping beside a tomb in another garden: *Genesis* 3 conflated with *St. John* 20 and with the psalmist's 'walk through the valley of the shadow of death'.

As MacNeice's poem, 'Autobiography', continues the story:

> When I was five the black dreams came;
> Nothing after was quite the same.
>
> *Come back early or never come.*
>
> The dark was talking to the dead;
> The lamp was dark beside my bed.
>
> (CP 183–4)

We know from *The Strings Are False* who 'was talking to the dead':

When I was in bed I could hear [my father's] voice below in the study – and I knew that he was alone – intoning away, communing with God. And because of his conspiracy with God I was afraid of him.[5]

With Mrs MacNeice's departure – to a mental home – in 1913, the most important presence in the garden became, for her children, the gardener so lovingly described in her son's autobiography:

Out best antidote to ... terrors and depressions was the gardener Archie, in whose presence everything was merry. My father did not think of him in that way, as Archie, whose professional pride was easily wounded, would sometimes absent himself for weeks out of pique. But for us nothing that Archie could do was wrong and he cast a warm glow upon everything he touched.[6]

He is presented as the presiding spirit of the innocent garden as opposed to – and opposed by – the Rector, presiding spirit of the nightmare-haunted house. Where the one lived by the Good Book and was the embodiment of Truth, the other could neither read nor write and was given to 'as my father called it, romancing'.

At school in England, the Rector's son went the way of the gardener rather than his father. His first headmaster, Littleton Powys, remembered him as a dormitory story-teller to be second only to that of his brother, John Cowper Powys; and, in a Marlborough College magazine,[7] there is an anonymous story – called 'Death' – that could only come from one hand. It opens in a cemetery in which a woman comes to the narrator's side. He says:

I could not see her face and I could not hear her footsteps on the gravel, but I heard her weep. 'They buried me,' she said, 'they buried me. But I did not love him then' and then she disappeared into the laurels.

The desolate words the schoolboy puts into his mother's mouth – 'I did not love him then' – can only refer to the husband who banished and (in 1914, literally) buried her; but, she said 'they buried me'. The plural pronoun would seem to implicate the son, who would later write to a friend: 'My birth was managed so rottenly that my mother had eventually to have a hysterectomy; after which she was ill off and on till she died'.[8]

When the scene in her 16-year-old son's story shifts to a dream conflation of Marlborough College Chapel and St. Nicholas' Church, Carrickfergus, there enters a figure resembling his father:

He was dressed in long white robes as a priest but, somehow, he seemed more heavenly. A shudder came over me, my heart gave a leap as he fixed his eyes on me and came towards me; quite definitely he wanted me to follow him. All was quiet save for an occasional cough and the inane stammerings of the prefect. I arose and followed him, the bench creaked but no one looked at me. We walked down the aisle together and none of the sleepy boys even glanced at us.

When we were out in the rainy night he said to me 'We are going to my Garden' and in silence I walked by his side across the windy field towards the cemetery.

Priest and narrator (father and son) enter a Mortuary Chapel like the one in the Carrickfergus cemetery, where the narrator is told to wait. He thinks 'I longed for the man, in a way I loved him', as he watches him among the graves help the woman to her feet. Then together 'they seemed to go up to heaven fainter and fainter in the mist'. The story ends with the narrator saying – as MacNeice must often have said to himself:

'Do not think of it any more; shout for your house on the touch line, turn your back to his Garden, you will soon have enough of polished granite, a white cross or a broken pillar.'

Beyond the Carrickfergus Rectory garden lay the cemetery screened by a hawthorn hedge until, every spring, this was cut by Archie and 'a polished granite obelisk would reappear looking over at us. Then Archie would shake his fist, say "Thon's a bad ould fella"'. Flanking both garden and cemetery on the south side was a railway embankment along which, several times a day, ran a train. By the time trains made the first of their many appearances in MacNeice's poetry, they had gathered shadows from the cemetery: we see them first in a poem originally called 'Reminiscences of Childhood':

> Trains came threading quietly through my dozing childhood,
> Gentle murmurs nosing through a summer quietude,
> Drawing in and out, in and out, their smoky ribbons,
> Parting now and then, and launching full-rigged galleons
> And scrolls of smoke that hung in a shifting epitaph.
> Then distantly the noise declined like a descending graph,

Sliding downhill gently to the bottom of the distance
(For now all things are there that all were here once);
And so we hardly noticed when that metal murmur came.
But it brought us assurance and comfort all the same,
And in the early night they soothed us to sleep,
And the chain of the rolling wheels bound us in deep
Till all was broken by that menace from the sea,
The steel-bosomed siren calling bitterly.

(*CP* 3)

Written in 1926, this offers a map of the mythic terrain of the MacNeice country that was to remain essentially unchanged for the rest of his life. The trains that pass from the high ground to the west – from garden to cemetery – on their way to the low ground by the sea, have unmistakably feminine associations: 'threading quietly ... drawing in and out, in and out, their smoky ribbons'. Their gentle murmurs, 'Sliding downhill gently to the bottom of the distance', remind us that (in the poem 'Autobiography')

My mother wore a yellow dress;
Gently, gently, gentleness.

(*CP* 183)

The gentle murmurs of surrogate mother-comfort are succeeded by a silent 'shifting epitaph' of smoke, as one after another the trains seem to follow her underground, and the motherless child comes to bitter awareness: '(For now all things are there that all were here once)'. Remembering how the shipyard siren would waken him at dawn, the poet gives it a 'steel bosom' perhaps associated – at some subconscious level – with the harsh Ulster nanny who ran the household after his mother left. 'When she carried you off in disgrace', he wrote, 'your face would be scratched by the buckle on her thick leather belt'.[9]

The loveless child became a loveless public schoolboy and a loveless undergraduate who, in his second year at Oxford, gravitated to a more accommodating bosom. His first girlfriend, Mary Beazley, was herself the child of a loveless marriage, the daughter of a Jewish father – killed in the Great War – and a formidable mother, who then married the brilliant classical scholar, J.D. Beazley, to whom she had been attached for some years. Mary looked 'like a Japanese doll, slight and dainty, her hair very black and her skin very white'.[10] She was said to be the best dancer in Oxford, measuring her life by dance-cards kept in a lavendered box tied with ribbon. MacNeice did not dance, but he was handsome and amusing, a puntsman and a poet. During the summers of 1928, 1929 and 1930, they spent lyrical afternoons on the river Cherwell, attended by dancing mayflies whose brief lives MacNeice arrested and extended in an amber lyric.

His 'Mayfly' begins:

> Barometer of my moods today, mayfly,
> Up and down one among a million, one
> The same at best as the rest of the jigging mayflies,
> One only day of May alive beneath the sun.
>
> The yokels tilt their pewters and the foam
> Flowers in the sun beside the jewelled water.
> Daughter of the South, call the sunbeams home
> To nest between your breasts.
>
> (*CP* 13–14)

These images of lively plentitude are starkly counterpointed by an image of what lies beyond the mayfly lovers' moment:

> hours of stone,
> Long rows of granite sphinxes looking on.
>
> (*CP* 14)

It is hard to dissociate these woman-breasted onlookers from the buried memory of a woman buried under Irish granite and, at the poem's end, the shadow of her tombstone falls across the lovers:

> The show will soon shut down, its gay-rags gone,
> But when this summer is over let us die together,
> I want always to be near your breasts.
>
> (*CP* 14)

On the last day of his last summer term at Oxford, Louis and Mary were married and, soon after, they moved to Birmingham to continue their idyll in a flat she painted like a gipsy caravan. From that colourful love-nest, he looked back to monochromatic and loveless 'Belfast':

> Down there at the end of the melancholy lough
> Against the lurid sky over the stained water
> Where hammers clang murderously on the girders
> Like crucifixes the gantries stand.

[.... .]

> Over which country of cowled and haunted faces
> The sun goes down with a banging of Orange drums

> While the male kind murders each its woman
> To whose prayer for oblivion answers no Madonna.
>
> (*CP* 17)

The repeated charge of murder obviously relates to the internecine Civil War that had contributed to the darkness of his adolescence, but the statement that 'the male kind murders each its woman' is puzzling. Admitting no exception, it would seem to implicate those who buried Mrs MacNeice: the son whose birth broke her health, the husband who buried her.

Three years later, MacNeice wrote his 'Valediction', a poem that takes leave of Belfast in terms that suggest he is taking leave not only of Belfast:

> This was my mother-city, these my paps,
> Country of callous lava cooled to stone[·]
>
> (*CP* 52)

The past tense is telling, as is the characterization of his motherland – 'callous lava cooled to stone': 'callous' a word more often used in the sense of 'hard-hearted' than 'hardened'; mother and land alike losing the heat of lava (lover?), acquiring the coldness of stone. Addressing his mother-country – and mother as well as country, I suggest – he continues his indictment:

> I would call you to book
> I would say to you, Look;
> I would say, This is what you have given me
> Indifference and sentimentality
> A metallic giggle, a fumbling hand,
> A heart that leaps to a fife band:
> Set these against your water-shafted air
> Of amethyst and moonstone, the horses' feet like bells of
>   hair
> Shambling beneath the orange cart, the beer-brown spring
> Guzzling between the heather, the green gush of Irish
>   spring.
> Cursèd be he that curses his mother. I cannot be
> Anyone else than what this land engendered me[·]
>
> (*CP* 52)

Mother and country have given him 'indifference and sentimentality', rather than love, for which (his syntax implies) he would curse them but for the fact that such a curse would rebound on the curser. To avoid such hurt, such hatred, such vengeful impulses, he decides:

> I will exorcise my blood
> And not to have my baby-clothes my shroud
> I will acquire an attitude not yours
> And become as one of your holiday visitors,
> And however often I may come
> Farewell, my country, and in perpetuum[·]
>
> (*CP* 53)

Refusing to share the shroud of his mother-country, he concludes:

> Good-bye your hens running in and out of the white house
> Your absent-minded goats along the road, your black cows
> Your greyhounds and your hunters beautifully bred
> Your drums and your dolled-up Virgins and your ignorant
>   dead.
>
> (*CP* 54)

'A plague on both your Protestant and Papist houses!' he implies, but the terms of his 'Valediction' suggest that those 'ignorant dead' – principally, of course, the dead of the Troubles – may also include a woman buried under a stone in Carrowdore churchyard.

Her shadow falls more obliquely across MacNeice's first play, also written in 1934. Called 'Station Bell',[11] its action (or, to be more precise, its inaction) is set in a Dublin station buffet, where 'a large woman of about forty' proclaims herself Dictator of Ireland and sets up her headquarters. Her name, Julia Brown, may invite associations with Hitler's Brownshirts, but in that Ireland is traditionally personified as a woman, one is surely meant to sense a connection with Kathleen-ni-Houlihan, icon of Irish nationalism, celebrated in Yeats's play of that name. The icon is directly invoked in Act II of 'Station Bell', when the Dictatress's general introduces her to members of his Propaganda Corps and a mannequin explains: 'The General has asked me to represent Kathleen-ni-Houlihan, this coat and skirt is of the best patently shrunk Connemara tweed. This necklace is made entirely of local stones'. MacNeice's parents came from Connemara and his mother, in her Ulster exile, spoke of it so often that 'the very name Connemara' – her son would write in his autobiography – 'seemed too rich for any ordinary place'.[12] His juxtaposition of *Connemara* and *stone* suggests a subconscious association of Lily MacNeice with Kathleen-ni-Houlihan.

However, if, snug in his Birmingham love-nest, he thought with his 1934 'Valediction' and 'Station Bell' to have exorcised the ghosts of mother and motherland, 1935 was to prove him wrong. That November, the past came back to haunt him – with a vengeance – when without warning, it would seem, his Mary left him for another man, an American graduate student called Charles Katzman. Not only did she leave her husband but her son, their 18-month-old Dan. For the second time in his life, MacNeice was stripped of a love on which he had come to rely, and it must have been doubly bitter to see Dan doomed to relive his own loss of a mother. Further compounding the difficulties and distress of the situation, Mrs Beazley now revealed herself as a mother and mother-in-law from Hell. Having earlier done everything in her power to prevent Mary's marriage to Louis, she now embarked on a campaign to prevent her divorce and union with Katzman. She went to the American Embassy in London to acquaint the authorities with her daughter's 'moral turpitude' – one account of the story has her hinting at Mary's involvement with white-slave traffic – in an unsuccessful attempt to block her application for a US visa. Katzman left for America to find a job before Mary's visa had come through, but not before Mrs Beazley had written letters to Oxford and Harvard trying to blast his career. She commissioned an eminent rabbi to compose a lethal curse and asked one of her husband's most brilliant acolytes, Isaiah Berlin, to cross the Atlantic (all expenses paid) and deliver it to Katzman in person. Berlin told a friend of 'a séance lasting some 3–4 hours of uninterrupted Medea-talk. The combination of tigress, bore and femme fatale is really very odd?'[13] Her would-be messenger did not ask whether he was expected to deliver the curse orally or in writing, but kept out of the way until the storm had blown over. That, however, was not before she had hired a private detective to 'shadow' her son-in-law in the hope of catching him *in flagrante delicto* with Dan's nurse or a maid she had insisted on appointing. The harassed poet would eventually strike back with a bequest in 'Auden and MacNeice: their Last Will and Testament':

> And to the most mischievous woman now alive
> We leave a lorry-load of moral mud
> And may her Stone Age voodoo never thrive.[14]

The same document made a generous bequest to the wife who had abandoned him:

> Lastly to Mary living in a remote
> Country I leave whatever she would remember
> Of hers and mine before she took that boat,

Such memories not being necessarily lumber
And may no chance, unless she wills, delete them
And may her hours be gold and without number.[15]

In November 1936 Mary married Charles Katzman and, within weeks, her former husband had written a love-song – it was entitled 'song' at its first appearance in print – for the girl who had been 'the best dancer in Oxford':

The sunlight on the garden
Hardens and grows cold,
We cannot cage the minute
Within its nets of gold,
When all is told
We cannot beg for pardon.

Our freedom as free lances
Advances towards its end;
The earth compels, upon it
Sonnets and birds descend;
And soon, my friend,
We shall have no time for dances.

The sky was good for flying
Defying the church bells
And every evil iron
Siren and what it tells:
The earth compels,
We are dying, Egypt, dying

And not expecting pardon,
Hardened in heart anew,
But glad to have sat under
Thunder and rain with you,
And grateful too
For sunlight on the garden.

(*CP* 84–5)

We know the poem is ostensibly addressed to Mary because of its reference to dances, but its setting is a garden she probably never saw: the garden of the Carrickfergus Rectory. Paradise has been lost, and again the 'sunlight on the garden' yields to the petrifying shadows of the Carrickfergus cemetery. Almost a decade before, in the poem 'Child's Terror', MacNeice lamented: 'I have lost my swing/ That I thought would climb the sky'.[16]

Now he remembers the exultation of that flight challenging the dark message of his father's church bells and the shipyard sirens: that gravity will not be denied. 'We are dying, Egypt, dying'. But why should he speak of 'not expecting pardon'? Mary had betrayed *him*. The only woman from whom he might not expect pardon is the woman in whose company he first experienced 'the sunlight on the garden', the mother whose death he believed he had precipitated, the mother who haunts this poem and so many others.

From the coming of 'the black dreams' in the wake of her departure until the end of his life, MacNeice's nights were visited with fears that did not trouble his days. He was always to dislike sleeping in a room by himself. The first time he stayed with George and Mercy MacCann, and showed his habitual reluctance to go to bed, they solved the problem by moving a spare bed into their room.[17] The day he heard of Dylan Thomas's death, he organized an informal wake that ended – when everyone but an old friend and former mistress, Margaret Gardiner, had gone home – with him saying to her: 'Please stay a little longer. Please.' She realized (she wrote in her autobiography) that that was what he wanted.

He didn't dare to sleep that night, for sleep was too dangerously akin to death. He had to stay awake. So we sat and talked until a grey light began to trickle through the curtains and the first sounds of the wakening town could be heard, single and distinct before they gradually increased and merged into a general hubbub. It was after six; the night was over and I went home.[18]

Such a man was not likely to stay celibate any longer than he could help and, at the start of 1937, MacNeice met 'a girl called Leonora who was a musical actress, very tall, very blonde, all eye-veils, furs and egotism; dabbled in religion and poetry, mixed her conversation with French and German, and was painted by Royal Academicians'.[19] This was almost certainly Leonora Corbett, whose conquests included A.A. Milne in whose play, *Sarah Simple*, she was to play the female lead in May 1937. She is said to have told a fellow actor, Griffith Jones: 'No-one can accuse me of having got here by my acting'. The affair with MacNeice ended, dramatically, with Leonora throwing a tea-table at him. As the flying tea-leaves scribbled their prophecy on the wall, the ex-lovers 'exploded into laughter' – perhaps, Louis thought, 'our one real moment of communion'.[20]

Leonora was followed by Nancy Coldstream, a painter like

her husband, Bill Coldstream. Wystan Auden, then a guest in their flat, brought his friend MacNeice back to supper with them. Afterwards, and with characteristic candour, he said to Bill: 'Louis could be very convenient', keeping Nancy happy while he, Bill, got on with his painting. So it proved. When Louis was commissioned to write a travel book, following in the footsteps of Boswell and Johnson to the Western Isles of Scotland, Nancy went with him and illustrated his text. Their love-affair lasted into the autumn of 1938, by which time MacNeice had embarked on another journey, another journal, one that would chronicle an autobiographical journey from autumn into winter and perhaps beyond. It was to have everything that, in 1938, he asked of a poem: it would admit the impurities of the world, the flux of experience, in a documentary form that, for all its seeming spontaneity, would be directed into patterns on the page – as images fixed on film – by the invisible imagination. The resulting poem, *Autumn Journal*, owes something to another masterpiece of the period, the documentary film, *Night Mail*, on which Auden (who wrote the text) had collaborated with Bill Coldstream.

Autumn Journal is *The Prelude* of the Thirties, but it is a dramatic rather than a philosophical poem, sometimes recording emotions as they occur, sometimes recollecting them, but seldom in tranquillity. History is a river on which Wordsworth in *The Prelude* looks back to the rapids of the French Revolution, whereas MacNeice can hear the premonitory thunder of the Falls ahead. Memory is a structuring principle of both poems, but in *Autumn Journal* it is a post-Freudian, Proustian memory that flies back and forward like a weaver's shuttle, leaving past and present, public life and private life interwoven on the loom. It is a poem about many things, none of them more central to its structure than love: love of women and love of country and, as in so many other poems, their images become transposed. In section 16, after reading the recently published memoirs of Maud Gonne, for whom Yeats wrote his greatest love-poems and his play *Cathleen ni Houlihan*, MacNeice exclaims:

> Kathleen ni Houlihan! Why
>   Must a country, like a ship or a car, be always female,
> Mother or sweetheart? A woman passing by,
>   We did but see her passing.
> Passing like a patch of sun on the rainy hill
>   And yet we love her for ever and hate our neighbour

> And each one in his will
>> Binds his heirs to continuance of hatred.

(CP 132)

'Mother or sweetheart … passing … passing … passing like a patch of sun', the same sunlight that on the garden 'hardens and grows cold'. Mother and motherland generate love and hatred, to which the classicist poet returns at his section's end:

> *Odi atque amo:*
>> Shall we cut this name on trees with a rusty dagger?
> Her mountains are still blue, her rivers flow
>> Bubbling over the boulders.
> She is both a bore and a bitch;
>> Better close the horizon,
> Send her no more fantasy, no more longings which
>> Are under a fatal tariff.
> For common sense is the vogue
>> And she gives her children neither sense nor money
> Who slouch around the world with a gesture and a brogue
>> And a faggot of useless memories.

(CP 134)

After finishing *Autumn Journal*, MacNeice had a brief love-affair with a seventeen-year-old artist's model, Mary Hunt, 'the most beautiful English girl I ever saw', said the poet Ruthven Todd.[21] Her beauty had one blemish: an amputated lower leg, replaced by a tin substitute (held on by suction). She would later appear, I believe, in MacNeice's poem 'Christina':

> It all began so easy
> With bricks upon the floor
> Building motley houses
> And knocking down your houses
> And always building more.
>
> The doll was called Christina,
> Her under-wear was lace,
> She smiled while you dressed her
> And when you then undressed her
> She kept a smiling face.
>
> Until the day she tumbled
> And broke herself in two
> And her legs and arms were hollow

And her yellow head was hollow
Behind her eyes of blue.

...

He went to bed with a lady
Somewhere seen before,
He heard the name Christina
And suddenly saw Christina
Dead on the nursery floor.

(CP 174)

Truth, as so often, is stranger than fiction. What at first sight
appears a surrealist fantasy of love and death is almost certainly a
splicing of two memories: the first, of Elizabeth's doll; the second,
of Mary Hunt 'who took her foot off before she went to bed'.

In March 1939, saying goodbye to her and England, MacNeice
set off for America. There he met and would have married
another writer, Eleanor Clark,[22] but his love was not returned
and, in December 1940, he returned to England, the Blitz, and a
job at the BBC. In 1942, he met a vivacious red-haired singer,
called Hedli Anderson, who was then making a name for herself
in London. She had sung in the Group Theatre production of
Auden's play, *The Dance of Death*, and had created several roles in
the Auden-Isherwood collaborations, *The Dog Beneath the Skin* and
The Ascent of F6. Following her success as 'The Singer' in the
second of these, Auden and Britten together wrote a series of six
cabaret songs for her – including what came to be her theme-
song, the one popularly known by its refrain, 'Tell me the truth
about love'.[23] She and MacNeice were married in July 1942 and
spent much of their honeymoon on the island of Achill – off the
west coast of Ireland – that he had first visited with Mary thirteen
years before.

At the end of the war, the BBC granted him three and a half
month's sabbatical leave and, with Hedli and their two children,
he returned to Achill. His principal project – a radio play to be
called 'The Dark Tower' – determined his choice of the place in
which to write it. Based on Browning's poem, 'Childe Roland to
the Dark Tower Came', MacNeice's story is relatively simple. The
hero, Roland, is brought up by his mother to follow in the family
tradition, undertaking a quest that has claimed the lives of his
forefathers and five older brothers. He watches a sixth, Gavin,
trained by a Sergeant-Trumpeter to play 'the Challenge Call'
before he, too, is despatched by his mother on the quest. In due

course, a bell tolls for him and his name is added to the roll of honour. Roland, in turn, is trained by the Sergeant-Trumpeter and a Tutor, who tells him never to fall in love. He does – with Sylvie – but is sent off to talk to Blind Peter in a castle ringed by 'smothering yew-trees'. Peter tells him more about the Dragon he must seek and challenge, and more about his father:

> You're like your father – one of the dedicated
> Whose life is a quest, whose death is a victory.[24]

His training completed, Roland takes leave of Sylvie and receives his marching orders from Tutor, Sergeant-Trumpeter, and Mother who gives him a last message:

> Here is a ring with a blood-red stone. So long as
> This stone retains its colour, it means that I
> Retain my purpose in sending you on the Quest.
> I put it now on your finger.

(SP 128)

The Quester sets out and encounters and escapes a number of tempters: a drunk and barmaid in a tavern, the seductive Neaera on a luxury liner, and Sylvie, whom he would have married had not the voices of Blind Peter, Gavin, and his Father persuaded him to leave her at the altar. The tempters' voices pursue him into the Desert we recognize as the Waste Land, and are driving him mad, when suddenly the blood drains from the stone in his ring and he hears his mother say:

> On my deathbed I have changed my mind;
> I am bearing now a child of stone.
> He can go on the Quest. But you, Roland – come back!

(SP 143–4)

Ecstatic at his reprieve, Roland throws the ring away, but hears it strike a stone that proves to be a gravestone inscribed:

> 'To Those Who Did Not Go Back –
> Whose Bones being Nowhere, their signature is for All Men –
> Who went to their Death of their own Free Will
> Bequeathing Free Will to Others.'

(SP 144)

Uncertain whether to go forward or to follow his footsteps back ('Are these my footsteps? But how small they look!'), he hears the pounding rhythm of his heart and sees the mountains closing round him. On their peaks stand Blind Peter, his brothers, the

Sergeant-Trumpeter, his Tutor, and his Father. With their exhortations in his ears, the Dark Tower rising from the ground in front of him, the Quester replies:

> I, Roland, the black sheep, the unbeliever –
> Who never did anything of his own free will –
> Will do this now to bequeath free will to others.

(SP 148)

He then challenges the Dragon to 'Come out and do your worst' and sounds the trumpet call.

How are we to interpret MacNeice's dream of the Dark Tower? 'Roland, the black sheep, the unbeliever' – who learns Latin and ethics from a Tutor – is obvious enough. A note to the printed text tells us that 'The Mother in bearing so many children only to send them to their death, can be thought of as thereby bearing a series of deaths. So her logical last child is stone – her own death. This motif has an echo in the stone in the ring'. The Mother, associated with death, is as readily identifiable – on one level – as the dedicated Father, 'whose death is a victory': Bishop MacNeice, who believed with St. Paul that 'Death is swallowed up in victory'.

I have come to believe that *The Dark Tower* has another, public, level of interpretation underlying the personal one. The clue to this lies in an exchange between Roland and his sweetheart, Sylvie. When he tells her that he's about to leave on his quest, she replies:

> You go away because they tell you to.
> Because your mother's brought you up on nothing
> But out-of-date beliefs and mock heroics.
> It's easy enough for her –

ROLAND Easy for her?
          Who's given her flesh and blood – and I'm the seventh son!

SYLVIE   I've heard all that. They call it sacrifice
          But each new death is a stone in a necklace to her.
          Your mother, Roland, is mad.

(SP 126)

Remember the mannequin in 'Station Bell', who represented Kathleen ni Houlihan and wore a necklace 'made entirely of local stones'. Roland's mother is at once MacNeice's own mother and Kathleen ni Houlihan, who brings up her children on 'nothing/

But out-of-date beliefs and mock heroics'. Her sons may love and obey her, but throughout history she has trained them to be sacrificial offerings and sent them to their deaths.

Louis MacNeice, as a child, loved his mother and, as an adult, loved his mothercountry, but each it seemed to him had an unforgivable love-affair with death. As he grew older, their images coalesced, at once generating and darkening the love poems of one of the great love poets of this century.

LOUIS MACNEICE AND DEREK MAHON

RICHARD YORK

The succession from MacNeice to Mahon may appear a very neat one. MacNeice died in September 1963, when Mahon was 22, and Mahon's first verse dates from 1962 (his first volume being published in 1968). The first poem in his *Selected Poems* (and the third in his *Poems 1962–78*)[1] is his elegy for MacNeice, 'In Carrowdore Churchyard'. It looks very much as if Mahon has taken up the tradition from the death of his predecessor. Certainly critics have often noted the connection. Brendan Kennelly's fine article on 'Derek Mahon's Humane Perspective' quotes the Carrowdore poem as showing that 'Mahon's original self begins in his tribute to Louis MacNeice'.[2] Above all, one has to cite Edna Longley's review of *Night Crossing* in *The Honest Ulsterman*, in which she says of Mahon that 'he reacts to and against an environment which is the antithesis of poetry and therefore compels it at a deep level. In this respect he is the heir and disinheritor of MacNeice – starting at the point where MacNeice leaves off', and speaks of MacNeice and Mahon as sharing a 'comprehensive appreciation of the things of this world'.[3] Later, reviewing *The Snow Party* she commented that 'his style uniquely combines influences from Yeats and MacNeice into a kind of racy rhetoric, subjected to the highest degree of lyrical concentration'.[4] The characterisation of Mahon's writing seems to me very apt; but the phrase which should most engage our attention is, I think, the one about Mahon as MacNeice's heir and disinheritor. She implies a complex relationship of authority and challenge, and I think that is borne out by close consideration of Mahon's work.

Mahon himself, in his prose writings, refers very frequently to MacNeice, and always with respect and as a model. Notably in his *Sphere Book of Modern Irish Poetry* he raises the question of whether

MacNeice's Irish status is only 'an accident of birth', but goes on to point out that his reputation is stronger in Ireland than in Great Britain, and particularly that in Northern Ireland 'his example has provided a frame of reference for a number of younger poets'.[5] It certainly seems reasonable to assume that the number of younger poets includes himself – and then to wonder what exactly a 'frame of reference' amounts to. Most of these references contain little criticism, though there is a special bias which I think is quite illuminating. For instance, in reviewing a book of verse by C. Day Lewis,[6] Mahon goes out of his way, as it may seem, to compare him with MacNeice, on the curious grounds that Day Lewis was also the son of an Irish clergyman. His comment is that, 'Unlike Day Lewis, [MacNeice] never regressed to nostalgia, perhaps because he was more truly an expatriate son'. The expatriate relation seems to be what matters to Mahon: the retention of a link with Ireland and the clear, firm judgement of the outsider to Ireland. Mahon himself has, of course, followed a pattern of exile in some ways resembling MacNeice's and in some ways differing from it: unlike MacNeice he was at school in Northern Ireland and at university in Dublin, and returned to Northern Ireland for a spell as poet in residence at the New University of Ulster, a period which was personally apparently very unhappy but which was obviously a major poetic stimulus and produced many important works. Mahon's relationship to Northern Ireland (in particular) is therefore more crucial to his sensibility than MacNeice's was, and it is more complex – but it is not dissimilar in kind: it mingles a sense of belonging or quasi-belonging, of respect and concern, with a sense of restriction, of illiberalism and discomfort, of the need to be elsewhere. Mahon saw, obviously, in MacNeice, someone who had negotiated the difficult transition from Ireland to England, and in doing so had discovered a dual identity. This in fact is the major concern of Mahon's two sensitive and acutely observed papers on MacNeice's work, 'MacNeice in England and Ireland' in Brown & Reid's volume *Time Was Away*,[7] and 'MacNeice, the War and the BBC' in the volume of *Studies on Louis MacNeice*,[8] the second being published in part as a revision of what he then considered 'wrong-headed' in the earlier volume. Much of what Mahon has to say of MacNeice in the first paper is clear, pertinent and of general relevance: notably he speaks of his mordancy, his fascination with the fact of language (qualities Mahon intriguingly finds in another of his heroes, another expatriate Irishman, Samuel Beckett), his wish to recreate the surface of English life, his sense of the poem as documentary, his 'existentialism of the passing minute' – I add in passing that both MacNeice and Mahon have translated Horace's *Carpe Diem* ode, in very different ways – his empirical humanism. Few readers would fail to find these qualities in MacNeice and few would fail to find them also in Mahon – if the humanism, as we shall see, is more tenuous or taut in Mahon. Two features however need special attention in our context. Firstly, Mahon's emphasis on the way he responds to landscape: he responds with a painter's eye – and Mahon certainly has that himself, as is apparent in the rich precision of his descriptions and in his frequent reference to actual painters; but he also responds with a sense of significance, of the way that forms of life are expressed in the seen world: 'Variety and vividness of landscape immediately suggest the variety and vividness of human personality and experience'.[9] The word *landscape* is used widely, to include cocktail bars and football matches; what Mahon is concerned with is essentially the sympathy, alertness and curiosity of the poet as observer. Given that, we shall not find it difficult to see the link with his own work, albeit the landscape is often bleaker, less vivid and varied than in MacNeice: which suggests his bareness may be a matter of restraint, of self-discipline, rather than of mere apathy or dull incuriosity. The second point arises from the first. MacNeice's status as observer, his love of perceptual sensation and what Mahon tellingly calls his 'profound superficiality' proves to be very much linked with what Mahon considers to be his 'Irishness' – namely that he is 'a tourist in his own country'. Not, Mahon insists, an exile – which is why I have rather awkwardly been avoiding the word – but one who thrives on 'memory in apostasy'. The apostasy counts; it gives distance, irony, and a kind of romanticism. The paper ends by quoting 'Carrick Revisited' – 'And the pre-natal mountain is far away' (*CP* 225) – commenting that 'reality lay elsewhere', in an Ulster childhood and a life's work abroad. The alien, the previous, the lost: these, it seems, are what for Mahon underlie the hedonistic immediacy of so much of MacNeice's writing. Terence Brown quotes the same poem to speak of MacNeice as an exile who has chosen detachment, and who through his knowledge of conflicting social and cultural loyalties is led to scepticism, and separately goes on to reflect on his muted Romanticism;[10] what Mahon has done is to see the scepticism as very closely bound up with the Romanticism as a kind of alienation which allows freedom, honesty and immediacy of sensation and feeling. MacNeice, for Mahon, isn't quite either English or Irish: as an Anglo-Irishman he doesn't belong to the people of Ireland and we recall Mahon himself in his poem 'Going Home' (formerly 'The Return') wishing to become an English tree: 'As if I belonged here too' – and then recalling the bare, worn Ulster tree which merges into night 'As if it belongs there'. Wanting to belong and not belonging: that is where poetry comes from.

In the second paper, on MacNeice and the war, Mahon returns to MacNeice's 'human priorities', his love of 'things being various', and stresses rather more his sceptical qualities, his 'ironic and anarchic' manner. Again the stress is on the ambiguity of MacNeice's feelings, which Mahon (to my mind less convincingly) links with what he calls his Anglo-Irish cultural inclusiveness: this time the ambiguity lies in his fascination with the destructive disorder of the bombings together with his proper liberal anti-fascism. Afterwards, MacNeice found a home – in the features department of the BBC, and finding a home, in Mahon's view, was bad for him; what makes him a significant poet is the subversiveness that goes with his humane feelings, the sense that 'we can only discover / Life in the life we make': in other words the 'cultural inclusiveness' is the ability to stand outside any one culture and regard the value of life as still to be created, and as lying largely in the act of creation. He quotes MacNeice's poem 'The Casualty', in which the poet says to his lost friend:

> ... your whole life till then showed an endeavour
> Towards a discovery ...

> (*CP* 247)

Perhaps it is the endeavour that matters; the discovery has to be postponed or eluded.

Eluded, in this case, by death. And it is not surprising that one of Mahon's first major achievements is his reflection on the death of MacNeice in 'In Carrowdore Churchyard'. Not surprising because of Mahon's constant concern with loss, the precariousness of existence, distance, limitation, mortality: so that the volume of selected poems in fact opens with an elegy for MacNeice and ends with one for Camus – who had actually died earlier, so that this final poem is a memory of a loss perceived at great cultural and geographical distance, the Algerian's death as felt in a Belfast grammar school. The MacNeice poem is a masterly balancing of opposites: concentration and diffusion, nature and civilisation, past and future, poverty and suffering on the one hand and sensuous novelty on the other, solemnity and playfulness. The theme of balance and duality is put in two particularly striking passages. First Mahon talks of the alternation of the seasons:

> Locked in the winter's fist, these hills are hard
> As nails, yet soft and feminine in their turn
> When fingers open and the hedges burn.

The tone nicely captures some of the MacNeice manner (or *a* MacNeice manner): the relaxed rhythm delicately pointed by an elegant rhyme, the refreshing use of cliché in 'hard as nails' – which becomes almost surrealist with the hint of fingernails, the discreet echo of the classical rhetorical opposition of the closed fist of hard argument and the open hand of mild persuasion, the discreet assumption of the winter-spring dichotomy which actually underlies much of the thought of the poem, the lucid logical order that links this line with the following stanza. Mahon has learnt his lesson: he has inherited much from MacNeice, and this is a worthy tribute to the master. At most, one might suspect that this is made a little too clear, that the display of gratitude is a little too conspicuous and that there is just a hint of an attempt to take control, to take possession of his predecessor – and so, Edna Longley might say, to disinherit him. The hint of rivalry becomes clearer in the following stanza to which I have alluded, and which is much quoted because it so forcefully formulates the fascination with ambiguity which is vital to Mahon and to Mahon's view of MacNeice. The third stanza is about winter and (unnamed) spring. The fourth (and last) begins:

> The ironical, loving crush of roses against snow,
> Each fragile, solving ambiguity.

There are a great many things to say about this, and things to speculate about in it. For instance, what is the grammar of the second line: is each ambiguity both fragile and solving? Or is each rose fragile and a way to solve ambiguity? Or are both roses and snow fragile? Or is all this ambiguous? And, then there is the ironical, loving crush: that it is both ironical and loving is itself a further irony, as well as an anticipation of the fragile solving ambiguity. On top of all this, is there an echo of Rimbaud's 'foule des jeunes et fortes roses', a crowd of roses introducing a totally new cultural dimension to the dialogue with MacNeice? But the crucial issue has to be the reference to a passage in MacNeice. It is specifically the early poem 'Snow' (*CP* 30). The poem is one that Mahon quotes in the Caen paper to highlight MacNeice's appreciation of 'The drunkenness of things being various'. He

also includes it in the Sphere Book. It starts with the snow and
roses:

> The room was suddenly rich and the great bay-window was
> Spawning snow and pink roses against it
> Soundlessly collateral and incompatible;
> World is suddener than we fancy it.

The second stanza is about the drunkenness of things. The third
and last returns to the snow and roses:

> And the fire flames with a bubbling sound for world
> Is more spiteful and gay than one supposes –
> On the tongue on the eyes on the ears in the palms of one's hands –
> There is more than glass between the snow and the huge roses.

We need not, I think, have any reservations about the lucidity and
relevance of Mahon's choice of this image. We may well feel, too,
that the reference to MacNeice gives a whole background of the
sudden and miraculous, the incongruous, alien, almost hostile,
which actually enriches the Mahon poem – but enriches it in a spirit
of contestation. Mahon's poem is decorous, rational, witty,
conclusive; MacNeice's is a puzzled confrontation with an
inconsistent, 'incorrigible' reality, which itself puzzles the reader and
makes demands on him, with its shifting tones and rhythms (unlike
Mahon's orderly but flexible six-line stanza, learnt, no doubt, from
the later MacNeice). Mahon provides tenderness where MacNeice
gave wonder. MacNeice, according to Mahon, 'lie[s] / Past tension
now': death has eliminated the tension that is in the 'Snow' poem.
All this gives a dignity and calm, a sense of inevitability and value,
which is no doubt apt to an elegy; it diminishes the love of surprise
to which Mahon paid tribute in his prose paper.

A footnote is necessary here. The snow roses recur in
MacNeice's writing: in the last section of *Autumn Journal* he says:
'Sleep, my past and all my sins, / In distant snow or dried roses'.
MacNeice, himself, that is, has started to relegate snow and roses
to past and sleep.

This, I think, is characteristic of the way Mahon uses MacNeice.
He recognizes the plurality of sensation in MacNeice (the word
plurality is, of course, one I take from the title of MacNeice's most
explicit of philosophical poems); and he shares with him the sense
that there is no monolithic, authoritative pattern of things. In these
respects, one hardly need add, both stand against the dogmatic
conformism that is not uncommon in Northern Ireland, and both
explicitly denounce it (Mahon's 'Ecclesiastes' corresponding to the

justly famous XVI section of *Autumn Journal*). Mahon therefore learns from MacNeice the voice of liberalism: irony, wide cultural reference – especially to the classics but also to continental writers in Mahon, a conversational style which allows shifts between, for instance, argument, reflection, psychological analysis, symbolic vision and metaphysical abstraction, the sense of anti-climax. In particular he learns a mastery of verse form, not least through the six-line stanza with flexible rhyme sequences and a strongly marked but flexible rhythmic pattern, a form which combines freedom with decorum. And he learns playful or disconcerting verse forms: the rhyme on a foreign word, the rhyme on a preposition or other subordinate word. Mahon, in other words, learns from MacNeice to write in a gentlemanly style, a style of learning, balance, good humour and humanistic good will. But there is more to Mahon than this: I am inclined to say that this other dimension may well be influenced by the continental existentialism with which he is obviously familiar, but it may well be essentially simply a matter of personal disposition, perhaps enhanced by a deeper and more uncertain struggle to free himself from Northern Ireland. And this extra dimension is a greater sense of negativity, a greater feeling that freedom means not being committed and so, perhaps, not having full contact with people or things. Identifying the sense of otherness in MacNeice, Mahon seems to intensify it in himself.

This has many results on the level of poetic form and style. There is a greater sense of the visual and the static; one may for instance compare on one hand MacNeice's poems on the National Gallery, section XX of *Autumn Journal* and the postwar 'The National Gallery', which are about the livingness of painting, with 'the full mystique of the commonplace', and on the other hand a poem such as Mahon's very fine 'Courtyards in Delft' which is about the 'chaste / Perfection of the thing and the thing made' (though the argument here is extremely subtle, and one must certainly admit that the early 'A Portrait of the Artist' – on Van Gogh – is much more animated). There is the development of a thinner texture of verse, notably in the various poems in three-line uneven stanzas like this:

> Two years we spent
> down there, in a quaint
> outbuilding bright with recent paint.

> ('The Woods')

There is a greater concentration on a characteristic landscape of bare rock and water: one can usefully think of his 'Achill', where he

> consider[s] the glow
> Of the sun through mist, a pearl bulb containèdly fierce;
> A rain-shower darkens the schist for a minute or so
> Then it drifts away and the sloe-black patches disperse

while he remembers his absent family and thinks of Greece; and
one can compare this with MacNeice's poems on a visit to Achill
such as 'Littoral', which is about the sensuous richness of the sea;
'This hoary beach is burgeoning with minutiae'. The MacNeice
poem, like the Mahon one, goes on to distraction and loss:

> burgeoning with minutiae
> Like a philosopher
> Who, thinking, makes cat's cradles with string – or a widow
> Who knits for her sons but remembers a tomb in another land.

> (CP 222)

The distancing is there; but it doesn't veil the intensity of the
immediate world, with its

> Indigo, mottle of purple and amber, ink,
> Damson whipped with cream, improbable colours of sea ...

Still more important, there is in Mahon a greater sense of the
artificiality and precariousness of the persona. Mahon often uses
the dramatic monologue. His liking for the form may be derived
from MacNeice (no doubt along with other sources, such as
Lowell in recent times and, of course, Browning behind them all).
One might cite from MacNeice the IVth part of 'Day of Returning',
about the biblical figure of Jacob, especially because it is on what
were to be the typically Mahon themes of survival and return:

> They call me crafty, I robbed my brother,
> Hoaxed my father, I am most practical,
> Yet in my time have had my visions ...

> (CP 316)

The sense of a resigned, self-aware anti-climax, with the aptly
hesitant, reticent tone, both self-mocking and placidly reassured,
has much that is akin to Mahon. But I think that in Mahon the tone
is usually more radically ironic or ambiguous. An early example is
the forger Van Meegeren, who like Jacob is a former visionary
who 'sold [his] *soul* for pottage' but unlike MacNeice's character
seeks to present himself as an implausible saviour:

> And I too have suffered
> Obscurity and derision,

And sheltered in my heart of hearts
A light to transform the world.

('The Forger')

In later years Mahon turned from such relative faith in humanity to the bleak exile of 'Ovid in Tomis'; which is again about a hidden unachieved revelation. Ovid, rather in the style of Mallarmé, reveres the blank page:

Woven of wood-nymphs
It speaks volumes
No-one will ever write.

I incline my head
To its candour
And weep for our exile.

And soon after, one sadly has to say, the exiled Mahon seems to have fallen silent, at least as far as original verse is concerned,* making himself above all the voice of other people in his brilliant work as a translator.

To point the contrast: in MacNeice, experience if past is not wholly lost; the ordeal, once achieved, transforms the speaker and befits him for a place in history, calmly preparing a future:

No more a chooser, I have been chosen
To father the chosen, a full-time task –
With by-products perhaps such as shall we say honey –
Still on the whole I have little to ask
But that day should return, each day of returning.

(*CP* 317)

In Mahon, on the contrary, experience can be a disqualification, as with Bruce Ismay in 'After the Titanic', who had the shame of having survived the Titanic disaster, and can only relive it in memory; he does have something to ask, namely the reader's pity:

My poor soul
Screams out in the starlight, heart
Breaks loose and rolls down like a stone.
Include me in your lamentations.

There is, one may say, not so much an enrichment of experience through the personae as an elucidation of experience, and

---

*See now of course, since the writing of this paper, *The Hudson Letter* (Dublin, Gallery Press, 1995).

especially of the cost of experience and its ultimate cruelty. The distinction is one which I should like finally to explore in two very well known poems, which I hope will bring out the quality of both writers, and their similarities and differences. The first of the pair is MacNeice's 'Woods', which I think brings together a lot of the important features of his writing. It is autobiographical: it is about his father and himself, about his own Irish background and English experience; it is about the literary imaginative significance of England, the fictitious world of Malory, Keats, Shakespeare 'with their interleaving of half-truths and not-quites' set against his father's orthodox wish to spell out True and Good; it is about a fascination and the fantasized self-image that arises in fascination, as the 'dark / But gentle ambush' of the English woods leads the child MacNeice into the imagined adventures and romance of the picture-book. It is about the growth and continuity of the self, the grown-up preserving the excitement of the child. And it is about a withdrawal from fascination, a cautious approximation to the father's unromantic view, as the poet recognizes that woods are not wild but set in a human society, 'assured / Of their place by men', and imagines himself walking out of the darkness of the wood to 'An ordered open air long ruled by dyke and fence'. It ends with a vision of England which nicely balances cosy traditional-homes nostalgia with ordinariness, blatant ordinariness and literary sophistication:

> With geese whose form and gait proclaim their consequence,
> Pargetted outposts, windows browed with thatch,
> And cowpats – and inconsequent wild roses.

> (CP 231)

The geese have consequence but the roses don't, or perhaps it's the other way round, the pretentiousness of the geese being a charming literary conceit about their awkward movements, and the roses a deft literary recollection of Brooke's 'English unofficial rose', the roses moreover neatly rhyming with 'discloses', so that they appear as an apt culmination, an apt revelation of the ordinary. All this is very complex, and recounted in a tone of deceptive ease, varying elegantly from an immediate sense of the physical imagination in 'caterpillar webs on the forehead, danger under the feet', to an awareness of the imaginative slightness of all this in, for instance, the 'rain-filled hoof-mark coined / By a finger of sun from the mint of Long Ago' and eventually to a very adult good tempered, almost prosaic evenness of judgement:

> Yet in using the word tame my father was
> maybe right,
> These woods are not the forest.

The whole is a major achievement, giving clear mythic shape to a discovery of the value of fascination and fancy, and in doing so showing how far that shape itself is something that binds individual to nation and culture.

If we now turn to Mahon to look for something similar, we are certainly tempted to look first at a poem I have already mentioned, 'Going Home' with its contrast between the 'mild woods' of the home counties and the stony growths of Northern Ireland. But the analogy there is not the most interesting, fine as that poem is. The poem called 'The Woods' resembles MacNeice's work only in regarding woods as something 'familiar from the story books'. I should rather turn to a later poem, which is not about woods but about 'A Garage in Co. Cork'. There is one aspect of this poem which gives a precise echo of a detail in MacNeice. In *Autumn Journal* there are 'shining semi-circles of petrol pumps / Like intransigent gangs of idols'. In the 'Garage' poem Mahon imagines that a pair of pumps are an old man and his wife transformed by a grateful god, who gives them immortality in this form. The mythical-playful view of petrol pumps may be a conscious echo, but it would hardly be surprising if it were complete coincidence derived from their common familiarity with the classics. What is more important is the overall form. It is a poem of similar scope to 'Woods': eight 6-line stanzas (as against seven stanzas in MacNeice), with the usual flexibility of rhyme and rhythm; the tone is conversational, rising to literary fantasy and to a haunting quasi-philosophical conclusion, in which the poet speaks of the hinterland as tense

> Not in the hope of a resplendent future
> But with a sure sense of its intrinsic nature.

There is a very precise vision, conveyed in concrete terms, and at times through listing of the familiar:

> Building materials, fruit boxes, scrap iron,
> Dust-laden shrubs and coils of rusty wire ...

There is the sense of light, the 'sacramental gleam' of disused objects. There is wit, verbal inventiveness, playful exploitation of a sophisticated culture. The general manner then is akin to MacNeice's: some points suggest a more precise debt, notably the last stanza where the place is said to be 'unique in each particular' and – in characteristic oxymoron – 'serenely tense'. The whole movement, too, is one akin to MacNeice's style of imagination: it is a movement into fascination and a withdrawal from it into fancy and reflectiveness. The speaker, seeing the abandoned garage, recalls – imprecisely – having seen it in his 'nomadic youth', describes it in really rather surprising detail – with the trail of a snail and the cabbage white butterfly in the garden. But then, peering through the darkened window, he realises that a family must have lived there, imagines the children now in south Boston or Cricklewood – and imagines them imagining the pumps as he now sees them. And here, after four stanzas, a disengagement starts: firstly the speaker turns to the surrounding landscape, an uncultivated landscape 'such as Noah knew', with a blackbird 'disconsolate in the haze': he passes on to formulate intellectually the 'death-bed glow of picturesque abandon' that he finds in this, to playfully transform this into an Ovidian metamorphosis and finally to reflect on the real restrictiveness of place, tense in its intrinsic nature. An impressively complex poem, which, like MacNeice's, encapsulates a great deal of what we may feel about place, change, personal growth and culture, and does so through a dialectic of imaginative identification with the given scene and modest impersonal reflection. The differences are these: firstly, the poem is much less directly personal. It is not difficult to recognize the specific references to MacNeice's own career, his school in Dorset and especially his relationship with his stern and fierce father. Mahon on the contrary never even uses the first person singular, addressing himself as 'you' at the start and broadening out to what 'we' experience at the end. At most, there is a reminder of his 'nomadic youth', which has taken him quite a long way south. Secondly, the variety of perspectives in MacNeice is clearly interpersonal and intercultural: it lies between father and son, between Ireland and England, between ethics and aesthetics; in Mahon it is a much more solitary affair, lying between the young Mahon as he observed the futile reality, the older Mahon as he sees its museum-like charm and the nostalgia of the children whose existence Mahon both deduces and imagines, but who are deliberately kept remote: 'Somebody somewhere thinks of this as home'. Thirdly, the sophisticated culture of Mahon is less coherent: it is made up on one hand of old westerns, with their blatant unreality, so that a frontier store-front conceals thin air, and on the other of the urbane conventionality of Roman myth: the first faintly relevant to the 'thinly peopled hinterland', no doubt, but tending to convert it to arbitrary spectacle; MacNeice's on the contrary is fairly consistently a chivalrous romanticism apt to his boyish self. With this goes the feeling that the magic in MacNeice is inherent in the scene, but that in Mahon it is incongruously invented. Fourthly, the observed scene in Mahon is mostly not seductive but either trivially distasteful or even frightening, as the family

> watched the rain
> Dance clean and cobalt the exhausted grit
> So that the mind shrank from the glare of it …

this subtly counterbalanced by the scene in which

> A cloud swam on a cloud-reflecting tile.

The poems are both about a mastering of experience: in MacNeice the experience is of the culture's excitements, in Mahon it is of the threat of a non-culture. What all this adds up to, I think, is that Mahon has embraced a much bleaker vision of the outsider than MacNeice: Mahon is, one might say, the outsider of the 1960s, the negative sceptic who suspects that the world is really made up of random objects, piles of unused cement, soft drink ads and pools of oil. Whereas *Autumn Journal*, for instance, ends with a section deeply attuned to preparation for a future in which

> there will be sunlight later
> And the equation will come out at last
>
> > (*CP* 153)

'A Garage in Co. Cork' ends, as we have seen, 'not in the hope of a resplendent future' but with a sure sense of the present; and the way the poem avoids any sure and certain hope is part of its total bleakness, its casting of the outsider essentially as recorder of static observed fact.

One more comparison for the Garage offers itself. In 'Order to View' MacNeice visits an empty house, which he vainly remembers:

> But memory, weak in front of
> A blistered door, could find
> Nothing alive now …
>
> > (*CP* 169)

The house, with the dripping shrubbery, tarnished weather-vane, decaying garden, inoperative bell is, if anything, in worse decline than Mahon's garage (if more distinguished to start with):

> And the whole place, one might
> Have supposed, was deadly ill:
> The world was closed ...

But suddenly there is change: a tree shakes

> like a setter
> Flouncing out of a pond,

a horse neighs, the curtains blow out: 'the world was open'. The
opening is unpredictable, miraculous; but MacNeice, unlike
Mahon, expects miracles. Something similar is noted on the
historic level in 'The News-Reel':

>   the intrusions
> Of value upon fact, that sudden unconfined
> Wind of understanding that blew out
> From people's hands and faces ...

> > (*CP* 204)

Intrusions of value on fact are what a lot of poetry is about;
perhaps this is another way of putting what Mahon saw as
MacNeice's interpretation of landscape in human terms. Mahon
himself is preoccupied with such intrusions and with their
absence; MacNeice joyously welcomes them.

McKinnon has characterised two qualities in MacNeice to which I
think our reading of Mahon should make us specially attentive: one
is the tendency to solipsism and self-reflection; the other is his wish
to overcome otherness.[11] I am not sure how far this wish actually is
present in MacNeice. In Mahon there is a strong recognition of
otherness and, I would say, an acceptance of its inevitability. This,
with his solipsism, makes up a sense of the solitariness of the poet,
of the imagination as self-supporting and self-denying.

And this, finally, should make us aware of the immense
richness of MacNeice. That empty, life-evading seclusion is there
in him too; but it goes with the companionable hedonist, the lover
of ideas and sensations, the political optimist, the observer open to
the novelty of others. One way of putting this, which I think
would not be alien to Mahon, is that there is a little of Beckett in
MacNeice; that is something to respect, but is something to respect
all the more because it is balanced by his wit, humanity, concern
for the real quality of life; and the inflection Mahon gives to this
balance is something – at the least – that makes it new for us, that
helps us to see it as something attained with much effort of
sensibility and commitment.

LOUIS MACNEICE AND MICHAEL LONGLEY: SOME EXAMPLES OF AFFINITY AND INFLUENCE

MICHAEL ALLEN

I

My first examples of MacNeice's influence on Longley might equally be seen to illustrate the affinity between the two that fuelled Longley's interest in the older writer. They are both poets who displayed an immense range and variety of tone and voice from very early in their careers. They were both slow to develop a single self-integrative and uniquely recognisable stylistic mode in the manner associated by Harold Bloom with 'strong poetry':[1] it could be argued that MacNeice achieved this only in his last book, *The Burning Perch* (1963), which went to press when he was in his middle fifties and Longley not until *Gorse Fires* (1991) and *The Ghost Orchid* (1995) when he was around the same age. Instances of intertextuality, then, I would suggest, grow from Longley's encounters with a spectrum of subtle and versatile idioms in which he recognised some kinship to his own potential imaginative range.

I begin from two extremes of MacNeice's style. One is direct, vigorous and colloquial, making of the speaker's correspondent an exemplary alter-ego:

> Holidays should be like this,
> Free from over-emphasis,
> Time for soul to stretch and spit
> Before the world comes back on it ...
>
> So I write these lines for you
> Who have felt the death-wish too,

> But your lust for life prevails –
> Drinking coffee, telling tales ...[2]

('Postscript to Iceland')

The other is tense and involuted, a dialogic voice responding to the high Modernist sense of the self as endlessly converted into text:

> ... seen myself sifted and splintered in broken facets,
> Tentative pencillings, endless liabilities, no assets,
> Abstractions scalpelled with a palette-knife
> Without reference to this particular life.
> And so it has gone on; I have not been allowed to be
> Myself in flesh or face, but abstracting and dissecting me
> They have made of me pure form ...

('An Eclogue for Christmas', *CP* 33)

In the first case a version of MacNeice addresses a version of Auden in an unproblematic way: at the other pole, as Foucault puts it, 'What does it matter who is speaking?'[3]

The corresponding extremes of Longley's style can be found in 'Letters' (to three Irish poets, *An Exploded View*, 1973) and 'Obsequies' (*The Echo Gate*, 1979). Here first are some lines from the letter 'To Seamus Heaney':

> Till we talk again in Belfast
> Pleasanter far to leave the past
> Across three acres and two brooks
> On holiday in a post box
> Which dripping fuchsia bells surround ...[4]

Longley has variegated the mode of 'Postscript to Iceland' into three such verse epistles. Just as Auden's known demotic trenchancy becomes part of MacNeice's effect, so, successively, do the erotic libertarianism of James Simmons and the 'metaphysical unease'[5] of Derek Mahon become part of Longley's, as does Heaney's grounding of Irish history in a love-affair with landscape. Searching in each letter for a stylistic symbiosis with its proposed recipient is a project akin to the search for a new 'View' of the Northern Irish polity implied by the volume's title. The introductory epistle 'To Three Irish Poets' (printed first but written last)[6] aims at a corporate style built on cultural diversity.

At the other extreme, Longley's 'Obsequies' announces in its first line its textual autonomy, its stylistic distance from such direct concern with the ideological predicament of its readers:

'They are proof-reading my obituary now'. It is more starkly self-referential than its precedent in MacNeice's 'Eclogue' but just as insistently formulated in visual and aesthetic terms:

> They have set my eyes like two diamonds
> In the black velvet of another's head ...
>
> Meanwhile, back at the dissecting theatre,
> Part of me waits to find in sinks and basins
> A final ocean ...

(P 145)

Film (*Andy Warhol's Frankenstein*)[7] replaces Modernist portraiture[8] as a source of imagery to present this posthumous speaker, so comfortably recumbent in his tank of formalin. His fragmentation as subject into 'bits and pieces' is not without black humorous relevance to the Belfast of the late seventies. But the impact is at once resigned and robust: an alternative (and large-scale) pre-natal situation (and this is pure Longley) is hinted at when 'big fish in the aquarium' (l.8) is modified through the line-end placing of 'breathing' in line 5 and 'head over heels' in line 6:

> Were they to queue up to hear me breathing
> The chemicals, then head over heels
> All my lovers would fall in love again,
> For I am a big fish in the aquarium ...

(P 145)

The '[p]art of me' that 'waits' at the end of the poem could thus be a new being ready to 'surface' in other poems. (The inversion of adult and child roles, or parent and child roles, is one of Longley's most persistent configurations.)[9]

Another (and probably the last visible) instance of MacNeice's presence in Longley's increasingly autonomous enterprise can be seen in 'The Linen Industry' (which appears late in *The Echo Gate*). Like its source, 'Mayfly', it represents a midpoint in its author's stylistic range. But I want to return to consider this example and its implications for Longley's development later. The important thing to emphasise at this point is that, in these three cases, MacNeice's influence re-emerges eight to twelve years after his work had its maximum impact on the young Longley between 1962 and 1968 (Longley's first book, *No Continuing City*, was published in 1969). It is this earlier period that I want to consider next.

II

In 1966 at the 'Pig and Chicken' in Glengormley, Co. Antrim, there
was a reading to celebrate the publication in that year of E. R.
Dodds's new edition of the *Collected Poems*[10] of MacNeice. The
readers were Seamus Heaney, Derek Mahon (who since it was on
his 'home ground' probably arranged the event) and Michael
Longley. Both Heaney and Mahon were already forging very
distinctive ('strong') poetic voices for themselves, and in both their
readings there was evidence of what Bloom calls approvingly
'textual usurpation'.[11] Heaney, for instance, read MacNeice's 'The
Dowser' and was obviously not unaware of how completely he
had transmuted its central impulse into his own characteristic 'The
Diviner', published in *Death of a Naturalist* in that same year.
Mahon read 'Prayer Before Birth', undoubtedly conscious of its
imaginative reconstitution into his own 'An Unborn Child'. He
also read 'Snow', an allusion to which firmly establishes his own
place in the hereditary line of MacNeice at the end of his 'In
Carrowdore Churchyard':

> This, you implied, is how we ought to live –
>
> The ironical, loving crush of roses against snow ...

Both these poems of the early and mid sixties contributed to the
success of *Night Crossing*[12] which was to be a Poetry Book Society
Choice in 1968.

Longley's contribution to the reading in Glengormley showed
no trace of the urge or the readiness to rival and supplant the
literary father-figure, what Bloom calls approvingly, 'an act of
imposition, a declaration of property'.[13] Looking back, Longley
saw the momentary adoption of such a strategy when he began to
write as having triggered his knack as a young poet of imitating
the weakness of his models.[14] (In 1962 he had published and then
suppressed an imitation of MacNeice's over-ingenious exercise in
the variation of a one-word refrain, 'Entirely'; Longley's poem was
called 'Completely'.)[15] On this occasion in 1966 he read three
MacNeice poems relevant to his own work and one of these,
'Mayfly', had its main influence much later. The other two were
'Carrick Revisited' (appropriate since Carrickfergus was just
down the road) and 'Death of an Actress'. In both these cases, a
listener familiar with Longley's own poetry of the time would be
conscious of a frequent similarity of poetic voice, occasionally and
startlingly underlined by an intertextual echo. When Longley
read from 'Carrick Revisited' of

> ... the child's astonishment not yet cured.

> Who was – and am – dumbfounded to find myself
> In a topographical frame – here, not there – ...

(CP 224)

one would hear internally the Longley persona in 'Christopher at Birth' suddenly overwhelmed by his own kinship with the child he is holding:

> ... I, a spokesman of that world outside,
> Creation's sponsor, stand dumbfounded,

> Although there is such a story to unfold
> – Whether as forecast or reminder – ...

(P 51)

Formal syntax and Latinate vocabulary at such moments give the two voices a similarly unexpected angle on experience, but beyond such stylistic resemblance as one might attribute to their common education as classicists, there are surely repeated traces of influence. ('[N]either western Ireland nor southern England / Cancels this interlude' (*CP* 225) says MacNeice later in the same poem; 'Interim nor change of scene shall shipwreck / Those folk ...' (*P* 54) says Longley in 'Leaving Inishmore'.) In retrospect it is that word 'dumbfounded' after a syntactic hiatus that strikes me as decisive. What it pinpoints is the early fashioning of Longley's distinctive 'release into gentleness and into an affection which seems bewildered but always benevolent, always strange, always at an imagined angle to reality' (Douglas Dunn).[16]

This can be seen again when one compares two rather more demotic snatches of dramatised bewilderment which were first conjoined in my mind at that reading in 1966. '[B]efore the war before / The present one' says MacNeice in 'Death of an Actress', Florrie Forde had

> ... made a ragtime favourite
> Of 'Tipperary', which became the swan-song
> Of troop-ships on a darkened shore;

> And during Munich sang her ancient quiz
> Of *Where's Bill Bailey?* and the chorus answered,
> Muddling through and glad to have no answer:
> Where's Bill Bailey? How do *we* know where he is!

(CP 178)

Before Longley read this poem he mentioned (as he does in an essay he was writing at the time)[17] how, in wartime London, MacNeice had become more interested in ordinary people and in the music-hall entertainment they enjoyed. What Longley learned from MacNeice's 'Death of an Actress' is clear at the point where in his own 'In Memoriam' he breaks free from an over-literary elegiac vocabulary to see his dead father

> With your kilt, harmonica and gun,
> Grow older in a flash, but none the wiser
> (Who, following the wrong queue at The Palace,
> Have joined the London Scottish by mistake),
> Your nineteen years uncertain if and why
> Belgium put the kibosh on the Kaiser.
>
> (*P* 48)

In each case the swoop back to a precisely realised time and place hangs on the known cadence of a particular song.

III

The Glengormley reading was a celebration (by a new generation of Northern Irish poets) of MacNeice as either Irish poet or 'Ulster poet' and the ideological tensions implicit in such a purpose were as visible in Longley's choice of 'Death of an Actress' as in his own related poem. (Heaney read 'Turf-Stacks' as a way of finding a feasible cultural connection with MacNeice.) But it was noticeable that Mahon and Heaney departed very little from the accepted selective canon of MacNeice then current, the one authoritatively promulgated by W. H. Auden's influential Faber selection of 1964.[18] The three poems I have described Longley reading, on the other hand, were drawn from outside that selection. They tally with those he selected for discussion in his essay 'A Misrepresented Poet', published in the Spring 1967 issue of *The Dublin Magazine*:[19] the others mentioned there are 'Trains', 'Trilogy for X', 'Belfast', the Irish canto (XVI) of *Autumn Journal*, 'The Casualty', 'Day of Returning', 'Flowers in the Interval' and 'Charon'. All of these except the last had been excluded by Auden in 1964. Longley's selection represented a deep encounter with individual volumes of MacNeice's poetry, the 1949 *Collected Poems*, *Ten Burnt Offerings* (1952), *Visitations* (1957), *Solstices* (1961) and *The Burning Perch* (1963), books acquired as a student in Dublin between 1958 and 1964 and the acknowledged mainstay of his later writings on MacNeice.[20] Longley's reading and his *Dublin Magazine* essay together, then, provide the first articulation of a revised selective canon of MacNeice to be established collaboratively by himself and his wife Edna[21] (among others) between 1966 and 1988 (the date of publication of the new Faber *Louis MacNeice: Selected Poems* which he edited). There is, of course, still considerable overlap with Auden's *The Selected Poems of Louis MacNeice*.[22]

But Longley was unlike either his wife or other members of Trinity College literary circles of the early sixties like Mahon and Terence Brown (who both collaterally promoted the new canon) in the unprescriptiveness of his intertextual encounter with the older poet. Ideological resonances emerge when Brown in 1975 dubs MacNeice 'an Anglo-Irish poet, not simply an English one'[23] or Mahon, in the previous year, acknowledging these components in MacNeice's 'background' nevertheless calls him a 'Northern Protestant'.[24] In 1985, Edna Longley, in a book subtitled 'the Protestant Imagination in Modern Ireland' presents MacNeice as the Irish poet who is essential to Ireland if not committed to it[25] and elsewhere sees the nature of his Irishness as akin to that of Northern Ireland, the 'product of pulls in contrary directions.'[26] Longley shows himself aware of such issues in his various prose writings on MacNeice but reserves his deepest attention for areas of productive affinity between their respective imaginative drives. When he refers in 1988 to MacNeice's obsession with 'three conjunctions of time and place': the North of Ireland, the West of Ireland and the South of England,[27] one has only to look at his later poetry to see that he has made these his own three historical and geographical conjunctions also. Such a creatively conditioned version of what Edna Longley as critic called 'pulls in contrary directions' was already germinating when Longley was modelling his own 'The Hebrides' on MacNeice's 'Day of Returning' back in the 1960s.

IV

In the course of the latter poem, MacNeice's mythic protagonist rather shiftily changes his identity (from Odysseus to Jacob). But his initial situation on the seashore of a steeply terraced island and his preoccupation with a 'stiff climb for a tired mind / ... the terraces dissolved / In the clambering eye' (*CP* 314) surely prompted Longley's Hebridean ascent from 'the water line' via '[l]ast balconies / Above the waves' to a 'vantage point too high above the bay', fighting 'all the way for balance'. (*P* 40 and 43) MacNeice's concern with a '[h]ome beyond this life' (*CP* 314) and a 'Zion' which is 'always future' (*CP* 315) are matched in

Longley's protagonist who is 'so far from home' and yet '[i]n whom the city is continuing' (the Pauline quotation clinches this).[28] MacNeice's Odysseus wants to turn his craft

> To the earth that bred it, a new threshing floor
> Or setting up boundary stones, for even the best
> Neighbours encroach – and I like to have someone to argue with
> About my rights of grazing or wood-cutting
>
> (*CP* 316)

Longley probably anthologised this section of 'Day of Returning' in 1988[29] because it shows us the MacNeice who could momentarily envisage a return to his 'roots' as do some other lines which became favourites[30] of the younger poet:

> And because one feels that here at least one can
>   Do local work which is not at the world's mercy
> And that on this tiny stage with luck a man
>   Might see the end of one particular action.
> It is self-deception of course, ...
>
> ('Autumn Journal', XVI, *CP* 133)

But already, in 'The Hebrides', he is responding to MacNeice's (formally qualified) yearning for the return home by constructing an urban version of Ithaca (which can only be Belfast):

> Old neighbours, though shipwreck's my decision,
>   People my brain – ...
>
>   ... In their heart of hearts,
>   In their city I ran aground.
>   Along my arteries
> Sluice those homewaters petroleum hurts.
>   Dry dock, gantries,
>
> Dykes of apparatus educate my bones
>   To track the buoys
> Up sea lanes love emblazons
>   To streets where shall conclude
> My journey back ...
>
> (*P* 41–42)

Such pragmatic self-discovery in response to MacNeice's dealings with archipelagal, regional and local identity was, however, subordinated always by Longley to two central premises of his 1967 essay: the crucial importance of MacNeice's engagement throughout his career with the theme of childhood and the view that 'the hub of his work is his love poetry'.[31] Both propositions apply equally to Longley himself. And he brings the two propositions very close together in the Introduction to his selected *MacNeice* when he invokes that poet's 'first masterpiece', 'Mayfly' –

> But when this summer is over let us die together,
> I want always to be near your breasts –

and adds: 'These two beautiful lines disclose the nucleus of his imagination'.[32] When his wife similarly argued the canonical centrality of 'Mayfly' (lecturing to a teacher's conference in 1967),[33] a colleague demurred because of what she called the 'infantilism' manifested in the lines quoted above. But such old-style patriarchal Freudianism has lost ground to other psychoanalytic approaches since then and it may have become easier for readers to accommodate 'the dependence that all of us have vis à vis the maternal body'.[34] According to Julia Kristeva (who I am deliberately quoting here from one of her most accessible statements) 'the process of loss which is the result of paternal authority' is inscribed in a 'social code' which kills 'the maternal and the primordial link every subject has with the maternal'.[35] (Poetry, for Kristeva, restores that link.) MacNeice's poetic challenge to the 'social code' in question in some of his finest lyrics and Longley's long-term subversion of it[36] are perhaps easier to accept now than they would have been thirty years ago.

MacNeice's 'Leaving Barra', one of the first of his poems to influence Longley, confronts precisely that 'process of loss' to which Kristeva referred; so too, of course, do his 'Autobiography' and 'The Sunlight on the Garden': the irretrievable (mother, lover, holiday love-experience) is in all these poems associated with bright sunlight-colour. (The same is true of 'Mayfly'.) In 'Leaving Barra', agency is attributed to this brightness so that not the speaker but the 'dazzle on the sea' is 'taking / My leave':

> The dazzle on the sea, my darling,
> Leads from the western channel,
> A carpet of brilliance taking
> My leave for ever of the island ...

> (*CP* 86)

'... [T]aking / My leave...' echoes the rhythm of '...take / The winds of March with beauty'[37] while retaining something of the idiomatic courtesy of 'by your leave'. Such associative richness of language achieves metonymic potency, dramatising what the final stanza of the poem makes explicit:

... living like a fugue and moving ... .
... you are alive beyond question
Like the dazzle on the sea, my darling.

(*CP* 88)

MacNeice himself referred to the two stylistic extremes of a poem like this one as 'the velvet image, ... the lilting measure' on the one hand and

Such words as disabuse
My mind of casual pleasure
And turn it towards a centre - ...

('To Hedli, *CP* 191)

on the other. One is reminded by the first of these extremes that poetry for Kristeva involves a 'modality' akin to 'infantile babblings' and stemming from the repression within the subject of 'mother and child ... in a permanent stricture in which one holds the other, there's a double entrance, the child is held, but so is the mother'. This 'modality', she believes to be 'the source of all stylistic effort, the modifying of banal logical order by linguistic distortions such as metaphor, metonymy, musicality,'[38] One might, of course, prefer to believe with MacNeice that the sources of stylistic effort are 'incorrigibly plural' ('Snow', *CP* 30) and still find the 'modality' Kristeva describes illuminating at this particular intersection of two *oeuvres*.

V

Longley's 'Leaving Inishmore' is like 'Leaving Barra', in its combination of extremes of style. If MacNeice ends on an explicitly pragmatic note ('living like a fugue' leading to 'you are alive beyond question'), Longley begins on such a note, his '[q]uiet variations on an urgent theme / Reminding [him] now ...' of loss:

Rain and sunlight and the boat between them
Shifted whole hillsides through the afternoon –
Quiet variations on an urgent theme
Reminding me now that we left too soon
The island awash in wave and anthem ...

(*P* 54)

At the opposite stylistic extreme, the metonymic potency of MacNeice's opening ('The dazzle on the sea ...') resurfaces at the heart of the Longley poem as an antidote to '[w]intertime past cure':

> ... the girls singing on the upper deck
> Whose hair took the light like a downpour ...

The intertextual moment (hinging on the verb in the second quoted line) seems to me unmistakable. One poet's idiom is caught changing into another's, the latter to develop towards something like 'Light Behind the Rain' (*P* 189–191).

Two other echoes of MacNeice in this first book are pertinent to the younger poet's development. The first does perhaps have elements of 'textual usurpation'[39] on the Bloom model. The approaching dawn, the passing train which are harbingers of loss in 'Trilogy for X' (II) (*CP* 89) become occasions of triumph for the lovers in Longley's 'Epithalamion' (*P* 17–18). And in a similar metonymic context where short-lived insects epitomise human ephemerality, MacNeice's 'show' which 'will soon shut down, its gay-rags gone' ('Mayfly' *CP* 14) is valorised by Longley into

> ... remnant yet part raiment still
>   Like flags that linger on
> The sky when king and queen are gone.
>
> > (*P* 19)

The result is ornately beautiful, celebratory in almost an Elizabethan way. But it doesn't lead forward in Longley's work. And what is lost in the textual transaction is precisely that sense of the male lover's capacity for childlike vulnerability which is to be so inimitable a component of Longley's later love poetry. In contrast to this example I want to examine another in which Longley, more characteristically, avoids creative bravado through a close encounter with the source-text which is at once attentive and transformative.

MacNeice's 'Circe' associates the sorceress (from the bewitched sailor's point-of-view) with 'unfertile beauty':

> '... vitreamque Circen'

> Something of glass about her, of dead water,
> Chills and holds us,
> Far more fatal than painted flesh or the lodestone of live hair
> This despair of crystal brilliance.
> Narcissus' error
> Enfolds and kills us —
> Dazed with gazing on that unfertile beauty
> Which is our own heart's thought ...
>
> > (*CP* 19)

The word 'vitreamque' in the epigraph links Circe's beauty to the brilliance of light reflected off glass and by extension the visual effect of transparent water over flesh.[40] MacNeice acknowledges the second (and erotic) possibility, reinforcing his sense of the power of Circe's embrace with the internal rhyme, 'holds … enfolds'. But the poem's self-referentiality (anguishing about the aesthetic dimension of style which MacNeice was elsewhere to call '… the velvet image / … the lilting measure', 'To Hedli', *CP* 191) makes him lay heavy stress on the other possibility broached by the epigraph: the embrace is sterile like glass and consolidates the speaker's own self-love like a mirror. We have already seen MacNeice (in 'An Eclogue for Christmas') at once indulging and deprecating that extreme of his own style which is closest to the purely aesthetic. In *his* 'Circe', Longley, sensing this conflict in MacNeice, constructs a generous imaginative ratification for the aesthetic in the way he transforms the 'glass', the 'dead water', the 'crystal brilliance':

> when the torn sky confides
> Its face to the sea's cracked mirror, my bed
> – Addressed by the moon and her tutored tides –
>
> Through brainstorm, through nightmare and ocean
> Keeps me afloat. Shallows are my coven,
> The comfortable margins – …
>
> … My necklaces of sea shells and seaweed,
>
> My skirts of spindrift, sandals of flotsam
> Catch the eye of each bridegroom for ever.
>
> (*P* 32)

His first manoeuvre is to speak from Circe's point-of-view, a device which brings into play his considerable capacity for writing 'out of the anima of his personality',[41] to quote Douglas Dunn. The second crucial innovation (and this is the breakthrough for Longley's own forward development) is the phantasmagoric amplitude with which he celebrates the stylistic potency of Circe's embrace:

> … counting no man among my losses,
> I have made of my arms and my thighs last rooms
> For the irretrievable and capsized –
> I extend the sea, its idioms.
>
> (*P* 32)

The disproof of MacNeice's (temporary) attribution of 'unfertile beauty' to the aesthetic extreme of style is in the phantasmagoric continuum which those lines share with these:

> Dawns and dusks here should consist of
> Me scooping a hollow for her hip-bone,
> The stony headland a bullaun, a cup
> To balance her body in like water ...

('In Mayo', *P* 119)

VI

MacNeice featured one last time in Longley's development, his presence preparing the way for the integrated voice and realistic modes of *Gorse Fires* ('I am making do with what has been left me,'[42] says the speaker in that book's first poem). That there was an element of bravado in Longley's early 'marriage poems' is emphasised by the Gothic and phantasmagoric turn which he was soon to give to their reworked materials. In 'No Continuing City' the incipient bridegroom pastes 'new hoardings'

> over my ancient histories
> Which (I must be cruel to be kind)
> Only gale or cloudburst now discover,
> Ripping the billboard of my mind –
> Oh, there my lovers,
> There my dead no longer advertise.

(*P* 35)

But 'The Adulterer' in the poet's second book (*An Exploded View*, 1973) recognises the fragility of such concealment:

> when I bundled into the cupboard
> Their loose limbs, their heads,
> I papered over the door
> And cut a hole for the handle.

> There they sleep with their names,
> My other women, their underwear
> Disarranged a little,
> Their wounds closing slowly.

(*P* 68)

And these banned presences emerge as *belles dames sans merci* ('Belladonna', *P* 116, 'Dead Men's Fingers', *P* 181), as a series of maternally inspirational lovers ('Dreams', *P* 114, 'Patchwork', *P* 188, 'Light Behind the Rain', *P* 189–91) and penultimately as the exotic co-partner in love and artistic enterprise of 'The Linen Industry'. Thus successive iconic renderings of the source of exploratory style as Kristeva envisaged it ('one holds the other ... the child is held but so is the mother')[43] anticipate the disillusioned sailor of 'Sea Shanty' with his history of dozing 'on her breastbone' and mumbling 'into the ringlets at her ear / My repertoire of sea shanties and love songs'.[44]

'The Linen Industry' is a moment of crucial transition in the poet's dealings with 'the process of loss'. It is also an occasion of extraordinary textual confluence. At its high point, its diction is opulent in a way that recalls the influence of Hart Crane (and possibly Yeats) on the early work. But its overall precision of tone is rooted in a dour social history, assimilating a dimension of intimate Northern identity prompted by John Hewitt and nicely complementary to the sweep of Longley's Mayo poems. It combines three roles first stylistically released in *Letters* and strategically deployed in the poems of *Man Lying on a Wall* (1976) and *The Echo Gate* (1979): the myth-making nature poet (as in Heaney), the erotic adventurer (as in Simmons) and the posthumous speaker (as in Mahon). And to deepen this latter resonance Longley draws on MacNeice's sketch for a *Liebestod* at the end of 'Mayfly':

> It is we who pass them, we the circus masters
> Who make the mayflies dance, the lapwings lift their crests,
> The show will soon shut down, its gay-rags gone,
> But when this summer is over let us die together,
> I want always to be near your breasts.
>
> (CP 14)

One only needs to add the 'kingcups / Ephemeral' from earlier in MacNeice's poem to the 'mayflies', the lifted crests, the 'gay-rags' to recognise how MacNeice's continued presence is imaginatively fused with all those other intertextual strands:

> And be shy of your breasts in the presence of death,
> Say that you look more beautiful in linen
> Wearing white petticoats, the bow on your bodice
> A butterfly attending the embroidered flowers.
>
> (P 179)

The voice (obliquely reflecting on the making of a style as does the whole poem) is nevertheless inimitably Longley's own. We have a speaker who is verging on the knowing rather than the innocent, who may be death's surrogate or death itself, but who urges the beloved in equality of courage towards the realism of facing death alone. Longley's meeting with MacNeice shows again a gentleness and reciprocity which it can be seen in this example to share with his other intertextual relationships.

KEEPING THE COLOURS NEW: LOUIS MACNEICE IN THE CONTEMPORARY POETRY OF NORTHERN IRELAND

NEIL CORCORAN

I

In W. H. Auden's 'In Memory of W. B. Yeats', written shortly after Yeats's death in January 1939, he discovers what has since become a famous trope for the way a poet might survive beyond the grave: at the moment of his death, he says, Yeats 'became his admirers'. It is clear that to the poet Auden this process is neither necessarily consoling nor desirable, since the imagery presenting it is one of dismemberment, self-estrangement, castigation and, ultimately, alimentary transformation:

> Now he is scattered among a hundred cities
> And wholly given over to unfamiliar affections,
> To find his happiness in another kind of wood
> And be punished under a foreign code of conscience.
> The words of a dead man
> Are modified in the guts of the living.

There is an almost surreal element in the final metaphor there, in which the somatic process is made to bear the burden of an alien, non-somatic substance – 'words'; and the metaphor, a peculiar one, may well be derived from Hamlet's revelation of 'how a king may go a progress through the guts of a beggar'. Neither for the king nor for the poet is the process likely to be an altogether aggrandising one; and it is unsurprising to find Stan Smith, although not for this reason, persuasively discovering in this poem a virtually proto-deconstructive Auden.[1]

I shall return to Auden's view of Yeats later, since it is complexly involved in the issues I want to raise here; but clearly it is also a way of introducing my topic. The poet Louis MacNeice has 'become his admirers' in the recent history of poetry and criticism in Northern Ireland in a way quite unpredictable to anyone who grew up thinking of him as an English poet of the 1930s, in the shadow of Auden and only the prefix to that composite term 'Macspaunday'; and there may, indeed, be some irony in the loner and refuser of various affiliations in the 1930s being now so well plotted into the organising graphs of others' solicitations. The re-appropriation of MacNeice has, however, been virtually coterminous with the development of the poetry of Northern Ireland since the mid-1960s; and it represents a concerted and strategically successful form of accommodation and recuperation of a kind for which I can think of no contemporary parallel, making a strong case for what Edna Longley pleads as the 'special, living sense' of the term 'intertextuality' in relation to Northern Irish poetry: 'a creative dynamic working upon mechanisms of tradition and cultural definitions alike'.[2] It could also be claimed that the revision of MacNeice's standing and place is one of the clearest manifestations, a litmus test, of the present strength and authority of contemporary Northern Irish poetry and criticism.

In generously promenading MacNeice, contemporary Northern poets are – although certainly not in the conventionally melodramatic, oedipal, masculinist and capitalist Bloomian modes of struggle and swerve – registering attachment to a chosen precursor. The choice is individually self-interested as well as culturally propelled; and it is unsurprising to find MacNeice taking on different colours as he appears in the work of different poets. Derek Mahon, in a piece of wittily oxymoronic critical table-turning, admires him as *'profoundly* superficial' and famously discovers matter for celebration rather than derogation in his role as 'a tourist in his own country': 'of what sensitive person is the same not true?' he asks, with a certain engaging disingenuousness.[3] Mahon's own work as a deracinated cosmopolitan sophisticate is undoubtedly being signalled in that assumed solidarity of sensitivity, and a covert effort of self-definition is the subtext of this excellent essay, which he has characteristically subsequently derided in print.[4] This makes it strange to find him writing, in 'In Carrowdore Churchyard', his elegy for MacNeice, and the poem which pointedly opens his Viking/Gallery *Selected Poems* of 1991, a poem so apparently at variance with his customary zestfully ironic modes. Subtitled 'at the grave of Louis MacNeice', the poem has the gravity and good faith of the elegiac country churchyard tradition it inherits:

This, you implied, is how we ought to live –

The ironical, loving crush of roses against snow,
Each fragile, solving ambiguity. So
From the pneumonia of the ditch, from the ague
Of the blind poet and the bombed-out town you bring
The all-clear to the empty holes of spring,
Rinsing the choked mud, keeping the colours new.

These lines pay a lovingly recreative homage to several prominent
circumstances of MacNeice's life and work: to the poem 'Snow'; to
the pneumonia of MacNeice's own death; to the figure of the
'blind poet' which appears in MacNeice's elegy for Graham
Shepard, 'The Casualty', a figure Mahon ingeniously interprets in
his essay; to the poems of wartime London which MacNeice wrote
from the perspective of a fire-watcher; and to the many
significances of the word and concept of 'colour' in MacNeice's
poetry and criticism. Themselves taking on the colour MacNeice
has left in the poetic landscape, these almost palimpsestic lines
bring the poem's opening trope of *paysage moralisé* – 'Your ashes
will not stir, even on this high ground' – to appropriate resolution;
and they implicate Mahon himself, with a kind of intimacy and
warmth not characteristic of his work, in the essential effort of
dedication which the moralised and written-over graveyard is
punned into carrying: 'This plot is consecrated, for your sake, / To
what lies in the future tense'. This 'high ground' is cousin, it may
be, of that 'high star' shining at the end of MacNeice's 'Thalassa':
'By a high star our course is set, / Our end is Life. Put out to sea.'
(*CP* 546) What lies in the future tense of MacNeice's example and
effort is, that is to say, this poem itself, and, since it is the opening
poem of a large selected works, to some degree the rest of Mahon's
poetry too. Since the poem was written in 1964, one cannot really
make the point that the 'bombed-out town' was then the Belfast of
the Troubles as well as London, but occurring in a contemporary
Northern Irish poet's *Selected*, the collocation is surely irresistible,
and knowingly so on the poet's part.[5] The generosity of
recognition here is made particularly telling by Mahon's use of the
potentially grandiose or portentous vocabulary of the Christian
religion. The language of 'consecration' may seem not
inappropriate to this Christian graveyard, or to this son of the
episcopal palace, and it is indeed corrected by the 'humane
perspective' into which Mahon's poem eventually opens; but it
nevertheless appears less guarded, more confirmed in its generous
impulse, than we might expect from the usually tempered

intelligence of Mahon's poems, in which watchful discrimination and the subtleties of self-mistrust are the very air and ambience.

Mahon's elegy does, nevertheless, preserve a tact in relation to its elegiac reverence, knowing that to put a foot one step further on this high ground would be to fall onto the much lower ground of the sententious. I am not sure that Tom Paulin's earnest in the critical pieces on MacNeice in his collection *Ireland and the English Crisis* and the essay 'Letters from Iceland: Going North' of 1976 does not fall briefly onto such ground. Nevertheless, these essays offer original readings of a Paulin-like, or at least early-Paulin-like, MacNeice who brings an anti-pastoral instruction – rather dourly, it may seem – in the way poetry should be 'responsible, relevant and social'.[6] If the word 'relevant' – that clarion-cry of the Sixties – sounds out now with an almost charmingly dejected and old-fashioned pathos, Paulin's perception that when MacNeice describes the Icelandic landscape, he is implicitly writing about Irish politics and landscape too is a striking one. It supplies the relevance of Iceland to Ireland in Paulin's own early poem 'Thinking of Iceland' in *A State of Justice* (1977), where the way 1970s Donegal is imaginatively mapped onto 1930s Iceland is the originary instance of that resourceful and increasingly complex trope in Paulin of geopolitical and historical allegorising, analogising, juxtaposition and parallel, that sardonically investigative tracing of symptom and causation which has been the constant impulse of so much in his otherwise extravagantly protean poetic.

Mahon and Paulin, then, confess and parade the MacNeiceian affiliation at initiatory moments in their careers, seeking and confirming, or creating, a mentor or progenitor in the place of their earliest poems. Michael Longley identifies the necessity, and virtually proposes the initiation of the programme, in his essay 'The Neolithic Night: A Note on the Irishness of Louis MacNeice', published in 1975, where he writes that 'judgements would be more precise if the Northern Irish context were taken more into account';[7] and, when the programme has been long under way, he observes in his own finest contribution to it, the edited selection of MacNeice published in 1988, that 'a new generation of poets from Northern Ireland has helped to change perspectives. They have picked up frequencies in his work which were inaudible in Dublin or London.'[8] However, the picking up of such frequencies was easier for some Northern poets at early stages of their careers than it was for others. Mahon, Paulin and Longley share not only MacNeice's Ulster background, but also, to varying degrees, his

Protestant religious background and his English connections. Seamus Heaney, on the other hand, tells us in his second collection of critical essays, *The Government of the Tongue*, that he bought MacNeice's *Collected Poems* when he graduated, but felt them to derive 'from a mind-stuff and ... a cultural setting which were at one remove from me and what I came from'.[9] This is said, significantly, in a second essay on Patrick Kavanagh, to accompany the by then well-known and frequently-cited first in *Preoccupations*. What Heaney found exemplary in Kavanagh there, and what he manifestly himself wished to imitate, was the ability to raise 'the inhibited energies of a subculture to the power of a cultural resource'.[10] This has its denominational inflection: the subculture in question is of course that of the Catholic minority of the North. In the shared aim, then, Kavanagh is for Heaney recognition, confirmation and encouragement; MacNeice's 'mind-stuff' is clearly alien to the conditionings and trajectories of that ambition. MacNeice's poems are, however, the essay has the grace to admit, the focus of a more vaguely apprehended ambition: 'I envied them, of course', Heaney says, 'their security in the big world of history and poetry which happened out there'.[11]

Some influence may in fact be veiled by these remarks, since it is hard to believe that *Letters from Iceland* and in particular MacNeice's 'Postscript to Iceland', dedicated to Auden, did not play some part among the many intertexts of *North*, with its psychologising of the alien territory – 'the North begins inside' – and its culmination in the minatory moment 'before / The gun-butt raps upon the door' (*CP* 73–5). Nevertheless, it is only when Heaney himself becomes secure in that big world of poetry and history, and secure too in a cosmopolitan existence well beyond the scope of the original parish, that he finds adequate space for MacNeice in his criticism. In his essay 'The Pre-Natal Mountain', first published in 1989, MacNeice becomes the exemplar of potential new perspective: he 'positioned his lever in England', Heaney says, 'and from that position moved his Irish subject matter through a certain revealing distance'.[12] The fact that distance and its capacity for alternative revelation are much on Heaney's own creative mind at this later stage of his career is clear from the entire orientation of his books, *The Haw Lantern* and *Seeing Things*, where the interest in parable, in visionary transcendence and in the revisiting of earlier phases of the career in order to read them differently, are all elements of a newly individualistic self-assurance, a position from which authoritative judgement may be made, from which satisfaction may be expressed without complacency, desire without velleity. If there is MacNeiceian sanction for these new distances and perspectives, there are also more specific traces in particular poems. The title 'Parable Island', for instance, of a poem first published in a *festschrift* for William Golding, derives from a phrase MacNeice uses in his book *Varieties of Parable*, which concludes with a discussion of Golding.[13] The title 'A Postcard from Iceland' clearly alludes to *Letters from Iceland*, but also perhaps makes a graceful little bow of obeisance, a postcard being an altogether less significant missive than a letter. And 'The Disappearing Island' secretes an episode from the narratives of the voyages of St Brendan or Brandan, with which MacNeice was fascinated, and from which he derived a great deal of imaginative stimulus.

When Heaney speaks of MacNeice 'positioning his lever', he is employing one of those many classroom metaphors which figure in both his poetry and his critical prose: here the lever remembers the physics lesson. These metaphors are compelling in their childlike immediacy and aura of nostalgia, but they are also sly in their authoritative, tutorial panache, as they measure, weigh and balance. In his writing about MacNeice Heaney has something of a field day – one might say – with such figures. 'In "Carrick Revisited"', he says, 'the whole parallelogram of cultural and ancestral forces operating in MacNeice's life is discovered and thereby to a certain extent redressed'.[14] The geometrical metaphor here, which offers the sense of unwieldy properties and relations mapped and plotted into manageability by the effort of MacNeice's own work, is elaborately extended in Heaney's final lecture as Professor of Poetry in Oxford. He uses the authority of his platform here to offer his own new geometry of modern Irish writing, by developing a binarism between Joyce's Martello and Yeats's Thoor Ballylee which he has employed elsewhere in his criticism. In a figure of extremely self-aware re-mapping, he presents the idea of a 'quincunx' of literary architecture. The quincunx establishes in relationship a central 'round tower' of what Heaney calls 'prior Irelandness' located at MacNeice's 'prenatal mountain'; Spenser's Kilcolman Castle; Yeats's Ballylee; Joyce's Martello; and, finally and for the first time, 'MacNeice's Keep' – which is, of course, at Carrickfergus Castle. 'By writing his castle into the poetic annals,' Heaney says, '[MacNeice] has completed the figure'. But it is of course Seamus Heaney who has completed the figure, in a bravura act of new geometrical re-appropriation, this attempt to 'sketch the shape of an integrated literary tradition'.[15] The act of writing Carrickfergus Castle into the annals in this way, when Heaney began by excluding MacNeice in favour of Kavanagh, has involved painful re-orientation and re-alignment on his part too. If the re-orientation is in part a further exemplification of Heaney's self-image as a poet-chieftain 'Still parleying, in earshot of his peers' in the poem 'Terminus' in *The Haw Lantern* – and his career may well be read as a kind of elegantly self-revising parley – my word 'painful' for these re-orientations is no mere figure. This lecture which terminates with the geometry of the quincunx originates in a tellingly baffled account of Heaney's anxieties when he was housed in an Oxford college room normally tenanted by a British cabinet minister on the day of the death of one of the IRA hunger strikers in the Maze Prison, a man from a family well-known to Heaney. It is of course to the point – although it is not a point Heaney makes – that the accommodating quincunx is a figure constructed exclusively from military architecture: towers, castles and keeps.

II

I do not wish here to take up further these implications of Heaney's figure, apart from mildly wondering where other less military and possibly less imposing Irish literary architecture might appear in the surface area of this quincunx: Kavanagh's Farm, for instance, or Clarke's Villa in Rathfarnham, or, indeed, Heaney's own Cottage in Glanmore or even Office in Harvard. I want, rather, to turn to MacNeice again by remarking how, in one way, Heaney's identification of his work with the Castle, while it has its manifest ideological point, is strangely inappropriate in its suggestions of solidity and permanence. For all the differences of discovery and self-discovery which these later Northern poets articulate in their treatment of MacNeice, all are agreed on the essential fluidity of imagination and position in the work. Honourably a tourist in his own country, says Mahon; 'his imagination is essentially fluid, maritime and elusively free,' says Paulin;[16] Michael Longley, in 'The Neolithic Night', celebrates his empirical anti-systematising; Heaney himself, in *The Place of Writing*, reads him in terms of 'distance' and 'doubleness'. Heaney's geometry and architecture, then, have the effect of hardening flux into the permanence of manageable form and identity, of appearing to make the fluidity of the work cohere into more readily identifiable construct. This is at odds with the actual architecture of MacNeice's own poems, whose paradigm is the house of 'Variation on Heraclitus' where 'Even the walls are flowing', and where the variation proposes the theme that 'One cannot live in the same room twice.' (*CP* 502–3) I assume that it was this kind of architecture which prompted Hedli MacNeice's metaphor in her short but pregnant piece 'The Story of the House that Louis Built', where this house is imagined as 'a handsome house with thick walls. The windows on the west side looked towards Connemara, Mayo and the Sea. Those to the south scanned Dorset, the Downs and Marlborough – the windows to the north overlooked Iceland and those to the east, India'.[17] This impossible house is everywhere and nowhere, then, less the inscription of a geometry than the topography of opportunity: a good home for the imagination, but also, it may be, a good place for a younger generation to inhabit, offering possibility without foreclosure, invitation without domination. It is also a not altogether desirable house, perhaps, with a few broken windows and one or two bad views, since the notorious 'middle stretch' of MacNeice's career provides so much less threatening a challenge than the self-confident magisterium that is Yeats's progress.

To mention Yeats, of course, is to recognise that the recuperation of MacNeice in contemporary Northern Irish poetry is in part a strategy for coping with that authority and scope, as MacNeice himself had to cope with it. When Paul Muldoon brings Yeats, Auden and MacNeice into poetic focus, he situates them at the opposite end of the architectural scale from Carrickfergus Castle, in a poem titled for what was in effect a home for transients, '7, Middagh Street'. Placed in the poetic equivalent of 'no fixed abode', they become free to circulate and permutate in a self-conscious display of the way literary history actually produces its future; the texts are circulated and permutated by this reader, Paul Muldoon, who is also the writer 'making it new' in an act of critical reading which is hubristic and unjust but also, as an effect of pleasure, adroitly persuasive.

Before examining these issues further in '7, Middagh Street', I want to look briefly at the other major way in which Muldoon makes MacNeice, in the Poundian phrase, 'of present use', since this may supply a frame for what I say. This is of course the citation of his dialogue with F. R. Higgins which supplies the alternative to an introduction for his *Faber Book of Contemporary Irish Poetry*, published in 1986. The fact that no introduction is supplied has had its moment of notoriety; but its audacity, even its impudence – the genie vanishing to leave a great swathe of smoke above the lamp – has implications for the critical essay that is actually supplied in '7, Middagh Street'. The dialogue itself is manifestly intended to set Higgins up as fall guy to MacNeice, with his atavistic and potentially fascistic talk of poetry and the blood and so on, compared to MacNeice's sophisticated modernity, and Higgins does indeed, in the passages quoted by Muldoon, live up to the reputation devastatingly hung on him when Patrick Kavanagh said 'Almost everything about Higgins needs to be put in inverted commas'.[18] However, as Muldoon must know, the evidence is that this was not MacNeice's view of Higgins: in *The Poetry of W. B. Yeats* some penetrating critical remarks by Higgins are cited, and this in a book which cites no other authority on Yeats; and MacNeice also writes approvingly, if mutedly, there of the subtle elegances and excellent craftsmanship of Higgins's own poetry.[19] Seamus Heaney is astute when he points out that MacNeice's poem 'Suite for Recorders' has a kinship with Higgins, and when he goes on to observe that in fact Muldoon's own poetry, with its sustained recuperation of Irish legendary and mythological material, complicates the apparently simple dichotomies of the Higgins/MacNeice debate. In Heaney's reading of Muldoon 'the final irony ... is that it was the ironist himself who produced the goods capable of transfusing new life into that apparently doomed and simple vision.'[20] None the less, the ironist editor of the anthology is knowingly tipping the scales when he makes Higgins the name for utterly uncomplicated 'simplicities', even crassnesses, knowing that Higgins's inter-locutor in that dialogue himself had a more complicated view: which is presumably why he allowed himself to be a participant in the first place.

However, if the unfairness of this supplies a frame for what I shall propose of unfairness in '7, Middagh Street' too, it clearly derives from Muldoon's primary allegiance. If there is, as Heaney says, work of MacNeice's which may be held in the same sentence with Higgins, one element which makes him so exemplary for Muldoon is the 'odi et amo' feeling for Ireland which informs many of his Irish poems. In 'Carrick Revisited' the triangulation of Ulster, the west of Ireland and England plots a graph of affiliation and detachment; but the poem 'Valediction', in particular, with its tropes of enmeshment and escape, submission and release, seems to set a kind of template for numerous Muldoon poems. In it MacNeice actually articulates the desire to be, precisely, a tourist in his own country, as a way of coming to temporary accommodation with the disconsolate thought that 'the woven figure cannot undo its thread'. The poem's venomous repudiations are cut across by the poignancy of particular interests and affections; and it is an oddly oxymoronic valediction which actually promises to return. The 'woven figure' which 'cannot undo its thread' may be a good way of defining all those figures in Muldoon who are enmeshed in circumstance, domicile and parish – the emblematically named 'Brownlee' and 'Joseph Mary Plunkett Ward', for instance. But a Brownlee who has left, undoing the weave of his name, like those other mysterious disappearers in Muldoon, is also potentially coded into 'Valediction' in a figure of startling vivacity and originality:

> If I were a dog of sunlight I would bound
> From Phoenix Park to Achill Sound,
> Picking up the scent of a hundred fugitives
> That have broken the mesh of ordinary lives.

> (*CP* 54)

In '7, Middagh Street' Muldoon turns MacNeice himself, along with the other inhabitants of Auden's Brooklyn house on Thanksgiving Day 1940, into such a fugitive figure. There is, of course, a biographical compulsion behind Muldoon's affiliation with MacNeice: at the time Muldoon was writing the poem he had taken up residence in the US after quitting a job with the BBC in Belfast; MacNeice in the time of the poem was in America lecturing, but contemplating a return to wartime England to take up a propaganda post with the BBC in London. This reverse symmetry, and others in their respective careers, may be why MacNeice leaves 'by the back door of Muldoon's' at the end of the poem. '7, Middagh Street' has been much discussed, but too frequently as if Auden and MacNeice were its only personnel really to count. I shall myself return to them in a moment, but I want here to say something about the place of the other personnel of the poem too.

It is well known that the fiction of '7, Middagh Street' is developed in part from a few sentences of Humphrey Carpenter's biography of Auden, published in 1981. In 1940 Auden the expatriate was living in a house in Brooklyn which he described as a 'menagerie'[21] – a human and bohemian one which included, for brief periods, six of the characters Muldoon includes in his poem: Auden; Chester Kallman; Louis MacNeice; Carson McCullers; the striptease artist Gypsy Rose Lee; and Benjamin Britten. The character Muldoon includes who appears not to have spent time in the house, but who was actually in America later in 1940, is Salvador Dali. Each speaks a monologue; and the monologues are titled according to the forenames of the speakers – 'Wystan',

'Louis', 'Carson' and so on, in a way that may nod recognition to MacNeice's *Autumn Sequel*, which names some of its characters in mythologised versions of their forenames – 'Gwilym' for Dylan Thomas, and so on. The monologues are constructed as a kind of postmodern *corona di sonnetti*, that Italian form of seven interlinked sonnets which Donne uses in 'La Corona'. In Muldoon there are not seven sonnets but seven sections in variations based on the number 7 (all apart from one section, which I shall come to), as befits the house number of the poem's title; and each section is linked to the subsequent one by a line or phrase repeated, a quotation completed or travestied. The whole poem opens with Wystan's citation of the opening line of John Masefield's once well-known school anthology poem 'Cargoes' ('Quinquereme of Nineveh from distant Ophir') and closes with Louis's picking up of the reference. This device of echo may also owe something to the Renaissance 'echo poem' tradition, the kind George Herbert uses in 'Heaven', for instance, and also, significantly, the form Yeats echoes himself in 'The Man and the Echo', the poem Wystan cites in the sequence. The numerological precision and the playing with complicated traditional poetic structures and devices is very much a feature of Muldoon's finicky aesthetic. This would seem a Joycean element in him, except that in Joyce the structural complication is always an effort towards density; in Muldoon it seems rather an element of the poems' airy thinness, the guy ropes emphasising the way they are only just holding down the buoyantly wind-whipped canvas. In '7, Middagh Street' the implication of the corona is, I think, that the issues raised by the poem's seven characters are irresolvable. The corona form, its theme with variations, insists that they will maintain a constant circulation, from Auden and MacNeice in the 1930s and 1940s to Muldoon and his Northern Irish mentors and peers in the present moment.

Those critiques of '7, Middagh Street' which concentrate more or less exclusively on the 'Wystan' and 'Louis' sections concentrate, not surprisingly, on the issues of art and action which those sections raise in relation to Yeats; and this is of course a major element of the poem's interest. It is also, however, greatly preoccupied with issues of sexuality, in a way which may be thought to move into another phase and a newer complication the trope of sexual-political linkage which figures variously in many Northern Irish poems, notably by Heaney, Paulin and Muldoon himself. The fugitives gathered in 7, Middagh Street are not political fugitives, but fugitives from stiflingly conventional sexuality, or from sexual or emotional misery. Wystan is in New York for the sake of Chester, striking out for the new sexual frontier and the 'ghostly axe / of a huge, blond-haired lumberjack'; Gypsy is in love with the intellectual George Davis, finding him a way of escaping the grasping over-protectiveness and ambition of her mother; Ben is in love, and sharing his life for the first time, with Peter; Chester seeks out the sailors of Sands Street; Carson has left her husband and is in love with several women, including Erika Mann; and Louis, after a failed marriage, is having a relationship with Eleanor Clark. In '7, Middagh Street' America is the new-found-land of greater sexual permission.

This is why, I think, the ship that transports Wystan and Christopher at the opening of the poem is the 'Quinquereme of Nineveh'. Separate poems in Muldoon's individual collections sometimes conduct a dialogue among themselves, and in *Meeting the British* the poem 'Profumo' initiates the reference to Masefield's 'Cargoes'. A sort of companion piece in reverse gender to Muldoon's marvellous earlier poem 'Cuba', in which the attempted domination of a daughter by father and priest is the issue, 'Profumo' has a Muldoon-narrator forbidden by his mother even to mention the name of the erring cabinet minister, even though he knows she is secreting all the salacious details in the *News of the World* beneath her 'snobbish' hams. Her snobbery and prurience attempt to thwart his desired relationship with a girl called Frances Hagan:

> 'Haven't I told you, time and time again,
> that you and she are chalk
> and cheese? Away and read Masefield's *Cargoes*.'

The instruction is presumably offered as a sort of preventative measure or prophylactic. We know that it has been carried out by one of the artful formal jokes of Muldoon's work. The syntax of 'Profumo', like the famously static syntax of 'Cargoes', contains three noun phrases, lacking their copulas. If this is a mocking gesture by the poet-narrator at the presumptuous interference of the mother, subverting her instructions by turning them into a vehicle of ironising judgement, it is also a formally ironic insistence on the reduction of opportunity and the sexual and social repressions of this family. The noun-phrases lack their copulas just as narrator and Frances Hagan are prevented from anything remotely resembling copulation, in this poem in which even the name of the arch-copulator Profumo is occluded, present only in the hidden newsprint beneath the snobbish hams.

But 7, Middagh Street is the place where copulation thrives –
with, it might be said, a vengeance; and the act of vengeance is
performed by the occupation of the mother's safely prophylactic
poem and the turning of its gorgeous first seacraft into the vehicle
of alterity. Sexuality, as Ovid knew, is the most provocative agent
of metamorphosis – and, as John Kerrigan has shown in his
brilliantly synoptic essay 'Ulster Ovids', Muldoon is a deeply
Ovidian poet.[22] Wystan with Kallman becomes different from
himself and says 'I will not go back as *Auden*', and Salvador Dali
turns into 'O'Daly' in Louis's perception of him. These are the
paradigms of the poem's fluidly mobile figures and effects, one of
which is the adducing of Yeatsian poetic tags for sexual
behaviour: 'There's more enterprise in walking not quite / naked,'
for instance, according to the teasing Gypsy Rose Lee, and Carson
thinking of her new woman lovers as 'two girls in silk kimonos'.
In this intermingling of poetry and sexuality art becomes
manifestly the vehicle of one sort of action: even an old anthology
chestnut like 'Cargoes' can take you to a new-found-land.

This celebration of the metamorphic and the indeterminate is, I
think, the real reason why the surrealist Dali appears in the poem.
Kerrigan has made this one element of his critique of '7, Middagh
Street': 'Muldoon's work,' he says, 'thins in those texts which
summon other linguistic consciousnesses but which, honourably,
cannot accommodate their difference … . What is Dali doing in
Middagh Street, and why does he sound like Muldoon?'[23] This
seems to me an uncharacteristically literal-minded question. Dali
is there because this is a poem much preoccupied with
metamorphosis, and surrealism is the major artistic mode of
metamorphosis in our time, one in which Muldoon is himself at
times engaged, with his disciplined surreal of mimetic
hallucinogenic experience in such poems as 'Gathering
Mushrooms'. He is also there because the sexual, scatological and
political are merged in his major canvases of the 1930s, as at least
two of those categories are in this poem. And he is there because
his eventual 'trial' by André Breton provides a central instance of
the problematic relationship between art and politics with which,
particularly in the shape of Wystan and Louis, the poem is also
deeply preoccupied.

But Kerrigan means the question literally, of course. Dali was not
literally a guest at 7, Middagh Street, as far as we know, though he
could have been. But he can be a guest at the house supplied by the
poem because the poem punctiliously goes out of its way to make
room for him. When Gypsy, arbiter of the arts, establishes a

correlation between striptease and literature, she sets a programme for Muldoon himself: 'it's knowing exactly when to stop / that matters, / what to hold back, some sweet disorder ... / The same goes for the world of letters.' Gypsy is quoting Herrick here, his 'Delight in Disorder', a poem on the pleasures of déshabille:

> A sweet disorder in the dresse
> Kindles in cloathes a wantonnesse:
> A Lawne about the shoulders thrown
> Into a fine distraction ...
> Doe[s] more bewitch me, then when Art
> Is too precise in every part.[24]

Muldoon's numerologically punctilious poem structurally slips its sleeve from its shoulder too when the penultimate poem of the Wystan section has only twenty instead of the expected twenty-one lines; and it does so also, I think, by including a Dali who was not there precisely because he was not there. This poem is, that is to say, not in any sense a re-creation of the circumstances of 7, Middagh Street on Thanksgiving Day 1940, but a metamorphic re-invention of them, continuous with Muldoon's reinventions of Irish legendary and mythological material in such poems as 'Immram' and 'The More a Man Has the More a Man Wants'.

But why, being there, does Dali sound like Paul Muldoon? Surely because everyone in the poem does, and because this is really not an attempt to 'summon other linguistic conscious-nesses'. It is, rather, an attempt to write a *corona di sonnetti* to the recipe MacNeice gives for the lyric in his essay 'Experiences with Images' – 'your lyric in fact is a monodrama'[25] – and perhaps even more particularly to the specifications of MacNeice's poetic self-analysis in *The Poetry of W. B. Yeats:*' As far as I can make out, I not only have many different selves but I am often, as they say, not myself at all'.[26] If you combine that with a striking remark by Muldoon in an interview – 'One of the ways in which we are most ourselves is that we imagine ourselves to be going somewhere else'[27] – then you have clues to the provenance and preoccupations of '7, Middagh Street'. There are no 'other linguistic conscious-nesses' in '7, Middagh Street'; in '7, Middagh Street' Paul Muldoon is not himself at all, seven times.

There may indeed, in this, be a sardonic subliminal recognition of the ways in which some lyric poems and sequences may too readily presume to a ventriloquial dramatic ability: 7, Middagh Street is a long way from that other notable contemporary Northern Irish poetic address, Station Island, but it too is a communing with ghosts. It also contains, in its Dali section's references to Antaeus and a welded foot, one of those parodistic or revisionist allusions to Heaney which you now wait for in every new Muldoon volume as you wait for the cameo appearances of Hitchcock in his own movies: one of the stamps of authenticity, one of the signatures. If Heaney's posture is the humble one of bowing before the advice of masters – with a view, of course, to himself inheriting their mantles – Muldoon's is that of the impudent, presumptuous, disconcertingly brilliant pupil, self-interestedly and unfairly reading the work and careers of others (not exactly masters, or mistresses) as facets of his own self-recognition and self-development.

It is in this light, I think, that we should read the debate between Wystan and Louis about Yeats which has been the focus of most critical commentary on the poem. The relevant lines are well-known. Wystan, characterising Yeats as 'part-Rapunzel' and 'partly Delphic oracle', remembers Yeats's question in one of his last poems, 'The Man and the Echo', about the potential political effect of his play *Cathleen ni Houlihan* and asks:

> As for his crass, rhetorical
>
> posturing, 'Did that play of mine
> send out certain men (*certain* men?)
>
> the English shot …?'
> the answer is 'Certainly not'.
>
> If Yeats had saved his pencil-lead
> would certain men have stayed in bed?
>
> For history's a twisted root
> with art its small, translucent fruit
>
> and never the other way round.

At the end of the poem Louis, thinking of the fate of Lorca, whom he has been reading in the Wystan section, and of Auden's new quietism 'intent only on painting an oyster', replies that

> … poetry *can* make things happen –
> not only can, but *must* –
>
> and the very painting of that oyster
> is in itself a political gesture.

Edna Longley has observed that the Wystan lines are sometimes cited as Muldoon's last word, but that the Wystan and Louis sections are of course in dialogue.[28] This is quite true; but it is unsurprising that more emphasis has been placed on the Wystan lines since, whereas the Louis lines are a reasonably accurate transcription-cum-recreation of what he actually says, mild-manneredly, in his book on Yeats, the Wystan lines are much harsher to Yeats than even the voice of the prosecution in Auden's dialogue about Yeats, 'The Public v. William Butler Yeats', also written, like 'In Memory of W.B. Yeats', in 1939. The lines Muldoon gives Wystan have the panache of absolute memorability and the brazenness of unfair aggression. It is instructive and revealing that one of the readers who appears to take them at face value is one of Yeats's many recent editors, Daniel Albright, who, in his edition of Yeats, cites them without further comment in a footnote to 'The Man and the Echo'.[29]

But of course they are unfair. That Yeats is capable of posturing probably no one would dispute, and some even of his *Last Poems* may be thought to maintain certain kinds of arrogance and self-importance. 'The Man and the Echo', however, seems to me not one of these poems, and its self-questioning is neither crass nor rhetorical. It is undermined by the closeness of death, which is what the poem is partly about, and by the closeness, therefore, of whatever kind of judgement Yeats believed in. The question, 'Did that play of mine send out / Certain men the English shot?', is the anxious prediction of a possible posthumous judgement on his own behaviour and works. This is emphasised by a marked poignancy in the form of the poem, in which the 'echo', with its death-inflected responses, may propose that the Delphic voice is merely the projection of human will and desire, a kind of Forsterian 'ou-boum' of failed transcendence. And Yeats was not the only person to ask the question: Stephen Gwynn in his *Irish Literature and Drama in the English Language: A Short History*, published in 1936, just a few years before 'The Man and the Echo', noted the effect on him of seeing *Cathleen ni Houlihan*, with, of course, Maud Gonne in the title role: 'I went home asking myself if such plays should be produced unless one was prepared for people to go out to shoot and be shot';[30] and MacNeice concludes the penultimate chapter of his book on Yeats with an exactly comparable judgement, the one Muldoon revises into his poem: 'Yeats did not write primarily in order to influence men's actions but he knew that art can alter a man's outlook and so indirectly affect his actions. He also recognized that art can, sometimes intentionally, more often perhaps unintentionally, precipitate violence. He was not sentimentalizing when he wrote ...' the

celebrated lines.[31] In a review of the *Last Poems* MacNeice says of
'The Circus Animals' Desertion' what I would want to say of 'The
Man and the Echo': that 'In this excellent and moving poem a self-
centred old man rises above his personality by pinning it down for
what it is.'[32] 'The Man and the Echo' is not crass nor rhetorical nor
posturing: one may indeed say of it what John Berryman said
feelingfully, self-interestedly and finely of the Shakespeare of the
Sonnets: that 'when [he] wrote "Two loves I have," reader, he was
not kidding'.[33]

If Muldoon allows Wystan an intemperateness that
overshadows Louis's critical equilibrium, however, it is perhaps
because '7, Middagh Street' is a poem so radically opposed to the
kind of 'certainty' Wystan isolates and witheringly ironises:

> '... Did that play of mine
> send out certain men (*certain* men?)
>
> the English shot ...?'
> the answer is 'Certainly not'.

Wystan's query '*certain* men?' here takes up the ambivalence of
the word 'certain', one of those words, like 'quite', which
Christopher Ricks, in his book *Beckett's Dying Words*, defines as
'words of antithetical sense', noticing that Beckett makes much use
of them.[34] 'Certain', according to the OED, can mean either
'determined, fixed, settled; not variable or fluctuating; unfailing'
or it can be 'used to define things which the mind definitely
individualizes or particularizes from the general mass, but which
may be left without further identification in description; thus often
used to indicate that the speaker does not choose further to
identify or specify them'. Muldoon here uses the antitheses as the
vehicle of an antithetical condemnation. His interrogative,
parenthetical, italicised repetition of the word 'certain' draws
attention either to Yeats's refusal to specify, which makes the
phrase 'certain men' sound condescendingly patrician; or to
Yeats's assumption of the men's assurance, which seems
altogether too self-assured about the effect his play might have
had in provoking such 'certainty', and is therefore justly rebuked
by the definitive assurance of the negative riposte: 'Certainly not'.
In '7, Middagh Street' the certainty of certain men is the certainty
which concludes the poem in the sectarian exclusions of Louis's
final sonnet, in which the gorgeous quinquereme of Nineveh is
stationary in the shipyards of Harland and Wolff, and, given the
Cyclopian foreman in the works, not about to admit the presence

of a MacNeice. For this, of course, is the certainty that gets
everything wrong:

> 'MacNeice? That's a Fenian name.'
> As if to say, 'None of your sort, none of you
>
> will as much as go for a rubber hammer
> never mind chalk a rivet, never mind caulk a seam
> on the quinquereme of Nineveh.'

The quinquereme ends, in short, where it began: not at the
beginning of this corona-poem, as the gorgeous ship of self-
transformation, but in 'Profumo', where it is the agent of
prophylaxis and the emblem of exclusion: 'None of your sort will
chalk a rivet'; 'Haven't I told you, time and time again, / that you
and she are chalk / and cheese?' Masefield in the mouth of the
socially and sexually exclusivist mother and Masefield in the
mouth of the sectarianly exclusivist foreman bookend this poem
with insistences on those intransigent certainties which lie outside
the utopian space of the poem, that space in which sexual, social
and political categories circulate and slide.

III

In conclusion, I want to turn once more to John Kerrigan's
critique. He discovers in the poem 'an elaborate bookish whimsy
which promises a long way round to empty-handedness'.
'Everything,' he says, 'turns into something else through the
unrelenting lightness of fancy'.[35] As it happens, the specific lines
he has in mind when he says this, those at the very beginning of
the Louis section, do seem to me, more or less, to merit the
criticism. And such bookish whimsy is a danger sometimes lying
in wait for Muldoon's rarefied, light-footed and humoured
writing. I am not at all sure myself that he does not succumb in
Madoc, where the bookishness and the whimsy seem elements
of too great a knowingness, too ready an assumption of
understanding from an insider readership. For all its length and
scope, *Madoc* as a result already seems an almost disposable
element of the Muldoon *oeuvre*.

In '7, Middagh Street', however, the word one wants is not
'whimsical', but a neologism Muldoon once reached for, only to
deny himself, in an interview: 'whimful'.[36] Muldoon's capricious,
fanciful play with his reading is earthed in a sense of how reading,
the play of the intellect among the texts of a culture, is the agency
of transformation. The reading one does with the encouragement

of '7, Middagh Street' is ramifyingly suggestive and inclusive: for instance, the connections very lightly proposed between MacNeice, Whitman, Lorca and Dali – threads running through the poem, which I have not had the space to unravel here – are provocatively congruent with the poem's central interests, not merely decoratively adjunctive to them. There is instruction as well as delight to be gained here, however lightly; and the nature of '7, Middagh Street' as a poetic critical essay traces a suddenly vibrant and knowledgeable line back through Byron to Pope. The poem's transformative ingenuity, which culminates with Louis clocking in at Harland and Wolff, offers MacNeice one of the most 'unfamiliar affections' even Auden could have predicted for him; but the affection, drawing on a respect for what MacNeice managed to hand on in the way of usable potential, is wholly unwhimsical, the product not of fancy, but of fully engaged sympathetic imagination.

TRACING MACNEICE'S DEVELOPMENT IN DRAMA: A COMMENTARY ON THE PUBLISHED AND UNPUBLISHED PLAYS[1]

ALAN HEUSER

PRELIMINARY

In three decades, 1933 to 1963, MacNeice wrote over 40 dramas – some for stage, most for radio, one for TV.[2] This essay traces his development in drama through thematic clusters of plays, and provides roughly chronological summaries of plots, dramatic modes, styles and production details, together with relevant historical comment. History was a central concern to MacNeice – as seen in his long poem *Autumn Journal* 1938 (1939); and public events or topical issues inspired a variety of his dramas – along with personal, literary, artistic interests. Hence this survey will emphasize how MacNeice's varied dramatic output is regularly a response to issues raised by the course of contemporary history and by his individual relationship to it.

STAGE PLAYS: TRAGEDY, FARCES, TRAGI-COMEDY, 1933–9

In the later 1930s MacNeice becomes known as poet, critic, dramatist. He adapts his *Agamemnon of Aeschylus* for Group Theatre production, (London, 1936). By inventive techniques, he tries to reveal the pity and terror of authentic Greek tragedy: (1) by his initial talk on the hereditary curse in the House of Atreus stating the play's values (a moral law, sin and punishment, a moral God, human dignity); (2) by translating the tragedy into modern English verse, idiomatic, without clutter or archaism; (3) by adding at the end, the first chorus of *The Choephoroe* – second play of *The Oresteia* – to show tragedy ongoing. Rupert Doone, producer, asked him to read the Greek aloud at performances, though this proved distracting. Exaggerated dress and choreography, to imitate the Greek, were unconvincing. On first night, the Chorus of Elders wore dinner jackets, a shock of Doone's, later changed. Benjamin Britten wrote the music. In spite of 'Dooneries' (E. R. Dodds's term), MacNeice was successful in his translation for the stage, though Yeats found the production 'the death of tragedy'.[3] Dodds's successor at Oxford, Sir Hugh Lloyd-Jones, said MacNeice's *Agamemnon* was 'the most successful version of any Greek tragedy that anyone in this country had yet produced'.[4]

In 1933–7 MacNeice wrote two farces – *Station Bell* and *Out of the Picture* – on public topics. *Station Bell*, an Irish prose comedy, burlesques Fascism in Ireland, alluding to General O'Duffy and his Blue Shirts when de Valera first came to power. (Yeats was briefly involved with O'Duffy.) MacNeice's *Duce* is a plump woman, with reluctant doctor-husband, shabby general, hard-boiled captain, recruits – making speeches and trying to take over Ireland. Lively vernacular makes minor characters funnier than major ones: e.g. a lunatic cleric and an old deaf capitalist. The dictatress Julia, called 'Herself' behind her back, is saluted with 'Hails' (*Heils*) to her face; her Propaganda Corps performs music-hall stunts. She stops her plan to seize power (blowing up of a boat-train). Female ambition, Irish nationalism, folkways, slangways make for high-jinks in a devil-may-care manner like that of Denis Johnston. MacNeice took great risks: the farce, rejected by Doone as 'too Irish', was acted by amateurs of the Birmingham University Dramatic Society, one month after his *Agamemnon*.

The next farce, MacNeice's long-awaited Venus play *Out of the Picture* – close to Auden and Isherwood in its collage of verse, prose, song, in simulated broadcasts – was, after publication, taken on by the Group Theatre in 1937. It portrays three persons well: an inept artist and two women – loyal model and narcissistic film star (based on Greta Garbo), for whom the artist has a love-crush; the rest are stereotypes. The self-parodic artist loses his art work 'Venus' to bailiffs and deserts his model for the film star. She consults a quack psychiatrist. The artist, failing to recover his 'Venus' at an auction, goes to the film star's home to snatch it and shoots a statesman; the model gentles the artist to a love-death. Venus steps 'out of the picture' as *Dea ex machina*. Art, film, psychiatry and religion are mocked. Doone asked MacNeice to help him revise the text to quicken the pace. Good songs were cut (re-published in MacNeice's collections 1925–40, 1925–48) and the remaining lyrics were sung by a Chorus, with Benjamin Britten's music to accentuate rhythms. MacNeice's Irish gusto was largely lost; yet the production was a success. The play referred to many public issues – Olympics, Geneva – but focused on MacNeice's personal themes of art, love and death.[5]

After *Modern Poetry, Autumn Journal* and the translation of the first chorus of *Hippolytus (1938–9)*, MacNeice wrote the one-act *Blacklegs*, 1939, a socialist tragi-comedy in prose, leading like early O'Casey from seriocomic banter to tragedy, to more than a 'shadow of a gunman'. Two strike-breakers, professor and labourer, work on scaffolding around a steeple amid Dublin flats, to be joined by the young brother of the strike-leader. Reluctant scab, he *must* work, for his wife is expecting their first. There is a war on. The strike-leader (based on an IRA veteran) enters with a gun. He challenges blacklegs; lets the first two go; but shoots his brother. A young woman announces the dead man's wife has borne a son. Then the war is over and there is cheering below. A middle-aged woman asks the strike-leader to decorate the steeple for war's end. – Power struggle is not mocked, as in *Station Bell*; tragedy focuses on brothers of opposing loyalties: class solidarity vs. family values. The play, accepted by the Abbey though needing adjustments, was not staged: Yeats was dead, the Abbey under F. R. Higgins was in transition, and the war, often warned about, had arrived. MacNeice's early stage plays – Greek tragedy, Irish and English farces, Irish tragi-comedy – form a nucleus from which his range would expand widely through the war crisis, but in another medium.

RADIO – THE MEDIUM OF SOUND

After ten months in America, where he published *Poems 1925–1940* and wrote *The Poetry of W. B. Yeats* (1941), MacNeice joined the Features Section of BBC Radio Drama and Features, early 1941; he took a radio course with Empson and Orwell – placed in BBC Talks to China (1941–6) and to India (1941–3) respectively.[6] Laurence Gilliam (Features Head) promoted 'pure radio' experiments; Val Gielgud (Drama Director) promoted radio theatre. MacNeice was taken on as 'a Classic' keen on history. He learned to suggest place and time by shorthand, to observe a strict time-frame for each script, to use microphone and control panel; soon (1943) to choose his actors for voice and microphonic agility, to guide them gently or leave them alone; and (1944) to ask for suitable music from composers. He learned the distinctive craft of sound drama. Radio was a new art form, an opportunity to experiment, pioneering plays in sound without sets or costumes – using voices in dialogue, with music subordinate.

A radio dramatist addresses listeners' imaginations, for like blind men they cannot see what they are experiencing. It is parallel to Shakespeare's freedom from stage decor, but more radical: there are no visual clues whatsoever. This genre, distinct from stage and television drama, is called 'pure radio' (Gilliam) or 'theatre of the mind' (Esslin) – a verbal, not a visual form, suited to poets juggling words as sounds, using actors for oral abilities, with music as needed. A reader of radio drama therefore needs to listen by ear with an 'auditory imagination', or a good radio play might not 'live' as meant to. MacNeice's radio work may have been underestimated by those approaching it in 'poetic' terms – and particularly with only one of his plays known to the public today. Sound drama is written to be spoken, to be heard; whether in verse or prose it is not strictly 'poetry', but pure sound. MacNeice in fact invariably requested his actors to avoid 'the poetry voice'. For plays from 1944 on, he wrote music cues, to guide composers on musical motifs to be used, and their development and duration. As writer-producer, he chose actors and composers, conducted studio rehearsals towards recorded and/or live broadcasts.

In 1941, MacNeice's interests changed from tragedy, farce, love, strikes, to Hitler's War, heroism against defeat, freedom fights against tyranny, salutes to the Allies, portraits of heroes, of ordinary combatants, and of evil careers. This was history, modern history, the reason he had returned from America.

FIRST RADIO PLAYS OF THE WAR: EPICS 1941–1942

MacNeice launches his first radio plays on epic subjects in 1941–2: *The March of the 10,000, Alexander Nevsky, Christopher Columbus* – pieces commissioned for the war crisis, with Britain and the Free World endangered. *The March of the 10,000*, from Xenophon's *Anabasis*, tells mainly in prose – through soldiers, Lady, few voices – how Greek mercenaries under the Persian King Cyrus escape, after his defeat, on a long trek to the Black Sea, 400 BC. A verse ode to the North Wind pleads against its force. Written March 1941 – recalling Dunkirk 1940, expecting British evacuation from Greece, April 1941 – the short play turns military withdrawal into an epyllion of heroic retreat, to 'the sea, the sea' (*thalassa*). *Alexander Nevsky* puts visuals of Eisenstein's Expressionist film (1938) into verse. Sir Adrian Boult conducts Prokofiev's music. In the mid-1200s peasants talk of threats to Russia by German marauders. Prince Alexander returns home to lead the struggle to defeat Teutonic Knights, in the famous battle on a frozen lake. At the end the patriot-hero (Russian Orthodox saint) gives a rousing speech. The play in support of Russia was written after Germany invaded the Soviet, June 1941 – to remind Britons that its new ally had a heroic history against a common foe, Germany. It was revived in a new production, June 1944, with some music by Walter Goehr, on the third anniversary of the Soviet Ally's entry into the war.

The third epic play, *Christopher Columbus*, based on US Admiral Morison's biography, salutes America's entry into the war. Broadcast with William Walton's music on the 450th anniversary of Columbus' discovery of America, it made 'a sensation in artistic circles on both sides of the Atlantic'.[7] Characters include: defiant Columbus; Prior; obstinate high commissioner Talavera; Queen Isabella; Marquesa; Columbus' neglected mistress Beatriz; Martín Pinzón, seamen – in a work of eloquent speeches, flexible verse. Both acts are quests: One, Columbus' long search for a hearing and permission to sail to the West; Two, his first long voyage to America and triumphal return. The build-up in each act is carefully planned. BBC Radio uses its old seagull recording, soon to be outdated. Hauntings pursue Columbus, choric voices of Doubt and Faith (MacNeice's bishop-father died in April). In 1944–50 there were revivals: a stage excerpt, four school performances, broadcasts in translation; and two printings (1944, 1963) with two introductions. MacNeice matured rapidly in radio feature and radio drama, 1941–2.[8] His first war plays show risky struggles or tough victories, wrenched from near-defeat, to evoke patriotism in the fight against Nazism, for Greek, Russian and American Allies.

RADIO PLAYS 1943: DEATHS OF FREEDOM-FIGHTING POETS
In 1943 MacNeice became a producer: first, of plays on 'deaths of poets', an initiative related to his features on freedom that year. The plays focus on freedom-fights of political poets (Byron, Marlowe, de Bosis) leading through last days to death. *The Death of Byron*, broadcast on his death anniversary, shows a no-nonsense Byron, vexed with Italy, sailing with Trelawny, servant Fletcher, and pet dog, to Greece, to support Greek independence, and to die under medical attention. *The Death of Marlowe*, broadcast after his anniversary, is written in Elizabethan pastische. Kit visits Walsingham in his garden; is summoned to Council; overhears Greene, Shakespeare, actor Edward Alleyn reciting at length; ends at a tavern where he is stabbed – a free spirit gone at 29. Pastiche and many quotations make the Marlowe play a hurriedly written

failure. The first two poet-plays use (1) Irish song, (2) Irish narrator.

The Story of My Death, 'A tribute to an anti-Facist martyr', is prompted by his friend Lt. Graham Shepard's death at sea. Italian poet Lauro de Bosis, reared by his father on Italian and English poetry including Shelley – many quotations – learns to fly, prints anti-Facist leaflets, flies from Sicily to Rome, showers papers over the city and vanishes 'into the sea', October 1931. Broadcast on the death anniversary, *the play brings together flying, poetry, and Italy – where in 1943 Allied offensives were winning victories, launched from Sicily, against the Fascists. All three plays demonstrate how the BBC policy of observing anniversaries was useful to MacNeice in finding congenial subjects: poets dying for freedom – Greek, British, Italian.[9]

RADIO PLAYS 1944: LIFE-PORTRAITS WITH FLASHBACK

When the war turned around, after D-Day, MacNeice produced, with interest in the technical possibilities of sound drama, two biographies using flashback – *He Had a Date* and *Sunbeams in His Hat*, broadcast summer 1944. 'He Had a Date, or, What Bearing?', memorializes Lt. Shepard, and mixes in MacNeice's own experiences, in an experiment.

The hero Tom Varney, typical of his generation and (upper-middle) class, has enlisted for World War Two. Action opens and closes with a frame – naval man on watch on the bridge of his ship – and within that frame unwinds a newsreel flashback, birth to death, cross-cutting excerpts from the life of a man going his own way: giving up Oxford education, a 'suitable girl', naval commission – for socialist action, journalism, working-class girl. The frame returns at the end with a vengeance as a torpedo hits the ship: recalled voices are overheard by the drowning man. MacNeice uses such voices with more restraint in *Date* than in *Marlowe*. The weaving-in of popular songs begins here, a device he was to use later; composer Alan Rawsthorne arranges the music. The figure of the ordinary but unorthodox man proves useful to MacNeice, and recurs. His second production of *Date*, on Third (1949), uses a more mature, enlarged script, practised actors and the George Mitchell Choir to secure higher professional standards.

Sunbeams in His Hat, a life-portrait expanded from his earlier play *Dr Chekhov*, broadcast on the death anniversary, focuses on Chekhov's last day in Germany – from masseur in the morning to doctor in the evening – a day when the writer and his actress wife Olga share memories, prompting flashbacks: (1) his father's vain faith; (2) his visit to the penal colony Sakhalin to study conditions; (3) gambling at Monte Carlo; (4) confronting Tolstoy and Gorky; (5) Stanislavsky's direction of Chekhov scenes for his jubilee. These memories flow in and out, for a rounded portrait of a happy man – husband, writer, doctor, humanitarian – a portrait in laughter and dedication, challenging the notion of a melancholic Chekhov. Successful use is made of new devices: interrupted stream of consciousness and sinister dream. Fine actors and Russian folk tunes (on the balalaika) contribute to the popularity of MacNeice's production, and it is broadcast twice again in 1944. These radio portraits of navy man and Russian writer pioneer flashback – a device more effective, original than that of quotation in the poet-plays.

From the Blitz to summer of D-Day, 1941–4, MacNeice wrote many features, eight radio plays historically related – Propaganda Plus. As war eased, however, he was released to explore new kinds of dramas.

TRANSITION 1944–5: SATURNALIA, SCIENCE FICTIONS, PARABLE

In 1944–5, MacNeice completed new scripts. As the war came to an end, transition called for new things. A short radio play *A Roman Holiday* (1944) assembles a batch of Romans, in the year of Christ's birth, to celebrate the Saturnalia, and ends with an abused slave-girl's hope answered by Palestrina's *Hodie Christus Natus Est* – as MacNeice's Christmas Eclogue (1933) ends with the Christ-child. Antony Hopkins writes banal music for the banquet. (In 1944–8 MacNeice wrote three more Saturnalian plays.) Then he versified two science fictions: (1) *Pax Futura*, from Dallas Bower's film scenario, where in a late war scare of German buzz-bombs and rockets (called a second Battle of Britain) airmen fight for world peace in 1995 (too ambitious and expensive, it was filed by Rank as *Pax Aerea*); (2) *Eureka*, a stage take-off from Aldous Huxley's *Brave New World*, written in apprehension of a National Health Scheme, has a totalitarian state making a medical researcher use his serum to control unwanted men in 1955. It is also too ambitious. Yet the ideas in *Eureka* of the dangers of science and tyrannies of the State are explored successfully later. In Britain in 1945, Welfare State planning was discussed and feared: Utopia? Dystopia? MacNeice's friends in BBC Talks – Empson, Orwell (gone from BBC), Priestley (Overseas Service), survivors of the 1930s – had forebodings, e.g. Orwell's fable *Animal Farm* (1945). Looking forward into nightmare accurately reflects the thinking of the time. At the end of July 1945, BBC Drama and Features was subdivided, with Features becoming independent under Gilliam.

During MacNeice's long family holiday on Achill (1945), he wrote a strange, exciting play in verse – to many, his only play remembered at all. The horrors of Summer 1945 – full disclosure of the 'final solution' in Nazi death-camps, destruction of Hiroshima and Nagásaki by atom bombs – prompted him to write an allegory based on his rôle in the war. *The Dark Tower*, 'A parable play on the ancient theme of the quest', was produced January 1946 with Benjamin Britten's music; published with an introduction and four other scripts (1947); praised; produced again by MacNeice 1949, 1956, 1959 – all with rebroadcasts; congratulatory letters; translations; posthumous productions. MacNeice uses skeletal action and imagery from Browning's dream poem 'Childe Roland' – a quest through difficult terrain under sinister conditions to the Dark Tower. Roland, seventh son, trained but reluctant, is sent off on an ambiguous quest by mother, tutor, trumpeter, in the steps of father and six brothers, who have not returned; and is warned by Blind Peter about an evil Dragon. Delayed by drink, false love, gambling, failing to marry a true love, he persists, from a sea of delusions to a forest of hallucinations, to a desert where an unborn child's voice pleads. In psychomachia, he struggles and hears voices of his past while the Dark Tower rises and he blows the challenge. The play in a flexible verse medium, with personifications (as in the quests of Spenser's Red Cross Knight and of Bunyan's Christian), universalizes MacNeice's part in the war as a journey into the unknown, to fight Evil. The familiar English legend of St George and the pitting of knight against dragon are turned through Browning's dream poem into a haunting quest, making inventive and suggestive use of music, sound effects and a variety of sometimes overlapping voices. Britten's eerie score, for 31 strings, bells, gong, percussion, trumpet – conducted by Walter Goehr – begins and ends with an unforgettable trumpet call, the signature of the play – a parable play of 'doubleness in the action'.[10]

RADIO PORTRAITS OF EVIL: NEW VOICE DEVICES, 1946
MacNeice's next plays were prompted by the Nuremberg War Crimes Trials (1946), reckonings for the death-camps. The big question then was what makes a good man evil, a dictator or a criminal – a question publicly debated as Summer trials led to Autumn verdicts. *Enter Caesar*, broadcast three times (1946), to

mark 2,000 years from the Roman invasion of Britain, is a newsreel treatment of Julius Caesar becoming dictator – based on writings of Cicero, Plutarch and Caesar himself. The clever trick in making Caesar an enigma of evil is to suppress his voice entirely, to let other voices speak in a public pageant – Sulla, Crassus, Pompey, Cicero, Cato, women – ending with Caesar's triumphal entry into Rome after Egypt, and the Ides of March, 44 BC. The study of 'the first great dictator of the modern type' opens with a school lesson linking Caesar directly to Hitler; pageantry with Elisabeth Lutyens' music echoes Hitler's crowd excitements. Another play cuts close to war collaborators. *The Careerist*, broadcast four times (1946, 1948), traces the extreme career of Jim Human, 1900s to 1940s. Human – named for Humanity as in a medieval morality – cheats to get into Oxford, fools his tutor, marries for money, invests in a publishing firm; then in visits to Germany turns Nazi, and returns to England to publish a Nazi newsletter. He buys up publishers and books, to corner the market in paper, as war intensifies. Police track him down as traitor. Trapped, Human shoots himself. Yet Jim Human has had better qualities. His career into extremity is marked by quarrels among his inner voices personified, rendering a moral struggle between good and evil urges – a complex inner debate more pretentious than in *Columbus*. Competing psychic voices make the play a 'psycho-morality' (MacNeice's term), a parable. Music for flute and voices is by William Alwyn. *Caesar* and *Careerist* are portraits of evil – after the epics of 1941–2, the freedom-fight plays of 1943, and the life-flashback dramas of 1944. New voice-devices are tried: (1) suppressing one voice (Caesar) to present a chronicle through other voices; (2) rendering one outer and several inner voices of a character (Human) in a chronicle. At the end of September 1946, the Third Programme was set up, for greater opportunities in sound drama. From 1944–8 (from 1946 on Third) MacNeice attempted new modes: folktale, skit, satirical comedy, saga.

RADIO FOLKTALE PLAYS, WITH MAGICAL PLOT DEVICES, 1944–8, 1959

There are four tales. *The Nosebag*, 1944, renews an old Russian tale of a discharged soldier, generous to beggars, given a magic nosebag, by which he gets rid of devils from the palace of the Tsar and cures everyone of plague. Tricking Mistress Death but tricked in turn, he returns to Earth to fight in Russian wars – a salute to Russian soldiers winning the siege of '900 days' (Leningrad/St. Petersburg, January 1944). The tale 'Death and the Soldier', with comic supernatural machinery, especially devils, is developed into earthy fantasy, using recordings of Russian music. The next tale, *The Heartless Giant*, Christmas 1946, from the Norwegian 'The Giant who had no Heart in his Body', opens in parody of *The Dark Tower*. When six brothers fail to return in quest for brides, a seventh son, Boots, ventures out on an old horse. On the way he helps raven, wolf, salmon – animals who guide him to a giant's castle where he finds brother-princes and brides turned to stone. A castle princess helps Boots on a second quest, for the giant's heart; the giant is forced to yield hostages, and all brothers return to marry their brides. Light rhymes to open and close, light quips of sly animals, mark this prose play with comic good will, accented by light music of Antony Hopkins. MacNeice wrote a new version (1954), broadcast with Arthur Oldham's special music.

A third tale, *The Two Wicked Sisters*, broadcast twice on Third (1948), with music by Matyas Seiber, re-hashes 'Cinderella' into a modern skit, where all the sisters marry, and Cinderella's Prince must find a job. Too-clever jokes, however, turn story and magic into facetious parody. A fourth tale, *East of the Sun and West of the Moon*, 1959 (Norwegian, modernized from Andrew Lang's *Blue Fairy Book*), tells of a girl sold by greedy parents to a white Bear – revealed in his underground snow castle as a handsome Prince. Losing him to troll magic (Psyche motif), she goes in quest of him – helped by three crones and four winds (comically portrayed) – to reach an evil castle (Spenserian motif), outwit an assortment of ugly trolls and unite with her Prince in the North, where their love turns barrenness into flowers. Tristram Cary renders troll mischief and magical effects by electronic music. Ballad elements in MacNeice's folktale plays provide links with lyric poems such as 'Bagpipe Music', 'Nuts in May', 'The Streets of Laredo', 'Children's Games'.

RADIO SKITS: A LICENSED FOOL, TOPICAL JESTING, 1942–7,
1958

There are four topical skits written for April Fool's Day, in which MacNeice plays the licensed Fool to mock topics of the day. *Calling All Fools*, 1942, sends up a Fun Fair, Laissez-Faire, the Superman – in a wartime trifle. The next skits are take-offs on Lewis Carroll, in *The March Hare Saga* (pub. 1947): (1) *The March Hare Resigns* laughs at political canvassing via March and Madness; and (2) *Salute to All Fools* pokes fun at wanderings after 'Truth'. Antony Hopkins makes comic music for both skits. *All*

Fools at Home, 'A study in blackwash', 1958, jests about literary trends of the 1950s, seen by an Ulsterman come to London. The topical flippancy in the skits has dated.

RADIO PLAYS OF SATIRICAL COMEDY, 1944–8

A related mode jumps out of his myth-kitty in 1944–8: Saturnalian or satirical comedy – plays derived from Apuleius, Aristophanes, Petronius, with MacNeice as Lord of Misrule. He divides Apuleius' Latin novel into a picaresque, *The Golden Ass*, and a story within, the romance *Cupid and Psyche*, both November 1944, repeated 1945. *The Golden Ass* takes a man Lucius – changed into an ass, a believable human ass – through rough-and-tumbles, a robber's cave, treadmills, threatened auctions – until changed back after he prays to the goddess Isis. Racy characters use sharp dialogue, slapstick, magic, confidence tricks, earthy humour. Lucius is a foreign voice, 'a stranger in Thessaly', his ass brayings mimicked in music. Gielgud and Gilliam wrote MacNeice happy letters of congratulation. He gave *The Golden Ass* an enlarged production on Third, 31 December 1951; repeated twice, January 1952. Antony Hopkins conducts his music again (impudence with musical jokes). *Cupid and Psyche* is an old wives' tale on quarrelling deities and Psyche's miseries (with an inevitable BBC seagull) and Antony Hopkins' music conveys Apuleius' magicality. *Psyche* was given a new production, 1947.

In *Enemy of Cant*, 'A panorama of Aristophanic comedy', December 1946, MacNeice links up his verse paraphrases from the Greek – to expose the foulness of a war which Thucydides recorded in his *History*. MacNeice's character 'Aristophanes' satirizes the bitter long War between democratic Athens and totalitarian Sparta – parallel to the recent war – and the Athenian tyrant Cleon who prolongs it. Contemporary references are pointed. 'Cultural capers' are extended to women (Lysistrata), education, cloud cuckooland. Aristophanes remains throughout an enemy of cant, stupidity, and selfish imperialism. Antony Hopkins composes and conducts satiric music with 'blasphemous' musical jokes.

Then MacNeice dramatizes a chunk of Petronius' Latin *Satyricon* called *Trimalchio's Feast*, for Saturnalia, December 1948: a comic satire of bragging excesses, during Nero's reign, at a banquet given by a vulgar-rich freed slave, who parades wealth before freed guests, in regional and slangy dialogue. As with *The Golden Ass*, speech and situations are lively, grotesque, burlesques of old Roman life. Alan Rawsthorne writes incidental music.

These three plays are of 'the people', consistent with his BBC broadcast 'In Defence of Vulgarity' (1937) and 'Introduction to *The Golden Ass*' (1946), keys to his debunking attitude.[11] In *The Golden Ass*, *Enemy of Cant*, *Trimalchio's Feast*, MacNeice is Lord of Misrule, Master of the Revels, for Saturnalia, pagan antics carried into celebrations, pantomimes of the Christmas season. He becomes more than Fool – he is an Arbiter of low life: broadcasts 'improper' Classics for postwar merriment; debunks in racy spirit as he does near the end of *Autumn Journal IX*. The satirical comedies take seasonal licence to defy Mrs Grundy and a rump of puritans. After tragedies of War, they are satyr plays.

RADIO SAGA PLAYS: FEUDING AND OUTLAWRY, 1947
There is a fourth new mode: saga narratives written as dialogue plays (each broadcast three times on Third, 1947). Dasent's *The Saga of Burnt Njal* is divided into *The Death of Gunnar* and *The Burning of Njal*. Blood feud and the new rule of law (by Assembly or *Althing*) are bitterly opposed. Arnold Cooke's music, conducted by Alan Rawsthorne, renders: wind, rain, sea, creaks, crashes, a halberd singing; the BBC seagull gone at last. *The Death of Gunnar* (the Achilles of Iceland) opens with his unwise choice of wife, whose earlier husbands have died violent deaths; pivots on sage advice with bond, Njal to Gunnar, to avoid bloodshed and maintain peace; ends with Gunnar besieged, betrayed by his wife and killed in his homestead. *The Burning of Njal* starts with an eerie vision of Gunnar in his grave; turns on a contest between old gods and new; ends with Njal and his family burnt in their home. In both plays, The Watcher, like The Watchman in *The Agamemnon*, is a Choric voice. Bitter feuds follow a rigid code of honour to bring about inevitable crimes and killings.

MacNeice condensed *Grettir the Strong*, from Morris and Magnusson's translation, into a compact tragedy. The 'doomed tough' – seen in MacNeice's 'Eclogue from Iceland', 1936 – jokes defiantly too often, is struck by one ill-luck after another, until, outlawed several times over, haunted by a victim's eyes, driven farther and farther from habitation, he is killed in his fastness by witchcraft and storm. Prose speech is terse, verse in strong rhythms; there is choric commentary by saga voices and a strong supernatural element. Matyas Seiber composes the music. (Icelanders in London wrote in to the BBC: they agreed that the saga programmes were accurate, 'first-rate'.)

The three saga plays are primitive epics, written halfway between *Letters from Iceland* (1937) and 'Dark Age Glosses' on Njal and Grettir (1957). His love of Norse stories resembles his partiality for Homer and Malory, for doomed men of action, for hard sportsmen of skill. So after five years, 1942–7, MacNeice came back to epic heroes. He had grasped ritual tragedy in *Agamemnon* (1936); he would write epic tragedies on Saul and Brian Boru (1956, 1959) echoing these saga plays.

His best new modes through 1944–8 – folktale, satirical comedy, saga – are variants from originals, inventive adaptations in three distinct new styles. The skits and satiric fantasies have dated in topicality. Tales, satires, and sagas live on through believable characters and lively plots, dialogues and language.

In October 1948, MacNeice marked a poetic milestone by completing *Collected Poems 1925–1948* (London: Faber, 1949), rounded off after a first visit to India. At the same time, the end of the British Raj (1947), his plays extended to new territories during a period of foreign trips and assignments, at the start of the Cold War.

PLAYS OF INDIA AND GREECE: PANORAMA AND DREAM-QUEST, 1948, 1951

In 1947–51 MacNeice was sent by the BBC to India (for partition and independence – three months 1947), was commissioned to translate Goethe's *Faust* (six months 1949) and served the British Institute and British Council, Athens (eighteen months 1950–1). After visits to India and Greece, near the end of Empire, he wrote two sets of programmes, with two plays. The Indian play, *India at First Sight*, 1948, opening a series on India and Pakistan, is a panorama centred on Edward from England – crash-landed in India, advised by voices from home and hearing 'native' voices: 'India' personified, a 'still voice', early historic voices, 'outsider' religions, local poets. A lively travelogue of little action, it points to a finer play: *Nuts in May* (1957), a picaresque treatment of an extravert – of Empire and post-Empire.

MacNeice's Greek play, *In Search of Anoyia*, 'A dramatic exploration of a strange village in Crete', is a dream-quest (1951) based on his failure when in Greece to climb Mount Ida in Crete – which his friend Dodds and son Dan were able to do; MacNeice and Hedli left halfway (he visited Anoyia, Holy Week and August, 1951). Amateur archaeologist John, ill, passes a troubled night on the mainland, with wife Mary, son, Irish doctor, a book – naval officer Thomas Spratt's *Travels and Researches in Crete* (1865). John – wakeful in sleep, interrupted by 'Spratt', helped by Mary – dreams of reaching Anoyia, a village in the hills below Ida, to be joined later by his party, one by one. In dream, shepherds exchange with John rhymed couplets (*mantinades*) – as exuberant as the Cretan writer Nikos Kazantzakis. Anoyia, centre of Cretan resistance during the occupation, had been fired by Germans in August 1944, a fact bitterly recalled. Easter is celebrated; then the Assumption, as memorial for the war dead. That night, a dance re-enacts John and Mary's wedding. Waking, John tells Mary their marriage is bound in a ball of thread, from the labyrinth myth of Crete. The play was broadcast twice before Christmas 1951 on Third. The Indian panorama circles; but the Greek play advances, through wakings and dreamings, a quest of encounters, sound effects (sheep/goats, fireworks, crowd, antique bus), with a live shepherd's pipe and recorded music – Cretan and Byzantine.[12]

VAST DRAMA OF GOETHE, PARABLE PLAY OUT OF HOUSMAN, 1949

Between his Indian and Greek visits, MacNeice laboured to translate Goethe's vast poetic drama *Faust* – for Goethe's bi-centenary, BBC 1949 (six programmes). MacNeice relied on E. L. Stahl for the German, but cut one third. Translating line-by-line, he used Goethe's original metres, his own imitative rhymes. He could render Faust, Mephistopheles, Wagner, Gretchen, in Part One, because knowledge, irony, ambition, love-betrayal, were not alien to him. He found Part Two a puzzling allegory, based on Goethe's lofty Classical idealism: he had to render Helen idealized, a Homunculus, Byron as reckless Euphorion, etc. He cut, then freely adapted Goethe's allegory in his own bridge passage, leading into the remainder and conclusion. Matyas Seiber's music was valued – the basis of his later Faust Choral Suite (broadcast 1961). *Faust* gave MacNeice types: Scholar of ambition, Spirit of negation; later he would write on the dangers of power and of science. The BBC said *Faust* was his greatest achievement; a senior BBC friend (E. A. Harding) commissioned and produced it; it was published to acclaim (1951). MacNeice cut most of Part Two in his own two-programme production, 1962, with the Ambrosian Singers and the London Symphony Orchestra.[13]

When assigned to *Faust* in early 1949, MacNeice, in search of a myth, crossed Goethe's Helen and Mephisto with MacDonald's Lilith, via Housman's memorable lyric 'The Queen of Air and Darkness', to invent a story of perverted idealism: *The Queen of Air and Darkness*, 'A study of evil', 1949[14] – adding a magic mirror from 'The Lady of Shalott'. In 1948–9 Communist dictators not only dominated Russia and Eastern Europe but blockaded Berlin and took over China, threatening all of Asia. The prospect of world Communism spurred MacNeice to write a play on world tyranny, at the time of Orwell's *Nineteen Eighty-Four* (early 1949). In every generation a blind Queen in her lower world bewitches a tyrant in a world above to evil. She replaces an old tyrant with a young lover she chooses as dictator in turn. Adam, a commercial artist with a gift for hypnotism, despite finer feelings, rises to power ruthlessly by perverse idealism and puts dissenters into underground tunnels, as his predecessor had done. His wife leaves him; he takes a mistress; she betrays him. Sent to the catacombs, he is cursed by all his prisoners. Then a forgotten prisoner (former tyrant's widow) names the witch and points Adam to her mirror. He breaks mirror and spell and destroys the Queen, as Houseman's lyric is read. Walter Goehr conducts Elisabeth Lutyens' music. The play is repeated twice on Third. MacNeice's parable exposes tyrants and despots: Caesars/Kaisers/Tsars, Mussolini, Hitler, Stalin, now Chairman Mao. *Queen*, written in answer to requests for another *Tower*, is an experimental drama on an evil career, an innovative parable more ambitious than *Careerist*. MacNeice needed new simplicities, but didn't find them till after Greece, 1950–1. In his 'middle stretch', his working life clashed with his domestic one; and in his last decade he wrote fewer plays.

RADIO PLAYS OF ESCAPE: BROADCASTER AND PRISONER, 1952, 1954

After broadcasts from his poetry book *Ten Burnt Offerings*, 1951 (1952), MacNeice produced two radio plays of realism and of breaking from realism. *One Eye Wild*, 'A romance in commonplace' (1952), mocks a would-be hero with the Walter Mitty motif, escapist heroics.[15] Roger Mallaveen (Irish surname),[16] blind in one eye, frustrated romantic, is a sports writer and radio commentator on sport. So preoccupied, he neglects wife and son. After giving a cricket broadcast at Lord's, going to meet an RAF pilot (hero) but hurt in traffic, he is hospitalized and dreams while unconscious – his dreams undercut by mockers: parrots, wife, Joker (Mephisto). With a classic dream girl beside him – Heliodora – Roger dreams of sport heroics in escapist flashbacks: from 1914 (win at tennis) to the Middle Ages (three winning jousts for his lady) to ancient Greece (attempted seduction before an Olympiad) – receding pasts, further escapes. Husband and wife are reconciled at last, with cross-fade of her lullaby and his sport broadcast. In

One Eye Wild MacNeice debunks himself as broadcaster, womanizer, sportsman: Mittyesque daydreams are self-revelations that undercut him. The action is not extended into a chronicle career but contained within a single day, morning to night. After the extraordinary chronicle careers of Human and Adam, *One Eye Wild* reasserts the ordinary. MacNeice produced a new version in 1961, with the BBC Radiophonic Workshop.

After the Everest victory crowned the Coronation (May–June 1953). MacNeice adapted Goronowy Rees's *Where No Wounds Were* (on ironic interrogations at a British prison-camp) and followed it with his own play on British prisoners in a German prison-camp: *Prisoner's Progress*, 'A romantic fable of imprisonment and escape' (1954 award-winner). Under the control of Browns (Germans) are Greys (British): a Padre rehearsing Wilde's *Importance*, an English teacher Waters, a woman archaeologist, Scottish officer Mac, Irish pilot Regan, coloured cook singing ballads – Toralf Tollefsen improvising on accordian. Grey women find a passage-tomb; Grey men, digging a tunnel, stumble on the tomb. Mac plans escape from a map. With an air raid as cover, the escape succeeds, but Mac is killed below, Regan shot above. Climbing a mountain[17] promotes companionship between Waters and Alison: they share confidence, poems, learn to love each other, before they too are shot. The hero Waters keens his bastard fate by quoting Job, curses his father's betrayal and recites love poems with Alison. Tunnels point ahead to caves in plays on Saul and Hank (1956, 1963). These two plays of the early 1950s set up dilemmas realistically, then break through them by escapes – in dreaming, in climbing.

MacNeice suffered personal losses at end of 1953: W. R. Rodgers moved from London; Dylan Thomas died – MacNeice becoming a literary executor; then his son Dan left home at age 19 for his mother in USA – personal losses made worse by professional changes in BBC policy: the Third programme cut by half; TV favoured over Radio Features. MacNeice wrote a long poem as if to compensate: *Autumn Sequel* 1953 (1954); six excerpts were broadcast.

PLAYS ON POWER: A DOOMED KING AND A MODERN POET, 1956

MacNeice's radio dramas of 1956 focus on corruption of power or avoidance of power (biblical, classical) at a tense time in the Cold War. *Also Among the Prophets*, 'The career of a doomed king', from Samuel One, is written late 1955 after a visit up the Nile, when Arab-Israeli conflicts are leading to military invasion and the Suez War (1956). MacNeice, reminded of ancient battles nearby, focuses on the corruption of a primitive ideal. Last judge Samuel, asked by the people for a king, reluctantly transfers power to a big lout, Saul son of Kish, first king by anointing. Saul, driven to disobedience, is deserted by Samuel and struggles in interior monologues against poison within. David joins Saul, who is soothed by David's harp, yet rages in jealousy, until David has to flee for his life. MacNeice innovates with underground voices and echoes for: Saul's inner cave where an evil spirit lurks, caves where David hides or Saul sleeps and a cave where Saul seeks the witch of Endor. Typically MacNeice focuses on a bad leader, failed king, driven mad, suicidal. Matyas Seiber writes psalm music (choruses by the Dorion Singers) and harp variations (David calming the king, and, after Saul's suicide, lamentation).

Carpe Diem, 'A twentieth-century tribute to Horace' (1956), portrays a poet, in retreat from power, through a montage of flashbacks – poems, songs, memories. The modern poet Quintus, away from London, is like Horace away from the power-centre of Rome. Quintus, tended in his last illness by a last love, re-enacts Horace's end. He recalls a medley of Horatian poems – English verse anthology with Latin snatches – asks his love to play recordings of nostalgic songs and looks back to his Horatian father, to memories of 1912–16. The play shows a poet (MacNeice?) avoiding power (promotion?). It is more innovative than the Saul play, for it is not direct from the source, but indirect through a series of lenses, to render a statement of the modern poet. Both productions, of Saul and Quintus, were broadcast twice on Third. Their negative views of power show a king going mad, a poet bidding farewell to life. Meanwhile there were new crises: Suez and Hungary (1956), the H-bomb and the return to nuclear testing – protested and negotiated for years to come: 1956 tolled the end of Empire; the Cold War intensified.[18]

From India, Goethe, Greece to Saul and Horace, the plays of 1948–56 experimented with panorama, dream, hypnotism, flashback, cave echoes, montage. Crises at home and at work sent MacNeice out in search of new topics, travels, innovations. Television usurped the broadcasting field; but he clung to sound. In 1956 Gilliam called him 'the most distinguished writer in the BBC'.

PROBLEM PLAYS 1957–60: LOVE, DANGER IN FOREIGN LOCALES

In the later 1950s, when the entire Third Programme was at risk, when nuclear-testing and negotiations were prolonged, MacNeice continued to write plays, two for stage: *Traitors in Our Way* (put on by the Ulster Group Theatre, Belfast, 1957); *One for the Grave* (by the Abbey Theatre, Dublin, 1966, posthumously). The latter is considered near the end of the essay. MacNeice made *Traitors* into a teleplay, *Another Part of the Sea*, 1960, with Benjamin Britten's music. The germ was the reappearance of a Marxist friend.[19] A ship's passage (Mediterranean, Tropics, Arctic) and a love-triangle (nuclear physicist Tom, wife Portia, ex-colleague Roger – now Communist): these make up set and central personae. In the Eastern Med, during the Suez Crisis, Tom and Portia celebrate their first wedding anniversary with an Irish couple, when Roger, alias Haffer, boards in disguise and is seen by Tom, who detects the danger. Conflicting loyalties and betrayals arise: should Tom betray his old friend, or put friendship ahead of country? Should Portia stay loyal to Tom, or go back to her old lover Haffer? *Traitors/Sea* is a workable but stiff problem play on private love and public danger, loyalty and betrayal, among defined characters. It pivots on a master portrait – a traitor who, imprisoned, emerges more dangerous – its late religious allusions needing sensitive acting; the thriller-ending is left open. *Traitors* begins a series of problem plays: *Nuts in May*, *The Pin is Out* in foreign locales; *The Administrator*, *Let's Go Yellow* in home-settings.

Nuts in May, 'A tragi-comedy', 1957, takes an English extravert, happy-go-lucky army man, to India, Ireland and Antarctica – a pukka picaro confronting dangers of Empire during and after the Raj. Colloquialisms and rhymes are exploited: army jargon, slang, comic and sinister songs. A Syngean spirit[20] centres on the army playboy Tom Bowlby, who goes out to the Northwest Frontier, over-spends on polo ponies and defends the Raj in a brawl. In the War, hit in action in Burma, he is invalided out. There are interludes of carefree Anglo-Irish and Gaelic songs. After the atom bombs, Tom goes into advertising. Hesitating between English and Irish girls, he marries his Dublin girl too late: her children by an ex-husband are not his. In quest of action, he goes out to Antarctica and dies in a rescue attempt. As a man of action his 'ignorance' is the problem mulled over in the play, with post-imperial questions. A singer repeats the title rhyme 'Nuts in May' to link episodes and stress hero as victim, which Tom becomes: her refrain 'Who shall we get to bear him away?' is insistent. Naturalistic dialogue alternates with stylized songs. The play is fitted to early 1957, when Asian powers meet in New Delhi.[21] MacNeice innovating, responding to new circumstances, shows an 'uncomplicated' extravert entering a post-war, post-imperial world – an ordinary man happy only in action. Tom dies in a futile, noble gesture, a man of ignorant vitality.

MacNeice's next problem play *The Pin Is Out* is a lampoon of South Africa – written after his 1959 tour – when apartheid has led to the banishment of four ANC leaders and to the setting-up of African Homelands.[22] A nameless land is split into *Inners* (ruling political élite of settler whites), *Outers* (wealthy, ostracized class who never win elections), *Zeros* (countless voteless and subhuman blacks). A liberal journalist from England flying to 'Zeroland' faces stupid regulations and brutalities and gets dubious help from fellow-Englishmen. Christian racists justify apartheid – caricatured in leaders and people. In one public speech an Englishman declares the Good Samaritan obsolete: at this, the liberal journalist walks out, along with a rich female Inner, also liberal. Incredibly these two fall in love; they picnic on a cliff looking to the South Pole. She introduces him to Inner thugs, and to a young educated Zero whom she has helped. When Inners win rigged elections, the young Zero turns to kill them, including the woman. The lampoon, with dangers and absurdities, is a mixture of Kafka and Ionesco, as bitter as Orwell's satire of Communism; the lovers hide as in *1984*. *The Pin* remains in draft, 'refused by BBC on policy grounds 1960'. The Sharpeville Massacre may have dated MacNeice's ending – but not the entire play nor the racism satirized. Yet the play was rejected, and MacNeice turned half-yearly freelance.[23] The unbelievable love affair may be the weakest part of the play. In the last years of Features, 1960–4, as Gilliam's health failed, Features competed with a stronger Drama Department and with Television. MacNeice, if asked to head Features , did not become its Administrator.

PROBLEM PLAYS 1961: CAREER CHOICES IN HOME-LOCALES

In 1961 MacNeice wrote two problem plays on careers in home locales, refining his dilemma through dreams in *The Administrator*, through journalism in *Let's Go Yellow*. *The Administrator*, is a dream play working out a decision: Should Jerry, a nuclear scientist, compromise to become a bureaucrat? Or remain a creative researcher, avoid power? His wife and his research student urge him to be Director of the Institute. Action leads from evening through a night of interrupted dreams to morning when the postponed decision is to be taken. Dreams reveal: separate and joined pasts of husband and wife, guilts over ex-lovers, dreamings into each other's unconscious; sleight-of-hand scenes based on

Lewis Carroll; the wife's social ambitions but pre-marital pregnancy; a safari with a leper-boy (reminder of South Africa); nightmare of Jerry's car-crash changing to scientific command of an iceberg that collides with the *Titanic* – which strangely turns into a morning telephone call. Such free associations make the recurrent dream troubles convincing. The ending, dictated by the BBC, has Jerry accept the post; MacNeice's ending (published 1964) has Jerry make his own decision – creative research. MacNeice/Jerry declines promotion. The play was broadcast twice. MacNeice went on experimenting – here by sophisticated dream-distortions – in his third dream play after *In Search of Anoyia* and *One Eye Wild* (1951–2).

Let's Go Yellow, (first titled *The Press Gang*), 'The story of a reporter in a world of double-think' (Fleet Street), centres on a young newsman, Haman, joining a big daily newspaper, to be sent out to report on three stories: (1) a sportsman's widow (Haman fails to exploit her grief); (2) a peer's paedophilic visits (Haman gives hints, duly appreciated); (3) a rich lady's gambling (unaware, Haman names the son of a millionaire supporter of the paper). Stung by hypocritical rebukes of editors, Haman examines the gambling case further and turns up a scandal of large-scale heroin-smuggling, which earns him further rebukes at the paper. Disenchanted by double-think, Haman defects to write his story, for the BBC. Haman's biblical name, a man hanged for planning mass hangings of Jews (Book of Esther), refers to MacNeice's back-fired play *The Pin*: key to a personal fable. MacNeice does not indulge in self-pity, but produces a new play, a popular success.[24] His plays on human 'problems' – treachery, extrovert action, racism, compromise, double-think – are not simply thesis-plays.

EARLY IRISH PLAYS: BATTLE AND VOYAGE, 1959, 1962
After 1957 MacNeice looked for new subjects in early Ireland to be energized into plays.[25] *They Met on Good Friday*, 'A sceptical historical romance', 1959, sharpens the presentation of the Battle of Clontarf, AD 1014, with convincing lead-up scenes and battle details. Characters include Gormlai, King Brian's ex-wife, who sparks a Viking invasion to get a new husband under her blanket; to Sigurd Earl of Orkney, leading candidate for Gormlai, who summons Viking hosts; to High King Brian Boru, who in old age prays in his tent and sends out son and grandson to battle, where they are killed unawares with others on both sides, including unguarded Brian. The Irish win a Pyrrhic victory over the Vikings. MacNeice uses Choric voices: old woman, skald of alliterative

verse, poet of Irish metres, harper, and deploys epic verse to intensify battle action. Tristram Cary composes music – psalm-chant, Brian Boru's March, *musique concrète* – in his electronic studio.[26]

The Mad Islands, 1962 based on the Irish 'Immram Mael Duín' (Voyage of Malduín), modernizes a quest-fable. Muldoon, sent out by his mother to kill his father's killer (Lord of the Eskers), assembles a crew, with Skerrie the Seal-Woman (to warn and save him from misadventures); then sails past nine mad islands of temptation. His mother urges him on, till he finds his unknown father – a deceitful killer-hermit. Too late Muldoon sees parents turn into seals, with Skerrie and her mate. Left alone, he realizes the vendetta was a false quest. Skerrie's seal voice is in Highland Scottish accent; her seal-barks warn Muldoon against foolish errands ashore. For Muldoon as for Odysseus, all companions are lost. Satiric personae include: rival Welsh sisters Branwen and Olwen bewitching men into tom-cats; pitiless Miller of Hell grinding all to the West; incorrigible Alchemist turned Inventor and mad Nuclear Scientist, making explosions and catastrophes – *caveat* on nuclear testing. These dramas, broadcast twice each, energize old Irish traditions of battle and voyage in a sharp and satiric manner.

SUMMARY PLAYS OF LIVING AND DYING: EVERYMAN, ARTIST, 1958–63

Two autobiographies round off MacNeice's development in drama: *One for the Grave* for stage, *Persons from Porlock* for radio. *Grave*, 1958–61, was produced at the Abbey, 1966. MacNeice, annoyed at his BBC-TV stint in 1958 – as a man of sound, not of visuals – found a lively echo of his rage in Joan Littlewood's Theatre Workshop production of Brendan Behan's *The Hostage* (1958). The morality pattern of *The Summoning of Everyman* universalizes his predicament, as he satirizes television and 'isms' (simplistic solutions to human complexities), in indignation at his tormentors: the idiot box, domestic crises, consumerism, electronics, poor singers, the trendy remedies of psychoanalysis, politics, science, medicine, divinity – their superficial experts – within the story of an ordinary man defending himself at death in a Kafkaesque world he cannot understand, before a live television audience. The symbolic set is a TV studio: Production Gallery above with Director as God figure (obscure, abrupt); Floor below with Manager Morty. To the set Morty brings motley people – realistic or personified – taking Everyman in Act One from Career and Conscience, through his family of complainers, to Patria and Sacrifice in two world wars; in Act Two from Admom, Electronic Brain, Crooner, and a parade of hectoring experts, to the tomb where a strong, kind Gravedigger prepares him for death. Ballads set to mock-tunes punctuate Act Two, ending with a choric send-off for Everyman. The revue style of farce and skit is revived, bits of music hall, echoes of Littlewood-Behan's *Hostage*, extending morality into satiric medley. MacNeice returns to a vital Irish tradition – including Behan, Flann O'Brien, O'Casey, Swift – in outrageous attacks on outrageous nonsense. Reaching for Swift's 'savage indignation', he writes in self-defence against know-it-all moderns, high-ups (BBC bureaucrats), experts on everything. Everyman lends his modern namesake bewilderment, pathos, self-defence, authenticity.

MacNeice's last radio play *Persons from Porlock*, 'The story of a painter' 1963, broadcast while he was dying, is an apologia summing up life and art. Painter Hank muddles through life, love, art, against forces interrupting his painting: irresponsible absentee mother; war in Burma and remorse at killing a Japanese; detours to commercial art and alcoholism; juggling true and false loves; unsuccessful art exhibit; bailiff taking chattels – with the crisis driving the true girl to crash their car. At last Hank accepts a cure against alcohol. Long before, he has practised speleology with pals in Yorkshire. On a last outing at Skrimshank's Cave, he is caught. Stuck underground at the Stygian Trap with water rising, he drowns, hallucinating, hearing echo-voices – until the last voice, a Noble Person from Porlock (borrowed from Coleridge), Death himself, comes to say that his death will make his pictures sell – black humour, for Hank is dying. Voices overheard by a drowning man was a device in *Date*, but is fully developed here; many strange ghosts appear, disappear, re-appear. Cross-cutting episodes are brought to high art in sound: realistic scenes acquire symbolic import, until they reach an echo chamber of mocking ironies in a cavern, a trap. The lives-in-crisis of Everyman and Hank are resolved by a strong Gravedigger and a Noble Person, agents of death. These black moralities are among his strongest plays. His last dramas of 1957–63[27] explore strange twists like the strange ironies in his last poems.

CONCLUSION

MacNeice cannot be assessed as playwright when few of his plays are in print, and only one performed. He is a major Irish poet – his *Collected Poems* appreciated over 30 years. Though once Golden

Boy of Radio, he is now forgotten as a dramatist, except for *The Dark Tower*. Have we lost touch with the medium (Radio Features) and the message ('pure radio')? When Radio Drama took over, the message of Radio Features was forgotten. For a clear idea of MacNeice's plays beyond the few modes in print (Quest, Portrait/Life-Summary, Parable, Irish Play, Morality), more good dramas need to be published, performed – plays in modes not yet represented (Dream Play, Saga, Problem Play, Folktale, Satirical Comedy, Tragedy, Tragi-comedy). All the radio plays of Denis Johnston, Samuel Beckett, Harold Pinter and Tom Stoppard are published; MacNeice's radio plays in print are a fraction. Like O'Casey, MacNeice wrote some uneven plays. Yet MacNeice's originality, versatility, vitality in a dozen kinds, if performed in Features manner[28] and *heard*, if published and read *by ear*, would lead to recognition of his dramatic *oeuvre*, its development and great variety – and begin a true assessment of MacNeice as playwright.

NOTES

INTRODUCTION

Alan J. Peacock

1   Jon Stallworthy, *Louis MacNeice* (London, Faber and Faber, 1995).
2   Brendan Kennelly, 'Louis MacNeice: An Irish Outsider' in *Journey into Joy: Selected Prose*, ed. Åke Persson (Newcastle upon Tyne, Bloodaxe Books, 1994), pp. 136–7.
3   Peter McDonald, *Louis MacNeice: The Poet in his Contexts* (Oxford, Clarendon Press, 1991).
4   Edna Longley, *Louis MacNeice: A Study* (London, Faber and Faber, 1988).
5   Louis MacNeice, *Selected Poems*, ed. Michael Longley (London, Faber and Faber, 1988).
6   Alan Heuser (ed.): *Selected Literary Criticism of Louis MacNeice* (Oxford, Clarendon Press, 1987); *Selected Prose of Louis MacNeice* (Oxford, Clarendon Press, 1990); (with Peter McDonald) *Selected Plays of Louis MacNeice* (Oxford, Clarendon Press, 1993).
7   W.T. McKinnon, *Apollo's Blended Dream: A Study of the Poetry of Louis MacNeice* (London, Oxford University Press, 1971); D.B. Moore, *The Poetry of Louis MacNeice* (Leicester, Leicester University Press, 1972); Terence Brown, *Louis MacNeice: Sceptical Vision* (Dublin, Gill and Macmillan, 1975).
8   David Wright (ed.), *The Mid-Century: English Poetry 1940-60* (Harmondsworth, Penguin, 1965), p. 15.
9   Maurice Wollman (ed.), *Ten Contemporary Poets* (London, Harrap, 1963), p. 107.
10 *Selected Poems*, p. xxii.
11 Samuel Hynes, *The Auden Generation: Literature and Politics in England in the 1930s* (London, Bodley Head, 1976), pp. 369–70.
12 See however Hynes's later comments in 'Like the Trees on Primrose Hill', *London Review of Books*, Vol. 11, No. 5, 2nd March 1989, pp. 6–7, where it is recognised how 'For a time after his death his reputation sagged, perhaps because the myth of the Auden Gang was growing in the academies, and he had never really been a full-time gang member' and where a rounded, sympathetic and suggestive portrait of MacNeice as a poet is provided.

13   Francis Scarfe, *Auden and After* (London, Routledge, 1942), pp. 56 and 62.
14   Virginia Woolf, 'The Leaning Tower', *Folios of New Writing* 2, ed. John Lehmann (London, The Hogarth Press, Autumn 1940), pp. 11–33.
15   *Selected Literary Criticism*, p. 124.
16   G.S. Fraser, 'Evasive Honesty: the Poetry of Louis MacNeice', in *Vision and Rhetoric* (London, Faber and Faber, 1959), pp. 179–92.
17   Stephen Wall, 'Louis MacNeice and the Line of Least Resistance', *The Review*, No. 11/12, 1964, pp. 91–4.
18   *Auden and After*, pp. 66–7.
19   *Ibid.*, p. 65.
20   Conrad Aiken, 'Poetry as Entertainment', *The New Republic*, Vol. 104, June 16th, 1941, p. 831.
21   Louis MacNeice, *The Strings are False* (London, Faber and Faber, 1965), p. 125.
22   Louis MacNeice, *Modern Poetry: A Personal Essay* (1938), 2nd edn. (Oxford, Clarendon Press, 1968), p. 29.
23   *Selected Literary Criticism*, p. 25.
24   *Ibid.*, p. 4.
25   Seamus Heaney has notably commented on the importance to his generation of 'The Group' in *Preoccupations: Selected Prose 1968-1978* (London, Faber and Faber, 1980), pp. 28–29. Edna Longley has recently balanced the received picture by stressing, for instance, the importance of Trinity College, Dublin in the late 'fifties and early 'sixties for Michael Longley and Derek Mahon: *The Living Stream: Literature and Revisionism in Ireland* (Newcastle upon Tyne, Bloodaxe Books, 1994), pp. 18–20. Cf. also, e.g., the 'Special Feature on the Belfast Group' in *The Honest Ulsterman*, No. 97, Spring, 1994, pp. 3–26 (recalling the retrospect of No. 53, November/December 1976), for the continuing debate on the significance of The Group.
26   Derek Mahon, ed., *The Sphere Book of Modern Irish Poetry* (London, Sphere Books, 1972), p. 14.
27   G.S. Fraser, Introduction to *The Poetry of Louis MacNeice*, pp. 9–10. W.T. McKinnon's study had of course appeared in the previous year: cf. footnote 7.
28   *Selected Prose*, p. xiii.
29   'Interview: The Longley Tapes', *The Honest Ulsterman*, No. 78, Summer 1985, pp. 13–31. See p. 20.
30   Robyn Marsack, *The Cave of Making: the Poetry of Louis MacNeice* (Oxford, Clarendon Press, 1982).
31   Edna Longley, 'Traditionalism and Modernism in Irish Poetry Since 1930: the Role of MacNeice' in *The Crows Behind the Plough: History and Violence in Anglo-Irish Poetry and Drama*, ed. Geert Lernout (Amsterdam, Rodopi, 1991), pp. 159–73. See p. 159.
32   *The Faber Book of Contemporary Irish Poetry*, ed. Paul Muldoon (London, Faber and Faber, 1986).

33 Michael Longley, *Poems 1963-83* (Edinburgh/Dublin, The Salamander Press/The Gallery Press, 1985), pp. 106–7.

YEATS AND MACNEICE:
A NIGHT-SEMINAR WITH FRANCIS STUART

Robert Welch

1 W.B Yeats, *Collected Poems* (London, Macmillan, 1958), p. 338. All other references to Yeats's poetry are taken from this edition.
2 John Montague, 'Despair and Delight' in *Time Was Away: The World of Louis MacNeice*, ed. Terence Brown and Alec Reid (Dublin, Dolmen Press, 1974), p. 123.
3 Edna Longley, *Louis MacNeice: A Study* (London and Boston, Faber and Faber, 1988), p. 144 and *passim*.
4 Louis MacNeice, *The Strings Are False* (London and Boston, Faber and Faber, reprint 1982), p. 220.
5 *Selected Prose of Louis MacNeice*, ed. Alan Heuser (Oxford, Clarendon Press, 1990), p. 230.
6 *The Strings Are False*, pp. 39–40.
7 Louis MacNeice, *The Poetry of W.B. Yeats* (London, New York, Toronto, Oxford University Press, 1941), p.155.
8 *The Poetry of W.B. Yeats*, p. 117.
9 *Selected Prose of Louis MacNeice*, pp. 260–1.
10 *Selected Plays of Louis MacNeice*, ed. Alan Heuser and Peter McDonald (Oxford, Clarendon Press, 1993), p. 127.
11 *The Poetry of W.B Yeats*, p. 129.
12 *Selected Plays of Louis MacNeice*, p. 349.
13 *The Poetry of W.B. Yeats*, p. 157.
14 John Ennis, Prefatory Statement to poetry section in *Dedalus Irish Poets*, ed. John F. Deane (Dublin, Dedalus 1992), p. 206.

MACNEICE AND THE PURITAN TRADITION

Terence Brown

1 Louis MacNeice, 'Poetry To-Day', in *Selected Literary Criticism of Louis MacNeice*, ed. Alan Heuser (Oxford, Clarendon Press, 1987), p. 12. Henceforth *Criticism*.
2 *Ibid.*, p. 41.
3 Louis MacNeice, 'When I was Twenty-One', in *Selected Prose of Louis MacNeice*, ed. Alan Heuser (Oxford, Clarendon Press, 1990), p. 222. Henceforth *Prose*.
4 Louis MacNeice, *Zoo* (London, Michael Joseph Ltd., 1938), p. 79.
5 *Ibid.*, p. 78.

6   Louis MacNeice, *Collected Poems* (London, Faber and Faber, 1966), p. 17. Henceforth *CP*.
7   Louis MacNeice, *Zoo*, pp. 85–6.
8   Louis MacNeice, *The Strings Are False* (London, Faber and Faber, 1965), pp. 53–4.
9   *Criticism*, p. 80.
10 *Ibid.*, p. 81.
11 *Ibid.*
12 *Ibid.*, pp. 81–2. The terms in square brackets are taken from the editor's translation of MacNeice's use of terms in Aristotle's Greek.
13 *Criticism*, p. 58.
14 Louis MacNeice, 'John Keats', in *Fifteen Poets* (Oxford, Clarendon Press, 1941), p. 351.
15 *Ibid.*, p. 353.
16 *Ibid.*, p. 354.
17 *Ibid.*
18 Louis MacNeice, *The Strings Are False*, p. 220.
19 Louis MacNeice, *The Poetry of W.B. Yeats* (London, Oxford University Press, 1941), p. viii.
20 Louis MacNeice, 'To Hedli', *Collected Poems, 1925-1948* (London, Faber and Faber, 1949), p. 9.
21 MacNeice, 'John Keats', p. 354.
22 *Prose*, p. 72.
23 *Criticism*, p. 39.
24 *Prose*, p. 188.
25 See my 'MacNeice's Ireland' in *Literature and Nationalism*, ed. V. Newey and A. Thompson (Liverpool, Liverpool University Press, 1991), pp. 225–38.
26 *Prose*, p. 71.
27 Louis MacNeice, *Varieties of Parable* (Cambridge, Cambridge University Press, 1965), p. 30.
28 *Ibid.*, p. 31.
29 Louis MacNeice, *The Dark Tower and Other Radio Scripts* (London, Faber and Faber, 1947), p. 72.
30 *Prose*, p. 188.

'WITH EYES TURNED DOWN ON THE PAST': MACNEICE'S CLASSICISM

Peter McDonald

1   Louis MacNeice, 'Louis MacNeice Writes ...' [on *The Burning Perch*], *Poetry Book Society Bulletin* 38 (Sept. 1963), repr. in Alan Heuser (ed.), *Selected Literary Criticism of Louis MacNeice* (Oxford, Clarendon Press, 1987), p. 248.

2 W.H. Auden,'Louis MacNeice', in *We Moderns: Gotham Book Mart 1920–1940* (New York, Gotham Book Mart, n.d. [1939]), p. 48.

3 Louis MacNeice, 'In Defence of Vulgarity', *The Listener* 18/468 (29 Dec. 1937), repr. in Alan Heuser (ed.), *Selected Prose of Louis MacNeice* (Oxford, Clarendon Press, 1990), pp. 43–44.

4 See MacNeice's 'Note' to *Autumn Journal*, *CP* 101: 'I am aware that there are over-statements in this poem – e.g. in the passages dealing with Ireland, the Oxford by-election or my own more private existence. There are also inconsistencies.'

5 Louis MacNeice, 'Translating Aeschylus', *The Spectator* 154/5576 (10 May 1935), repr. in Heuser, *Selected Literary Criticism*, pp. 9–10.

6 Holograph MS, deposited among miscellaneous uncatalogued MacNeice MSS in 1985 in the Bodleian Library, Oxford.

7 Louis MacNeice, *Modern Poetry: A Personal Essay* (1938), 2nd edn. (Oxford, Clarendon Press, 1968), pp. 48–49.

8 Louis MacNeice, Introduction to *The Golden Ass of Apuleius* (London, John Lehmann, 1946), repr. in Heuser, *Selected Literary Criticism*, p. 131.

9 Louis MacNeice, *The Strings Are False: An Unfinished Autobiography* (London, Faber and Faber, 1965), p. 91.

10 Louis MacNeice, review of *Journal and Letters of Stephen MacKenna* ed. E.R. Dodds, in *The Morning Post* 4 Dec. 1936, p. 19.

11 Louis MacNeice, *Carpe Diem* (broadcast 8 Oct. 1956), TS copy in BBC Written Archives Centre, Caversham, p. 19. For an acute discussion of this play, along with the whole issue of MacNeice's relation to Horace, see Alan J. Peacock, 'Louis MacNeice: Transmitting Horace', *Revista Alicantina de Estudios Ingleses* 5 (1992), pp. 119–30.

12 Kevin Andrews, 'Time And The Will Lie Sidestepped: Athens, The Interval', in Terence Brown and Alec Reid (eds.), *Time Was Away: The World of Louis MacNeice* (Dublin, Dolmen Press, 1974), p. 109.

13 Edna Longley, *Louis MacNeice: A Study* (London, Faber and Faber, 1988), p. 167.

'SOMETHING WRONG SOMEWHERE?': MACNEICE AS CRITIC

Edna Longley

1 Alan Heuser (ed.), *Selected Literary Criticism of Louis MacNeice* (Oxford, Clarendon Press, 1987), p. 58.

2 *Selected Literary Criticism*, p. 145.

3 Louis MacNeice, *The Poetry of W.B. Yeats* (1941; London, Faber and Faber, 1967), p. 16.

4 *Poetry of W.B. Yeats*, p. 26.

5 Louis MacNeice, *Modern Poetry* (Oxford, Clarendon Press, 1938, 1968), p. 78.

6 *Poetry of W.B. Yeats*, p. 18.
7 *Selected Literary Criticism*, p. 13.
8 *Poetry of W.B. Yeats*, p. 23.
9 *Selected Literary Criticism*, p. 167.
10 *Selected Literary Criticism*, p. 203.
11 *Selected Literary Criticism*, pp. 167–8.
12 *Selected Literary Criticism*, p. 146.
13 See Edna Longley, *Louis MacNeice: A Study* (London, Faber and Faber, 1988), pp. 98–100; Peter McDonald, *Louis MacNeice: The Poet in his Contexts* (Oxford, Clarendon Press, 1991), pp. 222–9: and Longley, '"It is time that I wrote my will": Anxieties of Influence and Succession', in *Yeats Annual* 12 (London, Macmillan, 1996).
14 *Selected Literary Criticism*, p. 232.
15 *Selected Literary Criticism*, pp. 127–8.
16 *Selected Literary Criticism*, pp. 153–4.
17 *Selected Literary Criticism*, p. 212.
18 See Longley, *Louis MacNeice*, pp. 53–5, 101–3.
19 See Longley, 'The Room Where MacNeice Wrote "Snow"', in *The Living Stream: Literature and Revisionism in Ireland* (Newcastle-upon-Tyne, Bloodaxe Books, 1994), pp. 252–70.
20 *Modern Poetry*, p. 34.
21 *Poetry of W.B. Yeats*, Foreword, p. 11.
22 *Selected Literary Criticism*, p. 11.
23 *Modern Poetry*, p. 197.
24 *Modern Poetry*, p. 20.
25 *Modern Poetry*, p. 33.
26 *Ibid.*
27 *Selected Literary Criticism*, p. 166.
28 *Selected Literary Criticism*, p. 169.
29 *Selected Literary Criticism*, p. 143.
30 *Modern Poetry*, p. 2.
31 *Poetry of W.B. Yeats*, pp. 27–8.
32 *Poetry of W.B. Yeats*, pp. 29–30.
33 *Poetry of W.B. Yeats*, p. 18.
34 Louis MacNeice, *Varieties of Parable* (Cambridge, Cambridge University Press, 1965), p. 151.
35 *Varieties of Parable*, p. 8.
36 *Varieties of Parable*, p. 146.
37 *Modern Poetry*, p. 205.
38 'Broken Windows or Thinking Aloud', Alan Heuser (ed.), *Selected Prose of Louis MacNeice* (Oxford, Clarendon Press, 1990), p. 141.
39 *Selected Literary Criticism*, p. 22; *Selected Prose*, p. 189; *Selected Literary Criticism*, pp. 179, 203.
40 In conversation.
41 *Selected Literary Criticism*, pp. 25–6.
42 *Selected Literary Criticism*, p. 37.
43 *Modern Poetry*, pp. 204–5.

44. *Modern Poetry*, p. 189.
45. *Selected Literary Criticism*, pp. 75–6.
46 *Selected Literary Criticism*, pp. 99–100
47 (Ed.) Edward Mendelson, *The English Auden: Poems, Essays and Dramatic Writings 1927–1939* (London, Faber and Faber, 1977), pp. 370, 396.
48 *The English Auden*, p. 403.
49 See Longley, *The Living Stream*, pp. 264–6.
50 *Selected Literary Criticism*, p. 113.
51 *Selected Literary Criticism*, p. 57.
52 *Selected Literary Criticism*, p. 13.
53 *Selected Literary Criticism*, p. 120.
54 *Selected Literary Criticism*, p. 12.
55 *Modern Poetry*, p. 35.
56 *Selected Literary Criticism*, p. 141.
57 *Selected Literary Criticism*, p. 120.
58 *Selected Literary Criticism*, p. 207.
59 *Selected Literary Criticism*, p. 203.
60 *Selected Literary Criticism*, p. 70.
61 *Modern Poetry*, p. 35.
62 *Modern Poetry*, p. 78.
63 *Modern Poetry*, p. 77.
64 *Selected Literary Criticism*, p. 17.
65 *Poetry of W.B. Yeats*, p. 146.
66 *Ibid*.
67 *Selected Literary Criticism*, p. 17.
68 Gail McDonald, *Learning to be Modern: Pound, Eliot and the American University* (Oxford, Clarendon Press, 1993), p. 210.
69 *Selected Literary Criticism*, p. 166.
70 See note 19.

LOUIS AND THE WOMEN

Jon Stallworthy

1 *Studies on Louis MacNeice*, ed. Jacqueline Genet and Wynne Hellegouarc'h (Caen, Centre de Publications de l'Université de Caen, 1988), pp. 9–10.
2 Louis MacNeice, *The Strings Are False* (London, Faber and Faber, 1965), p. 37. Hereafter *SAF*.
3 Letter to 'My Dear Dad', dated 'Sunday evening' [1914 or 1915?].
4 *SAF*, p. 42.
5 *SAF*, p. 38.
6 *SAF*, p. 47.
7 *The Heretick*, 29 March 1924. See Stallworthy, *Louis MacNeice* (hereafter *LM*) (London, Faber and Faber, 1995), pp. 83–86.

8   See *LM*, p. 138.
9   *SAF*, p. 41.
10 *SAF*, p. 109.
11 See *LM*, pp. 164–5, for an account of this unpublished play.
12 *SAF*, pp. 216–17.
13 Sir Isaiah Berlin to John Hilton, undated. See *LM*, p. 176.
14 W.H. Auden and Louis MacNeice, *Letters from Iceland* (London, Faber and Faber, 1937), p. 245.
15 *Letters from Iceland*, p. 238.
16 Louis MacNeice, *Blind Fireworks* (London, Gollancz, 1929), p. 10.
17 *LM*, p. 262.
18 Margaret Gardiner, *A Scatter of Memories* (London, 1988), pp. 129–30.
19 *SAF*, p. 170.
20 *SAF*, p. 171.
21 *LM*, pp. 238–40.
22 *LM*, pp. 244–85.
23 *LM*, pp. 305–8.
24 *Selected Plays of Louis MacNeice*, ed. Alan Heuser and Peter McDonald (Oxford, Clarendon Press, 1993), p. 126. Hereafter *SP*.

LOUIS MACNEICE AND DEREK MAHON

Richard York

1   Derek Mahon, *Poems 1962–78* (Oxford, Oxford University Press, 1979); *Selected Poems* (London and Loughcrew, Viking/Gallery, 1991): all Mahon quotations are from the latter edition.
2   Brendan Kennelly, 'Derek Mahon's Humane Perspective' in *Tradition and Influence in Anglo-Irish Poetry*, ed. Terence Brown and Nicholas Grene (London and Basingstoke, Macmillan, 1989), pp. 143–152. See p. 146.
3   *The Honest Ulsterman*, No. 8, December 1968, pp. 27 and 28.
4   *The Honest Ulsterman*, No. 50, Winter 1975, p. 180.
5   Derek Mahon, *The Sphere Book of Irish Poetry* (London, Sphere Books, 1972), p. 14.
6   *The New Statesman*, 4 Feb., 1977.
7   Derek Mahon, 'MacNeice in England and Ireland' in *Time Was Away: the World of Louis MacNeice*, ed. Terence Brown and Alec Reid (Dublin, The Dolmen Press, 1974), pp. 113–122.
8   Derek Mahon, 'MacNeice, the War and the BBC' in *Studies on Louis MacNeice*, ed. Jacqueline Genet and Wynne Hellegouarc'h (Caen, Centre de Publications de l'Université de Caen, 1988), pp. 63–77.
9   *Time Was Away*, p. 119.
10 Terence Brown, *Louis MacNeice: Sceptical Vision* (Dublin, Gill and Macmillan, 1975), pp. 15 and 31.

11 William T. McKinnon, *Apollo's Blended Dream: a Study of the Poetry of Louis MacNeice* (London, Oxford University Press, 1971), pp. 57 and 110.

LOUIS MACNEICE AND MICHAEL LONGLEY: SOME EXAMPLES OF AFFINITY AND INFLUENCE

Michael Allen

1 ... Strong poetry is strong only by virtue of a kind of textual usurpation that is analogous to what Marxism encompasses as its social usurpation or Freudianism as its psychic usurpation. A strong poem does not *formulate* poetic facts any more than strong reading or criticism formulates them, for a strong reading *is* the only poetic fact, the only revenge against time that endures, that is successful in canonizing one text as opposed to a rival text.

There is no textual authority without an act of imposition, a declaration of property ...

Harold Bloom, 'Poetry, Revisionism, Repression', from *Poetry and Repression: Revisionism from Blake to Stevens* (New Haven and London, Yale University Press, 1976), p. 6.
2 *The CollectedPoems of Louis MacNeice*, ed. E.R. Dodds (London, Faber and Faber, 1979), pp 74–75. Subsequent references will be given parenthetically in the text, prefixed *CP*.
3 Michel Foucault, 'What Is an Author', in Josue V. Harari (ed.) *Textual Strategies: Perspectives in Post-Structuralist Criticism* (Ithaca, New York, Cornell U.P., 1979), p. 141.
4 Michael Longley, *Poems 1963–1983* (Harmondsworth, Penguin, 1986), p. 84. Subsequent references will be given parenthetically in the text, prefixed *P*.
5 Derek Mahon, 'Introduction', *The Sphere Book of Modern Irish Poetry* (London, Sphere Books, 1972), p. 12.
6 Dated MSS in my possession.
7 Directed Paul Morrissey, 1974.
8 Picasso in his cubist phase, perhaps:
 I who was Harlequin in the childhood of the century,
 Posed by Picasso beside an endless opaque sea,
 Have seen myself sifted and splintered in broken facets ...
 (*CP* 33)
9 See: 'In Memoriam' (*P*, 48-9); 'Christopher at Birth' (*P*, 51); 'Wounds' (*P*, 86); 'Love Poem' (*P*, 193); 'The White Butterfly' (*P*, 210); 'Laertes' (*Gorse Fires*, London: Secker and Warburg, 1991, p. 33); 'The Balloon' (*Gorse Fires*, p. 34); 'Poseidon' (*The Ghost Orchid*, London: Cape, 1995, p. 31); 'Snow Bunting' (*The Ghost Orchid*, p. 59).
10 London, Faber and Faber, 1966.
11 See note 1 above.

12 London, Oxford U.P., 1968
13 See note 1 above.
14 Michael Longley, *Tuppenny Stung: Autobiographical Chapters* (Belfast, Lagan Press, 1994) p. 34.
15 *Icarus* 37 (1962), p. 22.
16 Douglas Dunn, Review of Michael Longley, *Selected Poems, 1963–1980* (Winston-Salem, NC, Wake Forest University Press, 1981), in *The Times Literary Supplement*, 31 July 1981, p. 886.
17 'A Misrepresented Poet', *Dublin Magazine*, 6:1 (1967), pp. 68–74.
18 Louis MacNeice, *Selected Poems*, ed.W.H. Auden (London, Faber and Faber, 1964).
19 See note 17 above.
20 See: 'A Misrepresented Poet', pp. 72–74; 'Poetry', *Causeway: the Arts in Ulster* (Belfast, Arts Council of Northern Ireland, Dublin, Gill and Macmillan, 1971), pp. 97-98; 'Preface' and 'Introduction', *Louis MacNeice: Selected Poems*, ed. Michael Longley (London, Faber and Faber, 1988) pp. xi, xvii–xxii. Longley's only attentions to MacNeice which do not observe the qualities and the poem order of the individual volumes are in '"The Neolithic Night": a Note on the Irishness of Louis MacNeice', *Two Decades of Irish Writing*, ed. Douglas Dunn (Cheadle Hulme, Carcanet, 1975), pp. 98–104.
21 See note 20 for Michael Longley's contributions to this. Edna Longley's contributions include (as well as lectures at Queen's University, Belfast and elsewhere from 1967 on and items, documented in notes 25 and 26 below): 'Autumn Journal', *Honest Ulsterman* 73 (1983), pp. 56–75;'Louis MacNeice: *Autumn Journal*' and '"Varieties of Parable": Louis MacNeice and Paul Muldoon' in *Poetry in the Wars* (Newcastle, Bloodaxe, 1986) pp. 78–93, 211–243; 'The Room Where MacNeice Wrote "Snow"', *The Living Stream: Literature and Revisionism in Ireland* (Newcastle, Bloodaxe, 1994); pp. 252–270.
22 See notes 18 and 20 above for full details of both selections. Terence Brown drew attention at the Symposium to the contribution of Alec Reid, a lecturer at Trinity, to the canon-making in question.
23 *Northern Voices: Poets from Ulster* (Dublin, Gill and Macmillan, 1975), p. 113.
24 'MacNeice in England and Ireland', *Time Was Away: the World of Louis MacNeice*, ed. Terence Brown and Alec Reid (Dublin, Dolmen Press, 1974), p. 117.
25 'Louis MacNeice: "The Walls are Flowing"', *Across a Roaring Hill: the Protestant Imagination in Modem Ireland* (Belfast and Dover, New Hampshire, Blackstaff), pp. 99–123 .
26 *Louis MacNeice:. a Study* (London, Faber and Faber, 1988), p. 1.
27 *Louis MacNeice: Selected Poems*, p. xiv.
28 'For here we have no continuing city' (*Hebrews XIII*, 14), also supplied the epigraph and the title for Longley's first book.
29 *Louis MacNeice: Selected Poems*, p. 117.

30 See *Tuppenny Stung ...,* pp. 54–55.
31 'A Misrepresented Poet', p. 70.
32 *Louis MacNeice: Selected Poems,* p. xxii.
33 At Queen's University, Belfast.
34 See note 38 below.
35 ... the classical pattern of development leads us to a confrontation inside the Oedipal triangle between our desire for the mother and the process of loss which is the result of paternal authority... .
... often in the social code, in social communication, the basis for our identities which the semiotic forms within language is repressed, thrown into confusion, and the fact of not hearing it, of not giving it room, (thus in a way of killing the maternal and the primordial link every subject has with the maternal) exposes us to depression... .
Julia Kristeva, 'A Question of Subjectivity – an Interview' (Reprinted from *Women's Review,* no. 12, pp. 19–21), *Modern Literary Theory,* ed. Philip Rice and Patricia Waugh (London, Arnold, 1989) pp. 130–131.
36 For instance,

> You alone read every birthmark
> Only for you the tale it tells –
> Idiot children in the dark
> Whom we shall never bring to light ...
>
> ('Birthmarks', *P* 58)
>
> I remember your eyes in bandages
> And me reading to you like a mother ...
>
> ('Readings', *P* 75)
>
> Where is my father's house, where my father?
> If I could walk in on my grandmother
> She'd see right through me ...
>
> ('Second Sight', *P* 151)
>
> Now that my body grows woman-like I look at men
> As two or three women have looked at me, then hide
> Among Ovid's lovely casualties – all that blood
> Colouring the grass and changing into flowers, ...
> ... creating in an hour
> My own son's beauty, the truthfulness of my nipples,
> Petals that will not last long ...
>
> ('A Flowering', *The Ghost Orchid,* p. 14)

37 *The Winter's Tale,* IV, 4, ll.119–20.
38 ... a modality which bears the most archaic memories of our link with the maternal body – Of the dependence that all of us have vis-à-vis the maternal body, and where a sort of self-eroticism is indissociable from the experience of the (m)other. We repress the vocal or gestural inscription of this experience under our subsequent acquisitions and this is an important condition for autonomy,

Nevertheless there may be different ways of repressing this experience. There may be a dramatic repression, after which we are building on sand because the foundation has been destroyed, suppressed. Or there may be an attempt to transpose this continent, this receptacle beyond the symbolic. In other words after the mirror phase, and Oedipal castration. (The word 'chora' means receptacle in Greek, which refers us to Winnicott's idea of 'holding': mother and child are in a permanent stricture in which one holds the other, there's a double entrance, the child is held but so is the mother.)

At that point we witness the possibility of creation, of sublimation... .

... this experience of the semiotic chora in language produces poetry. It can be considered as the source of all stylistic effort, the modifying of banal, logical order by linguistic distortions such as metaphor, metonymy, musicality... .

'A Question of Subjectivity – an Interview', Rice and Waugh, pp. 130–131.

39   See note 1 above.
40   Horace, Ode 17. 1.20 from Book I of the Odes. See Charlton T. Lewis and Charles Short, *A Latin Dictionary* (Oxford: Clarendon, 1880) p. 2000 and Edward C. Wickham, *Quinti Horati Flacci Opera Omnia: the Works of Horace with a Commentary* (Oxford, Clarendon, 1891), I, p. 60. I am grateful for help here to Maureen Alden.
41   Dunn, TLS, p. 886.
42   'Sea Shanty', *Gorse Fires*, p, 1.
43   See note 38 above.
44   *Gorse Fires*, p. 1.

KEEPING THE COLOURS NEW: LOUIS MACNEICE IN THE
CONTEMPORARY POETRY OF NORTHERN IRELAND

Neil Corcoran

1   Stan Smith, *W. H. Auden* (Oxford, Basil Blackwell, 1985), pp. 2–4, 23–5.
2   Edna Longley, 'Introduction: Revising "Irish Literature"', in *The Living Stream: Literature and Revisionism in Ireland* (Newcastle upon Tyne, Bloodaxe Books, 1994), p. 51.
3   Derek Mahon, 'MacNeice in England and Ireland', in *Time Was Away: The World of Louis MacNeice*, ed. Terence Brown and Alec Reid (Dublin, The Dolmen Press, 1974), p. 117.
4   Derek Mahon, 'MacNeice, the War and the BBC', in *Studies on Louis MacNeice*, ed. Jacqueline Genet and Wynne Hellegouarc'h (Caen, Centre de Publications de l'Université de Caen, 1988), p. 64.
5   Terence Brown points out to me, however, that the Belfast of Mahon's (and his own) childhood was then too a 'bombed-out town' as a result of German air-raids during the war.

6   Tom Paulin, 'Letters from Iceland: Going North', in *The 1930s: A Challenge to Orthodoxy* (Sussex, The Harvester Press, 1978), p. 59. The essay was published earlier, in 1976, in the journal *Renaissance and Modern Studies*.

7   Michael Longley, 'The Neolithic Night: A Note on the Irishness of Louis MacNeice', in *Two Decades of Irish Writing*, ed. Douglas Dunn (Cheadle Hulme, Carcanet, 1975), p. 104.

8   Michael Longley, 'Introduction' to *Louis MacNeice: Selected Poems*, ed. Michael Longley (London and Boston, Faber and Faber, 1988), p. xxiii.

9   Seamus Heaney, 'The Placeless Heaven: Another Look at Kavanagh', in *The Government of the Tongue: The 1986 T. S. Eliot Memorial Lectures and Other Critical Writings* (London and Boston, Faber and Faber, 1988), p. 8.

10 Seamus Heaney, 'From Monaghan to the Grand Canal: The Poetry of Patrick Kavanagh', in *Preoccupations: Selected Prose 1968–1978* (London and Boston, Faber and Faber, 1980), p. 116.

11 *The Government of the Tongue*, p. 8.

12 Seamus Heaney, 'The Pre-Natal Mountain: Vision and Irony in Recent Irish Poetry', in *The Place of Writing* (Atlanta, Scholars Press, 1989), p. 43.

13 The poem was first published in *William Golding: The Man and His Books*, ed. John Carey (London and Boston, Faber and Faber, 1986).

14 *The Place of Writing*, p. 44.

15 Seamus Heaney, 'Frontiers of Writing', *Bullán: An Irish Studies Journal*, vol. 1 no. 1 (Spring 1994), pp. 11–14. The figure of the quincunx is derived from Sir Thomas Browne's *The Garden of Cyrus*, as Heaney acknowledged in the original lecture; I am grateful for this information to Peter McDonald. The lecture has since been published, in part, in *The Redress of Poetry* (London and Boston, Faber and Faber, 1995).

16 Tom Paulin, 'The Man from No Part: Louis MacNeice', in *Ireland and the English Crisis* (Newcastle upon Tyne, Bloodaxe Books, 1984), p. 76.

17 Hedli MacNeice. 'The Story of the House that Louis Built', in *Studies on Louis MacNeice*, p. 9.

18 Cited by Seamus Heaney in *The Place of Writing*, p. 37.

19 See Louis MacNeice, *The Poetry of W. B. Yeats* (London and Boston, Faber and Faber, 1967; first published 1941), pp. 142, 152, 183.

20 *The Place of Writing*, p. 53.

21 It did in fact include, Carpenter tells us, a trained chimpanzee and also someone who specialised in inserting a cigarette in his anus and puffing out smoke. I have always thought it odd that a poem by Paul Muldoon, of all people, finds no room for them. See Humphrey Carpenter, *W. H. Auden: A Biography* (London, Allen and Unwin, 1981), p. 304.

22 See John Kerrigan, 'Ulster Ovids', in *The Chosen Ground: Essays on the Contemporary Poetry of Northern Ireland*, ed. Neil Corcoran (Bridgend, Seren Books, 1992), pp. 237–69.

23 *Ibid.*, p. 252.
24 *The Poetical Works of Robert Herrick*, ed. L. C. Martin (Oxford, Clarendon Press, 1956), p. 28.
25 Louis MacNeice, *Selected Literary Criticism*, ed. Alan Heuser (Oxford, Clarendon Press, 1987), p. 155.
26 *The Poetry of W. B. Yeats*, p. 146.
27 John Haffenden, *Viewpoints: Poets in Conversation* (London and Boston, Faber and Faber, 1981), p. 141.
28 Edna Longley, 'The Room Where MacNeice Wrote Snow', in *The Living Stream*, p. 265.
29 See *W. B. Yeats: The Poems*, ed. Daniel Albright (London, Dent, 1990), p. 839.
30 Cited in A. Norman Jeffares, *A Commentary on the Collected Poems of W. B. Yeats* (London and Basingstoke, Macmillan, 1968), p. 512.
31 *The Poetry of W. B. Yeats*, p. 192.
32 'Yeats's Epitaph: *Last Poems and Plays*, by W. B . Yeats ', in *Selected Literary Criticism*, p. 119.
33 John Berryman, 'Despondency and Madness: On Lowell's "Skunk Hour"', in *The Freedom of the Poet* (New York, Farrar, Straus and Giroux, 1976), p. 316.
34 Christopher Ricks, *Beckett's Dying Words* (Oxford, Clarendon Press, 1993), pp. 133–4.
35 'Ulster Ovids', p. 253.
36 *Viewpoints*, p. 140 .

TRACING MACNEICE'S DEVELOPMENT IN DRAMA:
A COMMENTARY ON THE PUBLISHED AND
UNPUBLISHED PLAYS

Alan Heuser

1 I am grateful to English scholars, University of Ulster at Coleraine: Des Cranston, who read the 1994 draft; Kathleen Devine and Alan Peacock, editors. The draft was revised after I read Professor Jon Stallworthy's fine, full *Louis MacNeice* (1995), and after I consulted MacNeice files at BBC Written Archives Centre. For photocopies of scripts, I thank Archivists of: The BBC Written Archives Centre, Caversham Park; The Berg Collection, New York Public Library; The Humanities Research Centre, University of Texas at Austin. My grateful thanks to the Social Sciences and Humanities Research Council, Ottawa, for a research grant.

Faber published 11 plays, 1936–68; the BBC, four more plays 1969 – all out of print except a Faber paperback *The Dark Tower*. OUP published a new book of eight plays, ed. McDonald and Heuser (1993). Faber keeps in print MacNeice's *Collected Poems*, ed. E. R. Dodds, and his *Selected Poems*, ed. Michael Longley. In 1996 Faber reissues MacNeice's *Autumn Journal* and *The Strings are False*, Jon Stallworthy's biography, Edna Longley's MacNeice study.

Background: Asa Briggs, *The History of Broadcasting in the United Kingdom*, 5 vols (1961–95); Rayner Heppenstall, *Portrait of the Artist as a Professional Man* (1969); Douglas Cleverdon, 'Radio Features and Drama at the BBC', *TLS*, 26 Feb. 1970, 229–30.

Criticism: Essays by W. B. Stanford, E. L. Stahl, Alec Reid, R. D. Smith, Dallas Bower, *Time Was Away: The World of Louis MacNeice*, ed. Terence Brown and Alec Reid (1974), with Smith's bibliography 'Radio Scripts 1941–1963'; Barbara Coulton, *Louis MacNeice in the BBC* (1980); Christopher Holme, 'The Radio Drama of Louis MacNeice', in John Drakakis, ed., *British Radio Drama* (1981); Michael J. Sidnell, *Dances of Death: The Group Theatre of London in the Thirties* (1984); Alan J. Peacock, 'Louis MacNeice: Transmitting Horace', *Revista Alicantina de Estudios Ingleses 5* (1992).

2 Radio feature (documentary) and radio play may overlap in dramatic devices; but feature is factual, play fictive.

3 E. R. Dodds, *Missing Persons* (1977), 132.

4 Dodds, *Persons*, 116. MacNeice's *Agamemnon* was performed on stage again by the Birmingham University Dramatic Society, Dec. 1937; and produced twice on the BBC Third Programme – by Val Gielgud, 1946, and by Raymond Raikes, 1953.

5 Eugene O'Neill's *Mourning Becomes Electra* (1931), an American *Oresteia*, was performed, same month, same theatre as *Out of the Picture* (December 1937, Westminster Theatre): Sidnell, *Dances*, 224. (O'Neill had won the Nobel Prize for Literature 1936.)

6 Bernard Crick, *George Orwell: A Life* (1980), 281.

7 Asa Briggs, *History of Broadcasting*, III, 585.

8 In 1941 MacNeice wrote nine scripts for a Blitz series, *The Stones Cry Out*; in 1942, nine salutes or homages to Allies and the United Nations; as well as other features. With *Columbus* 1942, his radio plays began to be noticed. His propaganda dramas were often rhetorical, and yet poetic in conception.

9 In 1943 MacNeice wrote nine features on freedoms, and others.

10 The stage plays of Yeats and of Eliot may have suggested 'parable play' to MacNeice. Eliot defined 'poetic drama' as 'a kind of doubleness in the action' – 'John Marston' (1934), *Selected Essays*, 3rd enlgd. edn.(1951), 229. In his Clark Lectures 1963, *Varieties of Parable* (1965), MacNeice referred to all genres, not drama alone, defining double-level writing or 'parable' from the OED as any 'saying or narration in which something is expressed in terms of something else' (2). His lectures, 'From Spenser to Pinter', provide useful backgrounds for most of his plays.

11 'Vulgarity' (1937) in *Selected Prose* (1990), 43–8; 'Apuleius' (1946) in *Selected Literary Criticism* (1987), 127–32. MacNeice wrote for annual BBC celebrations: April Fool's, New Year's, Saturnalia (four times each), Christmas (two more).

12 MacNeice used discs of Cretan music lent by Patrick Leigh Fermor; recorded Greek music for Easter/Assumption; recorded Byzantine wedding music (by eminent musicologist, Simon Karas), *Selected Prose*, 184–6; Kevin Andrews played a shepherd's pipe. In Athens 1950, MacNeice directed Synge's *Playboy*; in New York 1954, Euripides' *Hippolytus* – coaching *Playboy* in Irish accents, *Hippolytus* in Greek: see Stallworthy, 378, 409–10. MacNeice began translating *Hippolytus* 1938 – the first chorus published in Tambimuttu's *Poetry London* (April 1939).

13 In 1948–9 E. R. Dodds prepared the Sather Lectures for Autumn 1949, at Berkeley, Calif. His *The Greeks and the Irrational* (1951) examined Classical Greek culture through mystery cults, shame, madness, shamans; the book had a shock effect. For MacNeice, close to Dodds, and translating *Faust*, Goethe's Classical idealism was problematic – for Dodds's scholarship confirmed his own sardonic view of Ancient Greece – definitely not ideal – see *Autumn Journal IX*.

14 MacNeice, *Varieties*, 111–12.

15 James Thurber's story, 'The Secret Life of Walter Mitty', *New Yorker*, 18 March 1939, was later made into a film vehicle for Danny Kaye 1947, remote from the original: Burton Bernstein, *Thurber: A Biography* (New York, 1975), 311, 391–2. MacNeice was teaching at Cornell University when the Thurber story appeared. In World War Two, American servicemen introduced their slang into the UK; American airmen popularized Walter Mitty phrases.

16 Cf 'Mullaveen', Co Westmeath: Edward MacLysaght, *More Irish Families*, new revd. and enlgd. edn. (Dublin, 1982), 144 – traced with the help of Kathleen Devine who recalled 'Mulveen's'. Mallaveen may well be a variant of Mullaveen – 'Mal' for 'evil, malign'?

17 MacNeice's commentary for Thomas Stobart's documentary film *The Conquest of Everest* (1953) – see *Autumn Sequel III* – suggested the mountain obstacle and climbing in *Prisoner's Progress*, 1954.

18 MacNeice produced two successful radio series in 1950s: (1) Spenser's *The Faerie Oueene* 1952 (12 sections chosen by C. S. Lewis) for Elizabeth II's accession, hope for a New Elizabethan Age in the Arts, hence Spenserian mythopoeia in his *Autumn Sequel* 1953 (1954); (2) Virginia Woolf's masterpiece *The Waves* 1955 (two programmes selected by MacNeice), recitative for six voices, with a death in India as a focus – timely after publication of Woolf's *A Writer's Diary* (1953). (*Waves* was later rebroadcast.)

19. When Guy Burgess and Donald Maclean disappeared behind the Iron Curtain, May 1951, MacNeice was stopped in Athens, mistaken for one or other. (He had known Burgess, Cambridge 1930s.) Burgess' re-appearance in Moscow 1955 provoked the play. See the recent book: Yuri Modin, *My Five Cambridge Friends*, trans. Anthony Roberts (1994). MacNeice made his traitor a nuclear physicist, to raise the stakes. The idea of his play was, not political, but the effect of a public issue on private lives: *Radio Times*. 2 Sept. 1960, 2.

20 MacNeice singles out, in Yeats reviews, Synge's 'astringent joy and hardness', 'all that has edge, all that is salt in the mouth': *Selected Literary Criticism*, 44, 186; a Syngean 'edge' appears in *Nuts in May*. MacNeice's play lacks rural Irish settings, but uses vernaculars, Dublin episodes, an Irish girl, a Welsh friend, and an extravert-playboy as ignorant, as lively, as mischievous as Synge's Christy Mahon. MacNeice often lectured on Synge; he successfully produced *The Playboy*, Athens, May 1950.

21 1957 was 'The Asian Year'. MacNeice's *Boy's Own* locales were topical for May 1957 when *Nuts in May* was broadcast: in 1956–7 India received and gave loans; de Valera returned to power in Ireland, 1957; the Northwest Frontier Province had been taken into West Pakistan, 1955; the Commonwealth Trans-Antarctic Expedition 1955–8 was in progress.

22 South Africa began apartheid 1913, legalized it 1948, set up African homelands 1959 when MacNeice visited for six weeks. 'Consciences' (Alan Paton, Nadine Gordimer, Trevor Huddleston) wrote against apartheid. The ending of MacNeice's lampoon, of blacks killing whites, was questioned by Sharpeville Massacre, March 1960, of white police killing 70 peaceful blacks. Gilliam supported MacNeice, but the BBC rejected the script in Aug.1960.

23 MacNeice's troubles in BBC Features increased 1953–61: (1) According to Cleverdon (*TLS*, 26 Feb.1970), the post-war BBC Administration was hostile to Radio Features, especially after world TV broadcasts of Coronation 1953; (2) the BBC harassed MacNeice over sums received from foreign broadcasters in 1950s; (3) BBC Drama sponsored young outside playwrights, such as Pinter, Simpson, Bolt, 1957–61, superseding Features, so Drama became stronger – Cleverdon, ibid.; (4) MacNeice was sent on BBC duty assignment, six months in TV 1958: Heppenstall reports that Features men returned from TV duty 'having got nowhere' *Portrait*, 64 – Gilliam said it was 'the bitterest experience' of his career; (5) In 1959 BBC Administration cut Features producers from 25 to 15, while Drama was favoured with recent European plays – Cleverdon, ibid.; (6) BBC refused to pay MacNeice for his written narration for the Dryden-Purcell opera *King Arthur* (broadcast June 1959) – his narration taken as 'high spot of the evening' by producer Julian Herbage; (7) His script *The Pin Is Out* (1960) and (8) proposed feature on Sam Thompson (1960) were refused on political grounds: Stallworthy, 458, 460; (9) His Arthurian proposal 'The Remorse of Sir Gawayne' 1961 was turned down – a subject close to him: *Selected Literary Criticism*, 52–4. By 1960 MacNeice, senior writer-producer, had suffered many set-backs from the BBC. His marriage, strained after Greece, broke up. He signed as free-lance 1961, working for BBC half a year 1961–3.

24 See MacNeice's comment, *Radio Times*. 14 Dec. 1961, 26; his letter, *Listener*, 4 Jan. 1962, 33.

25 MacNeice – Belfast born 15 years before partition, of Protestant
     stock in the South but distantly Catholic – had met in London 1957
     Irish-American playwright William Alfred of Harvard (Stallworthy,
     424–5), who talked of drama (The Poets' Theatre in Cambridge,
     Mass., 1954–9), devoutly of 'the old faith' (Catholicism). Alfred's
     Irish piety, with daily communions, may have turned MacNeice to
     early Irish subjects – Clontarf and Mael Duín?

26 Anthony Thwaite and MacNeice proposed adaptations of Homer's
     Odyssey by 12 living poets – produced by Thwaite 1960. MacNeice
     translated 'Hades' (*Odyssey XI*): Odysseus' journey to the
     underworld and his encounter with the dead – ghosts of his mother,
     Tiresias, etc. – in hexameters closer to Homer than pentameters of
     Ezra Pound's Canto I (also the 'Hades' episode). MacNeice had
     given up translation of the *Iliad*, 24 books, 1952–6. Success of the
     Odyssey project led him to propose an Arthurian play from Malory –
     'The Remorse of Sir Gawaine' 1961.

27 In 1963 two MacNeice drama projects were accepted, but he did not
     live to write them: George MacDonald's 'The Golden Key' and
     James Hogg's 'A Justified Sinner'. Two of his last proposals concern
     famous sinners: Gawaine remorseful, Hogg justified.

28 Cf. the recordings preserved in the BBC Sound Archives, to be
     heard at the National Sound Archive, 29 Exhibition Road, London
     SW7 2AS. The 25–30 surviving play-recordings show that
     professional production is the test of a play. A producer new to
     MacNeice needs to know devices specific to Radio Features and to
     MacNeice's radio experiments; a new composer, to suit music to
     each chameleon script; actors, to rehearse in ensemble. MacNeice's
     first actors include: Robert Donat, Laurence Olivier, Cyril Cusack,
     Richard Burton, Peter Ustinov, Peggy Ashcroft, Gladys Young –
     stars. Dylan Thomas plays eight character roles. MacNeice chooses
     singers (Hedli Anderson, Marjorie Westbury), suitable known
     actors (Stephen Murray, Howard Marion-Crawford, Mark Dignam,
     Denys Hawthorne, Catherine Lacey, Cecile Chevreau, Mary
     Wimbush), in ensemble acting with the BBC Repertory Company.
     His chief composers – Benjamin Britten (four times), Matyas Seiber
     (four times), Elisabeth Lutyens (three times), Antony Hopkins (five
     times), Alan Rawsthorne, Tristram Cary – render musical cues into
     scores, fitted by him into production.

NOTES ON CONTRIBUTORS

MICHAEL ALLEN teaches American and Irish writing and critical theory at Queen's University, Belfast. He has written on American, English and Irish fiction but of late his main interest has been contemporary poetry. He recently edited an anthology of critical essays on HEANEY and is preparing a book on LONGLEY'S poetry.

TERENCE BROWN is Professor of Anglo-Irish Literature at Trinity College, Dublin where he is a Fellow of the College. He is also a member of the Royal Irish Academy and of the Academia Europaia. He has published and lectured widely on the subject of Anglo-Irish literature. He is currently at work on a critical biography of W. B. YEATS.

NEIL CORCORAN has taught at the Universities of Sheffield and Swansea and is now Professor of English at the University of St Andrews. His publications include *Seamus Heaney, English Poetry Since 1940*, and *The Chosen Ground: Essays on the Contemporary Poetry of Northern Ireland. After Yeats and Joyce: Reading Modern Irish Literature* will be published in 1997.

ALAN HEUSER was educated at McGill and Harvard and has taught twentieth-century British and American literature at Princeton and McGill. He has published poems and two radio plays in verse. He is now Professor (Post-Retirement) at McGill University. He has published *The Shaping Vision of Gerard Manley Hopkins*, (1958), and is the editor of *Selected Literary Criticism of Louis MacNeice* (1987), *Selected Prose of Louis MacNeice* (1990) and co-editor (with PETER MCDONALD) of *Selected Plays of Louis MacNeice* (1993).

EDNA LONGLEY is a Professor of English at Queen's University, Belfast. Her publications include: *Poetry in the Wars* (1986), *Louis MacNeice: A Study* (1988) and *The Living Stream: Literature and*

Revisionism in Ireland (1994). She has also co-edited, with Warwick Gould, *Yeats Annual 12:* YEATS and his Irish Readers: 'That Accusing Eye' (1996). She is an editor of *The Irish Review.*

PETER MCDONALD is Senior Lecturer in English at the University of Bristol. He is the author of two volumes of poetry, *Biting the Wax* (1989) and *Adam's Dream* (1996). His study *Louis MacNeice: The Poet in his Contexts* was published in 1991 and he co-edited MACNEICE'S *Selected Plays* with ALAN HEUSER in 1993. He has written widely on modern poetry, and his book on contemporary Northern Irish poets, *Mistaken Identities,* was published in 1997.

JON STALLWORTHY is a Fellow of the British Academy and Professor of English Literature at Oxford. He has published eight books of poetry – most recently, *The Guest from the Future,* two critical studies of YEATS'S poetry, and biographies of WILFRED OWEN (which won the Duff Cooper Memorial Prize, the W.H. Smith & Son Literary Award, and the E.M. Forster Award) and LOUIS MACNEICE (which won the Southern Arts Literature Prize); and he has edited OWEN'S *Complete Poems and Fragments, The Penguin Book of Love Poetry, The Oxford Book of War Poetry,* and HENRY REED'S *Collected Poems.*

ROBERT WELCH is Professor of English at the University of Ulster. He is the author of several books on Irish literature, novels in English and Irish and collections of poems. He is the editor of *The Oxford Companion to Irish Literature* (1996).

RICHARD YORK is Head of the School of Languages and Literature at the University of Ulster. He was educated at Emmanuel College, Cambridge and University College, London. He is the author of *The Poem as Utterance, Strangers and Secrets: Communication in the 19th Century Novel,* and several articles on French and English literature. His chief research interest is in literary language and style, especially in 19th and 20th century poetry and fiction.

INDEX

Page references in **bold** indicate complete articles.

THE IRISH LITERARY STUDIES SERIES
ISSN 0140-895X

19. *O'Casey the Dramatist.* Heinz Kosok
    ISBN 0-86140-168-9 xiv, 410pp. 1985
20. *The Double Perspective of Yeats's Aesthetic.* Okifumi Komesu
    ISBN 0-86140-158-1 200pp. 1984
21. *The Pioneers of Anglo-Irish Fiction, 1800-1850.* Barry Sloan
    ISBN 0-86140-205-7 xxxvi, 278pp. 1986
22. *Irish Writers & Society at Large.* Edited by Masaru Sekine
    (IASAIL-Japan Series 1)
    ISBN 0-86140-226-X x, 252pp. 1985
23. *Irish Writers and the Theatre.* Edited by Masaru Sekine (IASAIL-Japan Series 2)
    ISBN 0-86140-234-0 viii, 246pp. 1986
24. *A History of Verse Translation from the Irish 1789-1897.* Robert Welch
    ISBN 0-86140-249-9 xii, 200pp. 1988
25. *Kate O'Brien, A Literary Portrait.* Lorna Reynolds
    ISBN 0-86140-239-1 133pp.+8pp. illus. 1987
26. *Portraying the Self; Sean O'Casey & the Art of Autobiography.* Michael Kenneally
    ISBN 0-86140-250-2 xvi, 268pp. 1988
27. *W.B. Yeats and the Tribes of Danu: Three Views of Ireland's Fairies.* Peter Alderson Smith
    ISBN 0-86140-257-X 350pp. 1987
28. *Theatre of Shadows: from* All that Fall *to* Footfalls. *Samuel Beckett's Drama 1956-76.* Rosemary Pountney
    ISBN 0-86140-407-6 xx, 310pp. 1998 pbk of 1988 ed.
29. *Critical Approaches to Anglo-Irish Literature.* Edited by Michael Allen and Angela Wilcox
    ISBN 0-86140-285-5 x, 194pp. + 8pp. illus. 1988
30. *`Make Sense who May': Essays on Samuel Beckett's Later Works.* Edited by Robin J. Davis and Lance St. J. Butler
    ISBN 0-86140-286-3 x, 176pp. 1989
31. *Cultural Contexts and Literary Idioms in Contemporary Irish Literature.* Edited by Michael Kenneally (Studies in Contemporary Irish Literature Series 1)
    ISBN 0-86140-230-8 viii, 370pp. 1989
32. *Builders of My Soul: Greek and Roman Themes in Yeats.* Brian Arkins
    ISBN 0-86140-304-5 xxii, 242pp. + 4pp.illus. 1991
33. *Perspectives on Irish Drama and Theatre.* Edited by Jacqueline Genet and Richard Allen Cave
    ISBN 0-86140-309-6 xiv, 184pp. 1991
34. *The Great Queens: Irish Goddesses from the Morrigan to Cathleen ní Houlihan.* Rosalind Clark
    ISBN 0-86140-290-1 x, 278pp. 1992

35. *Irish Literature and Culture*. Edited by Michael Kenneally
ISBN 0-86140-313-4 x, 196pp. + 8pp. illus. 1992
36. *Irish Writers and Politics*. Edited by Okifumi Komesu and
Masaru Sekine (IASAIL-Japan Series 3)
ISBN 0-86140-237-5 viii, 350pp. 1991
37. *Irish Writers and Religion*. Edited by Robert Welch (IASAIL-
Japan Series 4)
ISBN 0-86140-236-7 xiv, 242pp. 1992
38. *Yeats and the Noh*. Masaru Sekine & Christopher Murray
ISBN 0-86140-258-8 xviii, 182pp. + 16pp. illus. 1990
39. *Samuel Ferguson: the Literary Achievement*. Peter Denman
ISBN 0-86140-326-6 viii, 230pp. 1990
40. *Reviews and Essays of Austin Clarke*. Edited by
Gregory A. Schirmer
ISBN 0-86140-337-1 xx, 388pp. 1995
41. *The Internationalism of Irish Literature and Drama*. Edited by
Joseph McMinn
ISBN 0-86140-339-8 x, 362pp. 1992
42. *Ireland and France, A Bountiful Friendship: Literature, History and
Ideas*. Edited by Barbara Hayley and Christopher Murray
ISBN 0-86140-341-X xii, 222pp. 1992
43. *Poetry in Contemporary Irish Literature*. Edited by Michael
Kenneally (Studies in Contemporary Irish Literature Series 2)
ISBN 0-86140-310-X xvi, 460pp. 1995
44. *International Aspects of Irish Literature*. Edited by Toshi
Furomoto, George Hughes et al. (IASAIL-Japan Series 5)
ISBN 0-86140-363-0 xii, 430pp. 1996
45. *A Small Nation's Contribution to the World*. Edited by Donald
E. Morse, Csilla Bertha, and Istvàn Pàlffy
ISBN 0-86140-375-4 xiv, 248pp. 1993
46. *Images of Invention. Essays on Irish Writing*. A. Norman Jeffares
ISBN 0-86140-362-2 xii, 352pp. 1996
47. *Literary Inter-Relations: Ireland, Egypt, and the Far East*. Edited
by Mary Massoud
ISBN 0-86140-377-0 x, 440pp. 1996
48. *Irish Writers and their Creative Process*. Edited by Jacqueline
Genet and Wynn Hellegouarc'h
ISBN 0-86140-384-3 viii, 150pp. 1990
49. *Rural Ireland, Real Ireland?* Edited by Jacqueline Genet
ISBN 0-86140-385-1 246pp. 1996
50. *Mrs S.C. Hall: A Literary Biography*. Maureen Keane
ISBN 0-86140-394-0 viii, 260pp. 1997

DATE DUE

DEMCO 38-297